GEOFF SAMMON

Exploring English Grammar

Anglistik · Amerikanistik

studium kompakt

theory
practice

Cornelsen

studium kompakt Anglistik • Amerikanistik

Exploring English Grammar

Die Hochschulreihe studium kompakt Anglistik • Amerikanistik wurde von den Verfasserinnen und Verfassern in Zusammenarbeit mit der Verlagsredaktion entwickelt.

Verfasser:	Geoff Sammon
Verlagsredaktion:	Dr. Blanca-Maria Rudhart
Layout:	Gisela Hoffmann
Technische Umsetzung:	Ingo Ostermaier
Umschlagsgestaltung:	Bauer + Möhring grafikdesign, Berlin
Zeichnungen:	Christina de la Mare, Berlin

Die Deutsche Bibliothek – CIP-Einheitsaufnahme:
Sammon, Geoff:
studium kompakt Anglistik • Amerikanistik:
Exploring English Grammar/Geoff Sammon. –
1. Aufl. – Berlin: Cornelsen, 2002
ISBN 3-464-37131-x

Cornelsen online
http://www.cornelsen.de

1. Auflage Druck 4 3 2 1 Jahr 05 04 03 02

Druck: CS-Druck Cornelsen Stürtz, Berlin

ISBN 3-464-37131-x

Bestellnummer 371310

Gedruckt auf säurefreiem Papier,
umweltschonend hergestellt aus chlorfrei gebleichten Faserstoffen.

Contents

Preface

Eliza Doolittle, the Cockney flower-seller in Shaw's *Pygmalion*, says in Act II, 'I don't want to take grammar. I want to talk like a lady.' Many people would have a similar attitude. Grammar is often regarded as boring. There are so many 'rules' which don't work in practice, or they have so many exceptions that the learner is confused: grammar sometimes appears to be a dusty collection of incomprehensible prohibitions. Or there are the 'rules' which have little to do with the way people normally speak and write. These are often passed on to foreign learners by native speakers who were taught them at school. A good example of these is the myths surrounding the concept of case (see Chap. XI). Yet in fact grammar is simply a description of the structure of a language, in all its fascinating complexity. If we can find beauty in the structure of a snowflake, surely we can appreciate the beauty of that much more complex phenomenon, a language? What is more, a knowledge of the structure of the target language, in this case English, and of the structure of the learner's native language, i.e. for most users of this book, German, is essential if we wish to grasp why people use two languages differently. We hope, therefore, that users of the book will not only find it useful as a means of improving their English, but also as a way of expanding their understanding of the language. Hence the title, *Exploring English Grammar*.

Aims

1 Target group: advanced learners

The main aim of this book is to improve the English of advanced learners at university level. It can be used either for self-study or with a teacher. It aims to concentrate on specific fields which are normally problematic for German-speaking learners. It is not, therefore, meant to be a comprehensive grammar covering every field. For this type of coverage, the learner can consult Quirk 1985, Lamprecht 1989, Swan 1995, Ungerer 2000, or Hoffmann 2001.

2 English compared

To illustrate the structure of English the book often compares it with other languages, either German or those which users of the book may know (e.g. French, Russian), or those most closely related to English, i.e. other Germanic languages. Similarly, along the time dimension Modern English is compared with earlier forms of English to show how English has changed. This is not intended as an excursion into an academic ivory tower. In many respects earlier forms of English, had a grammatical structure which was closer to Modern German. Thus, a comparison between English now and English then often highlights similar differences to those which emerge from a synchronic comparison of English and German. The historical dimension is also vital in reminding us that language is constantly changing. Furthermore, changes occur within language at different speeds. Informal, colloquial usage changes faster than usage in formal register. Consequently, innovations usually spread from informal to formal register, which tends to reflect an older, more conservative pattern. Colloquial English, for instance, uses the Progressive Form more and *whom* less than more formal English. In many ways it gives a glimpse of what English will be like in the future.

3 The structure of English
Because a major aim of the book is to outline the structure of English, it also needs to use the terminology of linguistics in order to be precise. Wherever possible, the meaning of these basic linguistic terms is briefly glossed in the text, with a more detailed explanation of key terms in the linguistic glossary in the appendix. Users who need more help should turn to a standard linguistic handbook, e.g. Kortmann 1999, or the dictionary of linguistic terminology, Crystal 1999.

4 A grammar in English
Since the book is aimed at learners with university-level competence, it is written in English. Explanations have been kept as simple as possible, where the complexity of the subject matter permits this.

Structure

The book contains two main elements, a theory section and a section with exercises, to give practice in using the insights gained from the theory. Both are equally important. In our experience university-level learners are reasonably fluent in English. Their English is, however, to a greater or lesser extent influenced by German. Advanced learners could do better than this, but will only succeed if they revive and expand the often only dimly remembered grammar learnt at school. The theory section is intended to support this spring-cleaning process. However, theory alone is not enough. It needs to be tested in practical contexts. Hence the exercises.

1 Theory

One common defect of grammars is that the user cannot see the wood for the trees. We have attempted to solve this by dividing each theory section into three sub-sections:

I Overview provides a general outline, including definitions of key terms, comparison with other languages and historical background.

II Normal pattern gives details of the standard patterns in the grammatical field dealt with in the chapter.

III Exceptions lists important exceptions to the normal pattern.

Where possible, we have tried to explain why English patterns in the way it does, and why there are exceptions to the rules. In many cases, of course, linguistics cannot give a simple, easy answer, or even an uncontroversial one, but it is better to try to make sense of linguistic patterns and fail than not to try at all. Learners who would like a more comprehensive overview of how English differs from German are recommended to read Leisi/Mair 1999. Please also note the following important points:

- **Rules:** Usage rules are basically a kind of shorthand – they are a handy way of making generalisations about which patterns are possible. The more concrete and specific a rule is, the more reliable it is. Thus a rule involving a signal word, e.g. 'The Perfect cannot be used with *yesterday*', is more reliable than a general, abstract rule such as 'The Perfect is used to link an event in the past with its consequences in the present', since the abstract rule can easily be misinterpreted, resulting in incorrect sentences like *'Columbus has discovered America' (the learner's argument being that America is still known to us). However, there is often no alternative to abstract rules. In such cases the rules can be made more reliable by consciously linking them to specific examples to demonstrate actual usage.
- **Examples:** The examples used to illustrate points of theory are taken from both formal and informal register. We have tried to make them lively and useful. They reflect usage in British English.
- **British and American English:** The grammatical differences between British and American English are relatively slight and are explained wherever this is important. This grammar can therefore be used by speakers of either variety. Other varieties of English are broadly similar to these two. Speakers of American English should remember that the sentences in the examples contain vocabulary and

spelling which is normal in British English, but may not always be current in American English.

2 Exercises
The exercises in each chapter normally progress from easier to more difficult exercises. The easier exercises are often designed to practise specific patterns, since even advanced learners frequently have grammatical 'blind spots'. Underuse of the Progressive Form in the Passive is an example of this. There is a wide range of different types of exercise: variety is the spice of life. Some exercises have the specific objective of getting learners to compare usage in German and English to make readers more aware of both languages. Many exercises test the learner's use of grammatical patterns. Others aim to stimulate linguistic creativity. Additional exercises can be accessed at:
www.uni-bonn.de/Anglistik/samgram

3 Key
The key gives suggested answers to the exercises. In some cases only one answer is correct. In other cases the answers given are the ones most, but not necessarily all, native speakers would give. Both British and American variants are listed.

Acknowledgements

A book such as this is not written in a vacuum. It builds on the achievements of others, e.g. Lamprecht 1989, Quirk 1985, and Swan 1995. Similarly, many exercises have benefited from the imaginative approaches to grammar in Low 1986, Murphy 1987 and Hewings 1999.

An invaluable part was played by students of the English Department of the University of Bonn, who *(sic)* I would like to thank for being the guinea pigs for large parts of this enterprise. In most cases they survived. I am also deeply grateful to my family, colleagues and friends for their support and helpful suggestions, in particular to Prof. Bernhard Diensberg, Dominik Eberhard, Prof. Jürgen Esser, Dr. Penny Franks, Prof. Friedrich-Wilhelm Gester, Linda Klinke, Prof. Wolfram Köck, Wolfram Leonhardt, Dr. Karen Ottewell, Jolie Taublieb, and Dr. Eckart Weiher. Needless to say, any errors are my own. I would be pleased to have feedback on this book. My e-mail address is:
geoffsam@t-online.de

Geoff Sammon

I Word Order

I.1 Overview

English is often described as a 'fixed word-order language' (Quirk 1985, § 2.14), where fixed word order is used to show the relationship between the main elements of a sentence, i.e. the subject, object or complement, and the verb. As with over 75 % of the world's languages, English is classed as an SVO language (Crystal 1997, p. 98), using the word order subject – verb – object, in contrast to languages such as Welsh and Irish, where the normal word order is VSO.

German is also an SVO language, but preserves greater flexibility in word order partly because of the survival of case endings which mark the difference between subject (= nominative) and object (= accusative). Compare:

statements

1 *Mein Bruder | mag | Katzen | nicht.*
S V O

object in front position

2 *Katzen | mag | mein Bruder | nicht.*
O V S

questions

3 *Mag | mein Bruder | Katzen | nicht?*
V S O

subordinate clauses

4 *Ich weiß, dass | mein Bruder | Katzen | nicht mag.*
S O V

In situations where case endings no longer distinguish between nominative and accusative, this flexibility in word order may occasionally lead to ambiguities:

ambiguity

5 *Die Frau mag die Katze nicht.*

In this case, is *die Frau* the subject, as in example 1 above, or an object placed in front position for emphasis, i.e. as in example 2 above?

History

Older forms of English, especially Old English, had more freedom in the choice of word order, with SVO common in statements, VSO or VOS in questions, and SOV in subordinate clauses (Mitchell 1982, § 143 ff). By the Middle English period (12th to 15th centuries) SVO became the norm. The pivotal position of the verb as second constituent of the main clause, which is still typical of other Germanic languages, including German, was lost by the end of the Middle English period. (König 1994, p. 137)

I.2
Normal pattern
auxiliaries

2.1 Word order in statements and questions

In discussing word order in modern English, it is useful to distinguish between two important parts of the verb phrase, viz. the auxiliary verb (Aux) and the main verb (Vb). The auxiliaries are *be, have, do,* modal auxiliaries are verbs like *can, dare, may, must, ought, shall, will.* In the complex verb phrase, the auxiliary has a largely grammatical or modal function, while the main verb carries the basic lexical meaning of the verb (hence the term 'lexical verb' often used for such verbs). In questions, the word order of subject and auxiliary differs from that of the statement, but the word order of subject – main verb – object remains the same as in a statement, i.e. SVO. Compare:

6 *Chris | is | buying | a new car.*
S Aux V O

7 *Is | Chris | buying | a new car?*
Aux S V O

The same pattern occurs with other auxiliaries, including modals:

8 *Michael | can | play | football | tomorrow.*
S Aux V O

9 *Can | Michael | play | football | tomorrow?*
Aux S V O

This helps us to understand why English makes the use of *do* compulsory in most questions: placing *do* in front of the subject shows that we are dealing with a question, but allows us to keep the word order SVO unchanged:

do & SVO

10 *Matthew | enjoys | a good joke.*
S V O

11 *Does | Matthew | enjoy | a good joke?*
Aux S V O

Compare this with the pattern still common in Shakespeare's day:

12 *Mean | you | his majesty? (Macbeth*, II, 3)
V S O

Inversion of main verb and subject, as in this Early Modern English example, is replaced in its Modern English equivalent by inversion of auxiliary and subject, leaving the standard SVO pattern unchanged:

inversion

13 *Do | you | mean | his majesty?*
Aux S V O

An important feature of English is that it does not normally tolerate adverbials in the position between main verb and object, whereas in German this is quite common:

adverbials

14 *I | play | football | on Saturdays.*
S V O Adv

15 *Ich | spiele | samstags | Fußball.*
S V Adv O

2.2 Fronted negative or semi-negative adverbials

A similar pattern to the word order used in questions occurs when adverbials with negative or semi-negative (restrictive) meaning are placed in front position in the sentence for emphasis:

16 *Never before | has | a government | shown | such incompetence!*
Adv Aux S V O

17 *Rarely | do | we | see | so much neglect of young children.*
Adv Aux S V O

Here too, use of the auxiliary enables SVO word order to be retained while emphasising the adverbial by placing it in front position. However, it should be noted that this use of inversion is normally only common in formal and literary style. Spoken informal language usually prefers the following alternatives:

18 *No government | has | ever | shown | such incompetence | before!*
S Aux Adv V O Adv

19 *We | rarely | see | so much neglect of young children.*
S Adv V O

Negative and restrictive adverbials causing inversion are listed below:

negative adverbials		restrictive adverbials
never (before)	neither.....nor	hardly.....than/when
nowhere (else)	at no time	little
no sooner... than/when	on no occasion	only + Adv (= erst)
not since	on no account	only if/when (= erst wenn)
not + Object	in no way	rarely
not until	under no circumstances	scarcely ... than/when
not only ... but also		seldom

20 *'Little do they realise that I have the means to blow up the entire world!' the mad scientist raved.*

21 *Only after the exam did she remember the answer to the last question.* (= *Erst nach der Prüfung ...*)

When it involves inversion of the auxiliary, *only* corresponds to German *erst*.

only with inversion = *erst*

22 *Only two weeks later were the police able to arrest two suspects.* (= *erst*)

Compare the alternative construction with the same meaning:

23 *It was only two weeks later that the police were able to arrest two suspects.*

Without inversion *only* is the equivalent of German *schon*.

only without inversion = *schon*

24 *Only two weeks later the police were able to arrest two suspects.* (= *schon*)

Compare the same sentence with a different word order:

25 *The police were able to arrest two suspects only two weeks later.*

When negative adverbials form part of a subordinate clause, inversion takes place in the following main clause. Contrast 26 with examples 27-29.

negative adverbials in subordinate clauses

26 *Not since March last year have we seen flooding on such a scale.*
27 *Not since Winston Churchill died have there been such massive expressions of popular grief as at Diana's funeral.*
28 *Not until Jim read her suicide note did he grasp how much she had loved him.*
29 *Only if these conditions have been met can we provide the funding you require.*

If both *neither* and *nor* are used as conjunctions introducing a clause, both clauses have inversion. Inversion also occurs if *neither* or *nor* are used separately. Compare 30 to 32:

neither, nor

30 *Neither was Don a good husband, nor was he an ideal father.*
31 *'We didn't go on holiday last year.' 'Neither did we.'*
32 *'I don't like Handel.' 'Nor do I.'*

Note

As with *only* (see 24 and 25 above), not every negative or restrictive adverbial in front position results in inversion. The crucial factor seems to be whether the adverbial refers to the whole sentence or only part of it (cf. König 1994, p. 554). In the former case, the result is inversion. In the latter, there is no inversion. Compare:

33 *At no time was he aware that he was actually committing a crime.*
34 *In no time she had solved the problem.*

Alternatively, the adverbial in 34 can be placed later in the sentence:

35 *She had solved the problem in no time.*

2.3 Cleft sentences

Cleft, i.e. 'split', sentences are sentences where what was originally a simple sentence consisting of one main clause is converted into a sentence containing a main clause and a subordinate clause in order to emphasise one part of the sentence. Cleft sentences occur in both English and German, but are more common in English (and French), because German often simply uses fronting to emphasise sentence elements. The two most common types of cleft sentences involve clauses beginning with *it* or *what*. In the examples below, 36 is the simple sentence, with 37 to 41 showing how cleft sentences are used for focusing on different sentence elements. The numbers below 36 show which elements the cleft sentences focus on:

36 *David often visits his girlfriend in London.*
37 38 39 40 41

37 *It's David, not Darren, who often visits his girlfriend in London.*
38 *What David often does is visit his girlfriend in London.*
39 *What David does is he often visits his girlfriend in London.*
40 *It's his girlfriend that David often visits in London, not his grandma.*
41 *It's in London that David often visits his girlfriend.*

German can use a cleft sentence similar to 40 to stress who is being visited:

42 *Es ist nicht die Oma, die David oft in London besucht, sondern die Freundin.*

However, German often prefers a simpler construction, placing the object in front position for emphasis. This is far less common in English, because it conflicts with the SVO tendency of the language:

43 *Nicht die Oma, sondern die Freundin besucht der David oft in London.*

Note

Note that in 43 the sentence is ambiguous without the clear case marker *der* in German. Only when (in colloquial German) *der* is used is it clear who is visiting and who is being visited.

I.3 Exceptions

3.1 Fronting

Fronting means placing an element at the beginning of a sentence which would not normally go there. In informal English this occurs fairly frequently with objects, though not as often as in German:

44 *Very good cake | you | made | yesterday!*
O S V

Fronting of adverbial phrases of place is also common in more formal style, especially in descriptions:

45 *Beneath the balcony | was | a rose bush in full bloom.*
Adv V S

46 *Along the road | trudged | a seemingly endless line of refugees.*
Adv V S

After *here, there* or a particle (e.g. *in, off, up*) at the beginning of the sentence or clause, inversion of verbs like *be, come, go* is used if the subject is a noun. Inversion here is a relic of the pivotal position of the verb as second constituent of the main clause, which was normal in medieval English (see I.1, History). This type is restricted to very few structures and only occurs with intransitive verbs:

47 *Here's your coat.*

48 *Here | comes | Johnny!*
Adv V S

49 *There goes your bus!*
50 *I got out of the car, and up walks this policeman.*

Note

Notice that inversion does not take place if the subject is a pronoun:

51 *Here* | *he* | *comes!*
Adv S V

3.2 Inversion with verbs of reporting

After direct speech, verbs of reporting are often inverted if the subject is a noun and the verb is fairly commonly used, e.g. *ask, reply, retort, say, suggest*. Inversion is typical of more formal style. Normal word order (SV) is always possible.

52 *'Are you coming with us?' asked Arthur.*
V S
53 *'Are you coming with us?' Arthur asked.*
S V

If the subject is a pronoun, SV word order is more common:

54 *'I don't like your tone of voice,' she said.*

Exercises

1 "Deutsche Sprache, schwere Sprache!"

Which German sentence could be ambiguous? Remember that it often depends on the intonation and sentence stress used. Translate the sentences into English to reflect the different meanings of the German sentence. Some vocabulary is given to help you.Then say briefly why the sentence is ambiguous or not, using the factors listed below.

Factors causing ambiguity	Factors preventing ambiguity
• neuter nouns or pronouns	• masculine nouns or pronouns
• feminine nouns or pronouns	• *ich, wir, du, ihr*
• plural nouns and *sie, Sie*	• sense
• names	

Example

Die Frau mag die Katze nicht.
a *The woman doesn't like the cat.*
b *The cat doesn't like the woman.*
c *feminine nouns*

Exercises

1 Katzen mögen Hunde nicht.
a ____
b ____
c ____

2 Das Mädchen konnte das Haus leicht finden.
a ____
b ____
c ____

3 Jennifer hat Tom auf einer Party kennen gelernt.
a ____
b ____
c ____

4 Die Ärztin guckte die Patientin skeptisch an.
a ____
b ____
c ____

skeptisch = *sceptical* (BrE)
= *skeptical* (AmE)

5 Das Mädchen findet die Wache süß.
a ____
b ____
c ____

Wache = *guard*
süß = *cute*

6 Frank mögen die meisten Frauen nicht.
a ____
b ____
c ____

7 Die Gangster haben Sie doch gesehen?
a ____
b ____
c ____

8 Berliner mögen Sie nicht, oder?
a ____
b ____
c ____

2 Shakespeare's Time Machine

William Shakespeare has landed in the 21st century in a time machine. He is not eligible for unemployment benefit and has therefore decided to write another play. Unfortunately he is still using Early Modern English grammar and vocabulary. Help him to get it right before he sends his new play to the publisher's. Don't worry about the metre: leave that up to him:

Exercises

Act II, Scene 3 – A room in the Palace
Enter Oswald and Sir Edgar
O: Why looks your Grace so seriously today?
E: The night was storm-toss't.
Strange cries were heard, and ghosts, men say,
Did walk abroad.
O: Aye, some say the earth was feverous and did shake.
Thus do the Fates betray the evil that men seek to hide.
Goes the king hence today?
E: I'faith, before the clock hath yet struck two.
O: Ride you with him this afternoon?
E: I do, if all goes well.
Enter a Servant.
S: O horror! Horror!
O & E: What's the matter?
O: How cam'st thou hither?
S: Know ye not the news? The king, the king, the king is dead!
Most foully murdered while he was yet abed! Awake! Awake!
Ring the alarum-bell! Murder and treason! Ring the bell!

3 SVO rules, okay?

Change the fairly formal sentences below involving fronted negative or restrictive adverbials into more informal sentences with normal SVO word order. Examples 16-19 and 22-23 in section 2.2. will help you.

Example

On no account should visitors to the zoo feed the animals.
→ *Visitors to the zoo shouldn't feed the animals on any account.*

1 'I don't like Tchaikovsky.' 'Neither do I.'
2 Only after the exam did she remember the answer to the last question.
3 Not until Tuesday did it become clear that the earthquake's death toll would run into the thousands.
4 'We didn't go on holiday last year.' 'Neither did we.'
5 Not since Winston Churchill died have there been such massive expressions of popular grief.
6 Not until Jim read her suicide note did he grasp how much she had loved him.

7 Only if these conditions are met can we provide the funding you require.
8 At no time was he aware that he was actually committing a crime.
9 Seldom have I experienced such crass stupidity!
10 No sooner had we entered the haunted castle when the lights went out.

Exercises

4 Rewriting a speech

You are working as an assistant to an Opposition politician in Britain. She has written the first draft of a short speech she is to hold at a party conference, but has asked you to make it more forceful by stressing specific elements, which she has underlined. You should emphasise these elements by fronting them, making the appropriate changes in word order.

Example

The government hasn't attempted to address this problem in any way.
→ *In no way has the government attempted to address this problem.*

Ladies and gentlemen,
This country has never been in such dire straits as under the present government.
The economy has not been neglected to the same extent anywhere else in the EU.
The number of multi-national firms leaving the U.K. has not been as high since the Wilson government of the 1970s.
And this is not surprising, either.
The present party had scarcely come into office when it began to frighten away foreign investors with its taxes on profits.
In the post-war period there has rarely been any party which has matched the government's hamfistedness in its timing and tactics.
It is my considered opinion that this will only change for the better if the government bites the bullet and sends the Chancellor of the Exchequer packing.
A large part of our financial problems would be solved in no time.
We would not only be rid of an incompetent administrator, we would also be saying a tearless farewell to a government minister who was better known for his love affairs than for his debating skills in the House.
He does not seem at any time to have been aware of the gravity of the country's financial situation.

Exercises

The government should not, therefore, under any circumstances, permit such a mediocre minister to remain one month longer in office.

5 Granny's hearing aid

During a visit to your grandmother you are telling her about your holiday plans. Supply the missing sections, using cleft sentences. The first section has been done to help you.

'Gran, how's your shoulder doing today?'
'Oh yes, I definitely feel older. You can't help it, you know, at my age.'
'No, gran, I said, 'How's your shoulder?' '
'Oh, my shoulder. Why didn't you say so the first time? Yes, it's not so good.'
'I'm going to Spain with my girlfriend next week.'
'Going to Paignton? Very nice.'
'No, granny, it's Spain we're going to, not Paignton[1].'
'Oh, I thought you said Paignton. I always used to go there with your grandad. We had a lovely time. Who's this Earl you're going with?'
'It's _____[2]. I don't know anybody called Earl. We're flying to Marbella next week.'
'Driving? That's a long way to drive, isn't it? And they drive on the wrong side of the road in Spain, don't they?'
'No, gran, what _____[3], not driving!'
'What's your girlfriend's name again? Marbella? That's a nice name.'
'No, gran, it's _____[4]. My girlfriend's name's Rachel. You've met her. She's studying speech therapy at college.'
'Ooh, beach therapy – I bet that'll come in handy when you're at the seaside in Spain. What is beach therapy exactly?'
'No, gran, what _____[5], not beach therapy. She's doing speech therapy at the same university as me, in Manchester.'
'Manchester? I thought you were at Keele?'
'No, gran. It's Bernie _____[6]. I'm at Manchester. Shall I get you your hearing aid? It would make things easier.'
'I don't need a hearing aid. What _____[7] a good cup of tea. That'll really perk me up. I can hear much better when I've had my cuppa. So go into the kitchen and make me one, will you?'

Exercises

6 Letter writing

You have been asked to help Heinz Katzenellenbogen, who is organising a trip to Oxford to visit the universities and schools there. Since his English is rather rusty, he has asked you to 'improve the style'. Correct his errors.

Example

Dear Professor Hogshead,

we are now putting the finishing touches to our program for Oxford. We have been very grateful for your kind offer to show us round your college and gladly accept. I have one or two questions. I was wondering wheather it would be convenient for us to come on the morning of Tuesday, 22 September. We are hoping to visit in the afternoon St. Edward's School, but not untill 2 p.m. we are going there, so that there will probably be enough time in the morning to visit your college. However, on no account you should change your plans if Tuesday is not convenient. We are very flexibel, except on Wednesday and Friday. The town Stratford-upon-Avon we are visiting on Wednesday. We have from 10 to 12 a guided tour round the Royal Shakespeare Theater, and the afternoon we will spend walking around the town and visiting Shakespeare's birthplace. Of course we will also see in Stratford a play from Shakespeare. We have bought tickets for 'The Merchant of Venice' in the evening. So we will have no time on Wednesday. And for Friday morning we have arranged a visit to Cheney School. In the afternoon we will be leaving for Germany. Please let me stress once more that under no circumstances you should cancel any plans you may have for Tuesday morning. I am sure we can fit most other times you suggest into our schedule. Looking forward to hear from you.

Yours sincerly,

Heinz Katzenellenbogen

II Tense & Aspect: The Progressive

II.1
Overview
definition: tense

1.1 Definition of 'tense'

By tense we mean morphological changes in the form of the verb which show the time when an action takes place. On the basis of this definition we can distinguish two tenses in English, viz. the past (e.g. *I lived, I ran*) and the present (e.g. *I live, I run*). Many linguists prefer the term *non-past* instead of *present* because it more accurately reflects the function of this tense:

1 *I live in Durham, where I run my own business.*

Here the 'present' tense of *live* and *run* also refers to the past and (probably) the future, not simply present time.

Note

Traditional grammars use the term *tense* not only for changes in the morphological shape of the verb but also for syntactic constructions expressing concepts related to time (see below, under *aspect*). This use of tense in traditional grammars is due to the influence of Latin grammar (see Crystal 1995, p. 196).

1.2 Definition of 'aspect'

definition: aspect

By aspect we mean 'a grammatical category which reflects the way in which the verb action is regarded or experienced with respect to time' (see Quirk 1985, p. 188). Compare:

2 *He was watching TV when the phone rang.*

Both actions occur in the past, but we view the action of watching TV as occurring over a period, whereas the ringing of the phone is felt to be brief.

English has two sets of aspectual contrast, the Perfective (see Chap. III), which expresses the concept of an action taking place during a period of time that is regarded as complete as opposed to incomplete, and the Progressive (see II.2 below), where the action is seen in terms of being in progress or not (i.e. durative versus punctual). This aspectual contrast is expressed by the Progressive Form (also known as the Continuous Form or Expanded Form) and the Simple Form, e.g. *I am/was going* versus *I go/went,* etc.

Note

A similar aspectual contrast between durative and punctual occurs in French between the imperfect and perfect *(passé composé)* and in Russian between the imperfective and perfective. Compare:

Il regardait la télévision quand le téléphone a sonné.
imperfect perfect

Он смотрел телевизор, когда зазвонил телефон.
imperfective perfective

Other Romance and Slavonic languages have similar aspectual contrasts.

History

The history of the Progressive Form is complex and unclear. A similar construction, consisting of *be* followed by the Present Participle, occurs as far back as Old English. Compare:

'Europe hio onginð... of Danai þære ie, seo is irnende of
'Europe (she) begins from Don the river, which runs from [the]
norþdæle... & seo ea Danai irnð þonan suðryhte...'
north... and that river Don runs from there due south...'

This example shows that the construction is similar in form to the modern Progressive, consisting of *is* and the Present Participle *irnende* (see Traugott p.187ff. in Hogg 1992). It also shows, however, that it is used differently from today's Progressive, since it refers to a general state, viz. the course of a river. In Modern English the Simple Present would be used. Furthermore, it alternates with the normal Present *irnð* within the same sentence. In Old and Middle English this construction is optional, and was simply a stylistic alternative to the normal verb (see Fischer p.254 in Blake 1992). During the Middle English period its use increased, being perhaps partly influenced by a similar construction with *be* followed by the preposition *on* and the Gerund, e.g. *he was on hunting* (cf. the German parallel *Ich bin am Überlegen*). It is only in Modern English that the Progressive becomes obligatory, though the present pattern is not established until the 18th century. For example, Shakespeare can still use the Simple Form where we would have to use the Progressive, e.g. in *Hamlet*, II.2:
'What do you read, my Lord?' (i.e. *What are you reading?*).
Since the 18th century the use of the Progressive has increased enormously (see Faiß 1989, §4.5.8.6.). This process is still going on and helps to explain some of the variations and anomalies in the current use of the Progressive (cf. Quirk 1985, §4.28, note).

II.2
Normal Pattern: Progressive Aspect

The Progressive Form indicates that a situation is in progress.

- It expresses temporary duration of the action.
- It can also imply that the action is incomplete.
- The Progressive often focuses attention on the action itself.

Compare:

3 *Judy works for a computer firm in Cape Town.*
4 *I live in Brisbane.*
5 *He wrote a letter last night.*
6 *Have you eaten all the cheese?*

7 *Mary's got a job for the summer. She's working as a waitress.*
8 *I'm from Brisbane, but I'm living in Sydney at present.*
9 *He was writing a letter last night between 8 and 10.*
10 *Ugh! You've been eating garlic!*

Whereas 3 and 4 describe habits, 7 and 8 refer to temporary situations.

Examples 5 and 6 show that the actions are completed, while 9 and 10 simply focus attention on the action, which may or may not be completed.

signal words

Some adverbs usually only occur with the Progressive or the Simple Form. These 'signal words' are normally a very reliable guide to which aspect should be used in a specific context.

The Progressive is used with the following adverbs of temporary duration: *at present, at the moment, currently, just.*

The Simple Form is used with the following frequency adverbs of habit: *always* (but see 3.2), *frequently, never, normally, occasionally, often, rarely, seldom, sometimes, usually.*

Note

The adverb *just* is only a signal word for the Progressive when it refers to present time, e.g. *Jane's just calling a taxi.* The adverb *just* is also used in the meaning of 'only', e.g. *I just wanted to ask if I could borrow your car.*

Some features of the distinction involved in the Progressive Aspect are more typical of specific tense or aspect combinations, as illustrated in 2.1 to 2.5.

2.1 Present Simple and Present Progressive

PRESENT SIMPLE

The Present Simple, more commonly known as the Simple Present, is mainly used for habits extending across the present, past and (presumably) future, whereas the Present Progressive refers to a temporary period in the present. Compare:

habits

11 *Usually I mow the lawn, but today John's doing it – I'm too tired.*
12 *We make sure that our car is serviced regularly.*
13 *Whenever I see them, they're arguing.*
14 *Every time we pop in on them, they're having tea.*

In 13 and 14 the subordinate clauses introduced by *whenever* and *every time* denote actions which keep occurring and therefore take the Simple Form in analogy with habits, while the Progressive in the main clause focuses on the temporary duration of the action on each specific occasion.

The Present Simple is also used for timeless general statements which are true for the past, present, and in some cases future (e.g. 16): general statements

15 *Water boils at 100° Celsius.*
16 *They say Indians eat a lot of spicy food.*

The Present Simple can be used to refer to future events (see also Chap. IV), where it is normally restricted to contexts involving time-tables. In general the use of the Present Simple in this way is only possible if there is clear reference to future time in the context, e.g. an adverbial: future events

17 *My train leaves at 5 pm, so I'd better get a move on.*
18 *The summer semester starts on April 3rd this year.*

The Present Progressive contrasts with the Present Simple in that it refers to a temporary situation. Compare examples 19 to 21 below with 15, 16 and 12 above: PRESENT PROGRESSIVE temporary situation

19 *The water's boiling!*
20 *What I'm saying is that spicy food may not be good for you.*
21 *My car's being serviced at the moment.*

The Progressive Form in 19 to 21 denotes a much shorter period, compared with the greater permanency implied in 12, 15 and 16. Notice the use of the Passive Progressive in 21.

Like the Present Simple, the Present Progressive can be used to refer to future events (see also Chap. IV). Normally it too requires an adverbial with future reference: future events

22 *I'm going to a disco on Saturday night.*
23 *We're buying a scooter next month, we've decided.*

2.2 Past Simple and Past Progressive

The Past Simple (also known as Simple Past) is the normal way of expressing past time reference, except when the situation in the past is seen as linked to the present. The situation takes place during a completed period of time: PAST SIMPLE completed period of time

24 *We met Gillian in town yesterday.*

25 *I grew up in a small town in Nova Scotia.*
26 *Every year the Johnsons went to Blackpool for a week's holiday.*

PAST PROGRESSIVE
temporary/completed

The Past Progressive is the marked (i.e. specific, non-neutral – see Glossary) form of the Past. It focuses on a situation of temporary duration taking place within a completed period of time:

27 *Ms Watson, what were you doing between 8 and 8.30 on the night of the murder?*
28 *Bert was being questioned by the police when his lawyer arrived.*
29 *The man who attacked the mayor was wearing a suede jacket.*

Notice the use of the Passive Progressive in 28. The Past Progressive often occurs in narrative descriptions, as in 29.

background situations

The Past Progressive frequently contrasts with the Past Simple when a main clause and subordinate clause of time are combined. While the Progressive is used to supply a background situation extending over a limited period of completed time, the Past Simple refers to events of very short duration:

30 *Mark was hiding in the tool shed when he saw his mother-in-law.*
In these cases, there are three possible combinations:

- Past Progressive and Past Simple
- Past Progressive in both clauses
- Past Simple in both clauses

Compare:
31 *The phone rang while I was having a bath.*
32 *Diane was ironing while Gerry was doing the dishes.*
33 *When he saw his mother-in-law Mark hid in the tool shed.*

In 31 the background situation *('having a bath')* forms the framework within which an event of short duration *('rang')* occurs.
In 32 two actions are taking place more or less simultaneously.
In 33 one action happens after another. When two verbs in the Past Simple are used in this way to denote one action following another, it usually implies that the first action was the cause of the second action. Contrast 30, which means that Mark happened to be hiding in the tool shed when his mother-in-law arrived, with 33, where Mark hid in the tool shed because he wanted to avoid his mother-in-law. Similarly:

34 *We were having tea when Alistair arrived.*
35 *We had tea when Alistair arrived.* (i.e. We waited till he came.)
36 *They were laughing when he entered the room.*
37 *They laughed when John entered the room. He had forgotten that he still had his girlfriend's skirt on.*

2.3 Present Perfect Simple and Present Perfect Progressive

The Present Perfect Simple is the normal, unmarked way of referring to past time when this is regarded as linked to the present. It often implies that the action is completed:

PRESENT PERFECT SIMPLE linked to the present, completed

38 *I've repaired my PC.* (i.e. It's fixed now.)
39 *She's learnt this poem off by heart.* (i.e. She knows it.)
40 *He's written a novel.* (i.e. It's finished)

The Present Perfect Progressive focuses on the action expressed by the verb during a period linked to the present. It also differs from the Present Perfect Simple in often implying that the action is temporary and may be incomplete: compare 38 to 40 with 41 to 43. It is commonly used with repeated actions (as in 44 and 45) or to express the idea that an action has taken place over the whole of a period of time (as in 42 and 45):

PRESENT PERFECT PROGRESSIVE linked to the present, temporary/incomplete

41 *I've been repairing the car. That's why I'm so dirty.*
42 *She's been learning this poem all day, but she doesn't know it yet.*
43 *He's been writing a novel.*
44 *Those boys have been kicking their ball against my wall again!*
45 *I've been trying to reach her all day. It's very frustrating.*

The fact that the Progressive focuses on the action is illustrated by 46 and 47, where the action is almost the only content in the sentence:

46 *Look! It's been snowing.*
47 *Have you been drinking?*

When the focus moves away from the action, for example to express an amount or to say how often something happened, the Perfect Simple is normal. Compare 48 with 47, and 49 with 45:
48 *I've drunk five pints of beer, but I still feel pretty clear-headed.*
49 *I've tried to reach her at least five times.*

2.4 Past Perfect Simple and Past Perfect Progressive

PAST PERFECT SIMPLE
pre-past

The Past Perfect expresses the idea of an event or state being completed before the situation expressed by the Past. The Past Perfect Simple is the unmarked way of referring to this.

50 *When I got there, the train had already left.*

PAST PERFECT PROGRESSIVE
limited duration

The Past Perfect Progressive is used to focus on limited duration of an action in a period leading up to the situation expressed by the Past. It thus tends to be preferred when we say how long the period lasted, as in 52:

51 *It had been raining hard. There were large puddles everywhere.*
52 *We'd been travelling for ten hours when suddenly I heard a shot.*

2.5 Infinitive and Progressive Infinitive

PROGRESSIVE INFINITIVE

Although the ordinary Infinitive (e.g. *to read*) is used in the vast majority of cases, in specific contexts a Progressive Infinitive (i.e. *to be reading*) occurs.

limited duration

The Progressive Infinitive occurs after modal verbs, the verbs *seem*, *appear* and some other expressions when limited duration of a situation is implied:

53 *He should be arriving any minute.*
54 *You might be wondering why I decided to leave the team.*
55 *The bus seemed to be stopping, but then it picked up speed.*
56 *He appears to be having difficulties with starting his car.*
57 *It's good to be talking to you again after so many years.*

In many cases use of the Progressive Infinitive is optional, e.g. in 53 and 57, where the normal Infinitive would be just as acceptable. In other cases, e.g. 54 and 55, the Progressive Infinitive is more common, and in 56 it is the only possibility.

II.3 Exceptions

3.1 Divergent patterns: Simple Form for Progressive

Verbs referring to actions sometimes take the Simple Form, despite a context implying temporary duration. If the Simple Form occurs where the Progressive would be expected, this is normally a survival of older usage, when the Simple Form was normal for any verb.

For a series of events, e.g. when giving instructions, the Present Simple is normally used: SERIES OF EVENTS

58 *To get to the post office you turn right at these traffic lights, then you go along Trinity Street and it's on the left-hand side.*

A similar type, also involving a series of events, is the fictional present, which is used for describing the plots of novels, films, etc.: fictional present

59 *Cathy, an unemployed social worker, falls head over heels in love with Ryan, a high school dropout. They leave Iowa and go to L.A., hoping to make the big time, but soon get involved in drugs ...*

The Present Simple is normal in performative utterances, i.e. utterances that 'act through words'. Performative verbs are often indicators of such utterances (cf. Levinson 1983, pp. 228-237). Some common performative verbs are listed below (for more examples, see Close 1975, §13.7d): PERFORMATIVE VERBS

accept, accuse, admit, advise, apologise, bet, deny, forbid, guarantee, hope, inform, name, predict, promise, recommend, request, resign, sentence, suggest, suppose, warn

60 *We apologise for being so rude last night. We were a bit drunk.*
61 *I bet you ten euros that horse won't win.*
62 *I won't accept this sort of treatment. I resign!*
63 *I hereby sentence you to six months' imprisonment.*

Utterances with performative verbs 'perform' the action they refer to: saying 'We apologise' is itself the act of apology. This performative use is normally associated with verbs in the first person and in the present tense. In other tenses they merely act as normal verbs, i.e. describe the action. Compare 60 with 64 below:

64 *We apologised for being so rude the previous night.*

The Present Simple is often used instead of the Present Progressive and Present Perfect in newspaper and magazine headlines to focus on the basic meaning of the verb: headlines

65 BUSH HEADS FOR EUROPE *(Mr Bush is going to Europe.)*
66 ARCTIC ICE SHRINKS BY HALF *(The Arctic ice sheet has shrunk ...)*

habit
repeated actions

3.2 Divergent Patterns: Progressive Form for Simple Form

Verbs denoting actions can use the Progressive when they refer to habit, provided they are accompanied by the adverbs *always, continually, constantly, forever*. It is used for repeated actions and often implies annoyance on the part of the speaker, as in 67 to 69, though not in 70:

67 *You're always interrupting me!*
68 *She's constantly forgetting her homework!*
69 *He was forever poking his nose into my affairs.*
70 *Uncle Bill's so generous. He's always buying the children sweets.*

3.3 Stative verbs: Simple Form

Stative verbs are verbs denoting a state, as opposed to dynamic verbs, which describe actions and events. Almost all the verbs highlighted in red or underlined in examples 1 to 70 are examples of dynamic verbs. The only exceptions are *have* (14 and 34) and *see* (30 and 33), which are stative. Examples of common stative verbs are listed in the table below. Stative verbs normally only take the Simple Form:

71 *Our new secretary is a Czech from Prague.*
72 *He hates getting up in the mornings.*
73 *I think we've made some progress at last.*

STATIVE VERBS: SEMANTIC TYPES

Type 1	states of 'being' and 'having': *be, apply to (= 'be true of'), belong, concern, cost, depend, resemble,* *have, contain, lack, own, possess, weigh (= 'have a weight of')*
Type 2	intellectual states (large class): *assume, believe, doubt, expect, forget, hope, imagine, know, notice, realise, remember, suppose, think (= 'be of the opinion'), understand, wonder*
Type 3	emotional states or attitudes (large class): *agree, consider, hate, intend, like, love, need, pity, prefer, regard, trust, want, wish*

Type 4 states of perception (closed class):
feel, hear, see, smell, taste; appear, seem

Type 5 states of physical sensation (small class):
ache, hurt, itch, tickle

3.4 Divergent Patterns: Stative verbs in the Progressive Form

In some cases stative verbs can take the Progressive Form to express temporary duration. Use of the Progressive where the Simple Form would be expected is usually a feature which is of (relatively) recent origin.

When the stative verb *be* is used to express temporary behaviour, it takes the Progressive, in analogy with dynamic verbs like *act, behave*. A typical feature of this use is that it is followed by an adjective or noun referring to a type of behaviour (e.g. *serious, a fool*):

TYPE 1
verbs *be* and *have*

74 *Are you being serious?*
75 *He's being such a fool!* (cf. *He's behaving so foolishly!*)

Similarly, when the stative verb *have* refers to an activity of limited duration, it takes the Progressive (see also examples 14 and 34):

76 *We're having a swim.* (cf. *We're swimming.*)
77 *They were having dinner when I arrived.* (cf. *They were eating* ...)
78 *She's having a baby.* (i.e. *She's pregnant*, in contrast to: *She has (got) a baby.*)

The stative verbs *feel, look, smell, taste,* take the Progressive when used in an activity sense. They answer the question *What is X doing?*:

TYPE 4
verbs of perception

79 *She's feeling for the switch. (cf. She's groping for the switch.)*
80 *I'm looking to see if she's home yet. (cf. I'm checking to see ...)*
81 *The dog was smelling at the meat. (cf. The dog was sniffing at ...)*
82 *I'm tasting the soup to see if it needs more salt. (cf. I'm trying ...)*

The perception verbs *feel, look, smell, sound, taste* usually take the Simple Form when the thing or person perceived is the subject, as in 83 and 84:

83 *You look much healthier nowadays.*

84 *This material feels wonderfully soft to the touch.*

However, with animate subjects, especially persons, the Progressive is now commonly used in contexts expressing temporary duration:

85 *You're looking much healthier this week.*
86 *How are you feeling today, Mrs Weatherspoon?*

When these five perception verbs are used with a personal subject, where the subject perceives something, the modal verb *can* is normally added in the Present, and often in the Past, particularly in British English:

87 *I can taste the garlic in this soup. How much did you put in?*
88 *Can you smell something burning? I'll swear I can.*

TYPE 5
verbs of physical sensation

These verbs, most of which denote the physical sensation of pain, differ from other stative verbs in permitting both the Simple Form and the Progressive to be used for temporary situations:

89 *Is your back still aching? = Does your back still ache?*
90 *My leg's hurting = My leg hurts.*

OTHER STATIVE VERBS

Some stative verbs are also used in dynamic senses, often in analogy with dynamic verbs of similar meaning. They then take the Progressive when the situation involves limited duration. Compare the dynamic use of *think* in (91) with its stative counterpart in (92), meaning 'to be of the opinion':

91 *'What are you doing?' 'I'm thinking.'*
92 *I think we should stop sending Christmas cards this year.*

Similarly:

93 *This car is costing me a packet.* (But: *This car costs £10,000.*)
94 *We're thinking of buying a boat.* (cf. *We're planning to buy one.*)
95 *How are you liking your stay here?* (cf. *How are you enjoying it?*)
96 *I'm just seeing Mr Jay to the door.* (cf. *I'm just taking him there.*)
97 *We've been hearing a lot about you.* (cf. *People have been telling me a lot about you.*)

Some stative verbs take the Progressive, implying a tentative attitude. This attitudinal use makes the statement or request sound less direct, and is thus often preferred as a more polite alternative to the Simple Form:

attitudinal use

98 *We're hoping that you will reconsider your offer.*
99 *I was wondering if you could help me.*

Exercises

1 A break-in at Pratt's

You are on the phone looking out of the office window when you see something suspicious happening at the factory opposite your office. Tell the friend you are ringing what is happening. Turn the key words into full sentences, using the correct form of the Present. The first one has been done for you.

Example

There's a man outside Pratt's factory.
he / climb / over / wall — *He's climbing over the wall.*

I / think / he / try / break / into / factory ______1
he / appear / have / difficulties ______2
security guard / shout / to him ______3
now / guard's German shepherd / run / towards / man ______4
man / run / away ______5
dog / pin / him / to the ground ______6
guard / seem / call / for help / on his mobile ______7

2 Marketing a product

Imagine that you work for an advertising agency. You need to invent a brand name and create a TV commercial for one of the products described below.

Product No. 25: mobile phone
Target group: age group 15-25
Marketing features: small size, inexpensive, wide range of colours

Product No. 72: soap
Target group: women aged 20-30
Marketing features: relatively expensive, uses only natural substances, was not tested on animals

3 Signal words in context

Fill in the gaps in the following, using Present Simple or Present Progressive, and taking care to put any adverbials in the correct position. Underline the signal word(s) in each sentence.

1 Normally I use the motorbike for work, but today Tom _____ (take) it.
2 Jane usually comes home around six, but today she _____ (work) overtime, so she probably won't be home before eight.
3 As a rule I get up early, but today I _____ (have) a lie-in for a change.
4 I _____ (rarely; use) public transport, but at the moment I _____ (take) the Tube or the bus because my car _____ (be repaired).
5 We frequently get pretty wet weather in the Shetlands in spring, but the weather _____ (seem) to _____ (get) better now.
6 Angie is a good friend of mine, but she _____ (often; have) these really wild ideas!
7 We _____ (always; recommend) this make of dish-washer to customers, because it's very reliable and value for money, but of course occasionally we _____ (come across) one which is faulty.
8 The government _____ (currently; appear) to _____ (experience) a crisis of confidence in its own ability to solve the country's economic problems.
9 It's really frustrating! Whenever I _____ (phone) Sue, she _____ (have) a bath.
10 If you could wait a minute, Mr Jones. Your car _____ (just; be given) a final check.

4 Something to hide

Anita Biggleswade, the rich heiress, has been murdered. Inspector Knacker is interviewing suspects in the study. She asks all of them the same question:
'What were you doing on the night of the murder between nine and half past nine?' None of the suspects are telling the truth. Fill in the bubbles below to show what the suspects said they were doing and what they were really thinking. Some vocabulary is given to help you. The pictures on the right show what the suspects were actually doing at the time of the murder.

get ready to go out • have a watch TV • make love to • read the paper • be in bed with sb. • listen at the door • have an argument with sb.

Exercises

Example

Mrs Blackstaff, the maid:

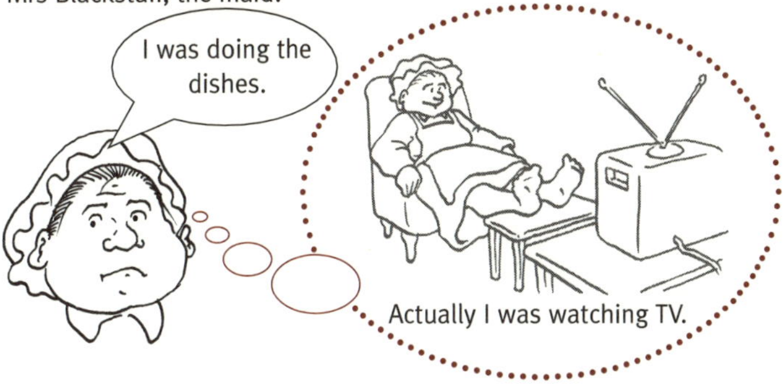

Simon Mander, Anita's handsome young private secretary and secret lover:

①

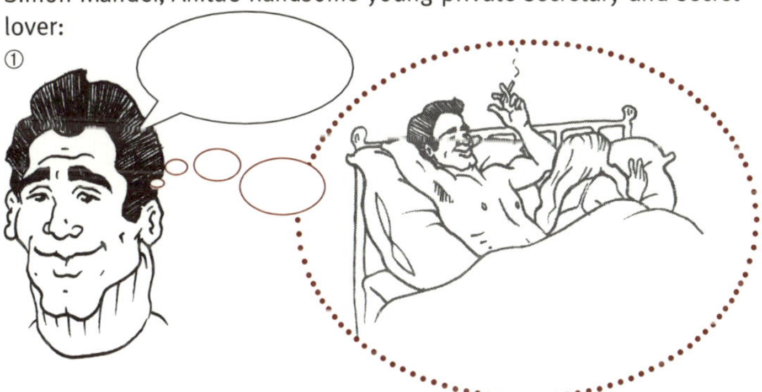

Sir Anthony, Anita's 60-year-old husband:

②

Exercises

Emma Barton, Anita's 22-year-old cousin:

③

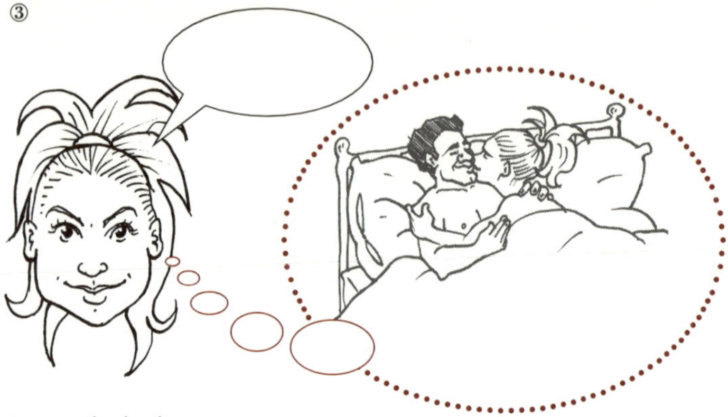

James, the butler:

④

5 Total chaos, but it was a brilliant party!

Complete the sentences using the verbs given in brackets. Put any adverbials in the correct position.

We _____[1] (have) a brilliant party last Saturday – totally chaotic, though. I had arranged to buy the food and drink, but just as I _____[2] (take) them to the car I _____[3] (drop) my car keys down a grid. So I _____[4] (run) home to get my spare car keys. When I _____[5] (get) home, Andrea _____[6] (phone) her boss. He had rung her to say that he _____[7] (want) her to pick up some work from the office. Then, while I _____[8] (prepare) the food, Dave _____[9] (ring) to say he couldn't come. Angie _____[10] (expect) a baby, and the contractions had started, so he _____[11] (take) her to hospital. Then Andrea _____[12] (come) back, so I _____13 (go) upstairs to have a shower and get changed. Just as I _____14 (get) out of the shower the first guests _____15 (arrive) – twenty minutes early – Andrea _____16 (still; put) the finishing touches to the salads! When Andrea _____17 (open) the door she _____18 (burst) out laughing. They _____19 (be) all in fancy dress – they _____20 (think) they _____21 (come) to a fancy-dress party. One of them _____22 (wear) a clown's costume, another one _____23 (pretend) to be a traffic warden – she _____24 (certainly; look) fierce enough. We _____25 (still; laugh) about it when the next guests _____26 (turn up). It _____27 (definitely; break) the ice, though. In no time at all we _____28 (swap) stories and jokes, and the party _____29 (really; take off) when the dancing _____30 (start).

Exercises

6 Focusing on recent actions

Form a question that fits into the situations described below.

Example

You see your sister Jane with jam on her mouth.
→ *Have you been eating jam?*

1 Your friend is wearing shorts and running shoes. His face is red and he is sweating.
2 Your father comes in out of the garden. He's wearing his old gardening clothes. They are muddy.
3 Your boyfriend calls at your flat. His breath smells of beer.
4 You drop in on your cousin Harry. He is dressed in old clothes and there are flecks of paint on his face and hands.
5 You have just arrived late at the disco, where your friend is waiting for you. He is looking at his watch.

7 Completed or not?

Underline the correct form of the verb in the following sentences.

Example

She's eaten / She's been eating five pork pies.
→ *She's eaten / She's been eating five pork pies.*

1 I've revised / I've been revising hard for my exams all afternoon.
2 Our team has won / has been winning the FA Cup three times.
3 I've read / I've been reading the book you lent me but I haven't finished / I haven't been finishing it yet.
4 Have you eaten / Have you been eating garlic again?
5 I've looked / I've been looking for that book the whole morning!

6 They've toured / They've been touring the US for the last six weeks. They've visited / They've been visiting ten major cities.
7 If you ask me, you're feeling off colour because you've worked / you've been working too hard.
8 Have you seen / Have you been seeing my wife anywhere?

8 Becoming a republic

Change the verb forms underlined into passive constructions.

Example

The country's foreign minister opposed the change.
→ *The change was opposed by the country's foreign minister.*

Jamaica's prime minister announced[1] yesterday that his country would become a republic in the near future. Several Commonwealth countries are considering[2] similar measures, as Britain's links to the EU become progressively stronger. They see[3] the Queen as an alien figurehead who no longer adequately represents their own societies. Many observers are predicting[4] that the number of Commonwealth countries opting for a republic will increase over the next few years. Barbados is also currently debating[5] a possible move to a republic, and although a majority of Australian voters rejected[6] republicanism in the 1999 referendum, political experts are assuming[7] that a change to republican status is only a matter of time. Buckingham Palace is monitoring[8] developments closely.

9 Eavesdropping

Fill in the blanks with the appropriate verb forms.

'Hey, Miranda. That _____[1] (look) like my ex over there, propping up the bar. _____[2] (you; see) who he _____[3] (talk) to?'
'No, but he _____[4] (seem) to _____[5] (have) a pretty lively conversation with the barmaid.'
'I _____[6] (feel) like getting closer to them to see what _____[7] (go) on.'
'Just stop it, Jane. You _____[8] (be) nosey again. You _____[9] (really; be) an inquisitive person!'

10 Mysterious Marek

Fill in the gaps in the text below, taking special care with the aspects. Put any adverbs in the correct position.

„Siehst du den Mann da drüben?“
'_____[1] *that man over there?'*

Exercises

„Meinst du den Mann mit dem Schirm, der an der Ecke steht?“
'_____[2] *the man with the umbrella, who* _____[3] *on the corner?'*

„Nein, der Rothaarige, der einen teuren Pelzmantel trägt.“
'No, the red-haired one, who _____[4] *an expensive fur coat.'*

„Ach ja, der Typ, der eine Zigarre raucht. Was ist mit ihm?“
'Oh yes, the guy who _____[5] *a cigar. What about him?'*

„Das ist Jessicas neuer Freund. Er nennt sich Marek und spricht
'That's Jessica's new boyfriend. He _____[6] *himself Marek and*

nennen = *to call*

mit einem starken ausländischen Akzent. Sie hat ihn vor einem
_____[7] *with a heavy foreign accent. She* _____[8] *him at a*

halben Jahr auf einer Party kennen gelernt. Da sprach er gerade
party six months ago. He _____[9] *to a friend*

kennen lernen = *to meet*

mit einer Freundin von ihr. Sie hat die beiden miteinander bekannt
of hers there. She _____[10] *the two to each other,*

jd. bekannt machen = *to introduce sb.*

gemacht, und Jessica fand ihn sehr attraktiv. Seitdem treffen sie
and Jessica _____[11] *he was very attractive. Since then they*

finden = *to think*
sich treffen=(here) *to see*

sich regelmäßig. Sie mag seinen aufwändigen Lebensstil – sein
_____[12] *each other regularly. She* _____[13] *his lavish lifestyle –*

schickes Auto, die Penthouse-Wohnung, die teuren Geschenke.
his fancy car, the penthouse apartment, the expensive presents.

Sie ist richtig verknallt in den Typ.“
She's really crazy about the guy.'

„Du scheinst aber nicht viel von ihm zu halten.“
'You _____[14] *to* _____[15] *much of him, though.'*

halten = *to think*

„Nein, da hast du Recht. Man sieht ihn oft mit zwielichtigen
'No, you're right there. You _____[16] *him with shady characters*

Gestalten im Rotlichtmilieu. Und Jessica hat mir erzählt, dass er
in the red-light district. And Jessica _____[17] me that he

sich benehmen = *to act*

sich in letzter Zeit ganz komisch benimmt. Er scheint sie im Augen-
_____[18] pretty strangely recently. He _____[19] to _____[20] her

meiden = *to avoid*

blick zu meiden, und wenn sie ihn zu Hause anruft, legt er – oder
at the moment, and when she _____[21] him up at home, he – or

Hörer auflegen = *to hang up*

jemand anders – den Hörer auf."
someone else – _____[22].'

„Das klingt alles sehr merkwürdig."
'That all _____[23] very weird.'

„Und ein guter Freund von mir meint, seine Firma Gasimport würde
'And a good friend of mine _____[24] his firm Gasimport _____[25]

unter die Lupe nehmen = *to investigate*

zurzeit von der Polizei unter die Lupe genommen. Auch Jessica
by the police at the moment. Even Jessica

überlegen = (here) *to wonder*

fängt an, skeptisch zu werden. Sie überlegt jetzt, ob sie nicht mit
_____[26] be sceptical. She _____[27] now if she

ihm Schluss machen soll."
ought to finish with him.'

III Tense & Aspect: The Perfective

III.1 Overview

definition

1.1 The Perfective Aspect

The Perfective consists of an aspectual contrast between Past and Perfect (for a definition of aspect, see Chap. II.1). The Past is used to express the concept of an action or state occurring during a period of time which the speaker sees as complete. By contrast, the Perfect is used when the period of time is regarded as incomplete. In English the categories Past and Perfect differ in their semantic functions and are therefore not usually interchangeable. The related Germanic languages Danish, Norwegian and Swedish have a similar distinction. Likewise, Spanish distinguishes between the *indefinido*, used for an event or state taking place during a completed period of time, and a Perfect implying that this is not the case.

History

This semantic contrast is relatively recent: in Old and Middle English the two tenses were often used interchangeably. Shakespeare, too, uses them in ways which are no longer acceptable (for examples, see Faiß 1989, p.303, Strang 1970, p.149 and Lass 1999, p.224f.). In the use of Past and Perfect with adverbials, some varieties of English such as American and Canadian English have retained greater flexibility than Standard British English, cf. *already, ever, just* etc. (see below, p.3, and Faiß 1989, p.304f.).

cf. German

In German the Past and Perfect are interchangeable in many contexts, the difference between the two tenses being largely stylistic. This is comparable to the pattern in French, where the choice of whether to use the *passé simple* or the *passé composé* (i.e. Perfect) is mainly stylistic. Similarly, in Italian *passato remoto* is restricted to formal, written language, while the *passato prossimo* is preferred in spoken and informal contexts. For German, compare:

1 *I saw him yesterday.*
2 *Ich habe ihn gestern gesehen.*
3 *Ich sah ihn gestern.*

formal/informal

Whereas in English the Past is used both in formal and informal contexts and in written and spoken usage, German prefers the Perfect for informal and spoken language, but the Past for formal and written language. In German the difference is also partly regional, with South Germans traditionally preferring the Perfect, whereas North Germans have been more likely to use the Past (cf. Rug 1993, p.66). This has resulted in geographically mixed types:

4	*Ich war gestern in Köln.*	('Northern' type)
5	*Ich bin gestern in Köln gewesen.*	('Southern' type)
6	*Ich war gestern in Köln gewesen.*	(mixed type, non-standard)

Past: completed period

In English, the Past denotes an action or state taking place during a completed period of time which is regarded as separate from the present. It is often, though not always, linked to the idea of definite time.

Perfect: past-present link

The Perfect indicates an action or state in the past which is seen as linked to the present. Many grammars describe this as 'current relevance'. It is also often associated with the idea of indefinite time, although this is not an essential feature of its meaning. Compare:

7	*I lived in Hull for 10 years.*	10	*I've lived in Cork for 10 years.*
8	*Did you ever see the Beatles?*	11	*Have you ever seen Madonna?*
9	*He never drank whisky.*	12	*I've never drunk whisky.*

Examples 7 to 9 denote a state, action and habit respectively during a completed period of time separate from the present. The Past in 7 implies that the speaker no longer lives in Hull, while 8 takes the Past because the Beatles no longer exist. In 9 the usual implication is that the habit is finished because the person referred to is dead.

By contrast, 10 to 12 refer to a state, action and habit which are linked to the present. In 10 this means that the speaker is still living in Cork. In 11 the sentence implies that it is still possible to see Madonna, e.g. because she is still performing. In 12 the Perfect shows that the speaker has not drunk whisky right down to the point of speaking.

same situation, different points of view

Past and Perfect can refer to the same situation, but they see this situation from different points of view, as in 13 to 16 below:

13 *I broke my ankle last week.*
14 *I've broken my ankle, so I can't go running.*

Example 13 describes an event taking place during a period of time which is completed, whereas 14 specifically states the result of the past event. This use of the Perfect is often known as resultative.

15 *We agreed to meet at six. Where were you?*
16 *Where have you been? I've been looking everywhere for you.*

In 15 the focus is on the plan to meet at six, which is a completed period of time. Hence the use of the Past, whereas in 16 the focus is on the location of the person addressed during a period of time leading up to the present.

signal words

Some adverbs usually only occur with the Past or Perfect. These 'signal words' are normally a very reliable guide on which tense to use in a specific context (see boxes below).

Box 1: Signal words for Past

The Past is used with the following adverbials of completed time:

ago	*on Monday*
at Christmas, at Easter, etc.	*once* (= einst, mal)
at 4 pm, at 6 o'clock	*the other day*
earlier this week, month	*until recently, until yesterday*

in 2002, in spring, in the afternoon	*when* (= wann?)
just now	*when* + clause (= als)
last week, last year, last Thursday	*yesterday*

Compare:

17 *Darren was playing in the park just a minute ago.*
18 *I could swear that was Elvis I saw just now in the supermarket.*
19 *We once had a Scotch terrier that could balance a ball on its nose.*
20 *Did you see that film about Cyprus on TV the other day?*
21 *Until recently I thought Prague was the capital of Hungary!*
22 *When did you last see your father?* (= wann?)
23 *When I was in Moscow, they were still renovating the Kremlin.* (= als)

Note

The conjunction *when* can also correspond to German *wenn*, in which case it can be used with the Perfect:

24 *It's always been raining when I've been to Bath.* (*when* = *wenn*)

Box 2: Signal words for Perfect

The Perfect is used with the following adverbials, which mainly express the idea of a link between past and present:

hitherto	*since* (= prep.)	*until now*
lately	*so far*	*up to now*

Compare:

25 *We haven't seen Rebecca lately. Have you?*
26 *She's been studying Russian since last October.*
27 *Until now I've always lived on my own.*
28 *We haven't had any problems with our new neighbours up to now.*

Note

The adverb of indefinite time *lately* is normally only used in questions and negative statements, but not in affirmative statements. In the latter case it is replaced by *recently*, which is not subject to any such restrictions. Note also that *recently* can collocate either with the Past or the Perfect, depending on its meaning in the context.

In England the Perfect is the normal tense used with the following time adverbs when the time referred to is not complete:

already	*just*	*not yet*
ever	*never*	*still*

In some cases they co-occur with the Past (see below, 3.1).
In other varieties, e.g. American English, they are used with both Perfect and Past. However, in recent years there are indications that usage in England may be changing, with speakers using the Past as well as the Perfect, at least in some contexts. This is probably due to the influence of American English in the British media, though regional factors (including influence from Scottish and Irish English) may also be involved. Compare:

29 *We've already discussed that. Let's talk about something else!*
30 *Have you ever been to Cologne?*
31 *The Kellys have just come back from a fortnight in the Bahamas.*
32 *Just imagine – she's never stayed in an English-speaking country!*
33 *I haven't finished my seminar paper yet.*
34 *Are you telling me you still haven't tidied up your room?*

Note

The adverb *just* can either be used as a time adverb or in the sense of 'only, simply' (cf. its use in example 17 above). In this latter case there are no restrictions on the tenses it can co-occur with. Compare:

35 *Sorry. I was just looking for my scarf.* (= *only looking*)

2.1 Past: Focus on past event or state

III.2
Normal Pattern

The Past is used when the focus is on a past situation which is seen as separate from the present. This can either be made specific by adverbials of completed time, e.g. *last week* in 36 below, or the context may imply it, because the emphasis lies on the past cause of a situation (37 to 40):

past cause of a situation

36 *I only spoke to her last week.*
37 *I bought these books in Edinburgh.*
38 *Where did you learn such fantastic English?*
39 *How did you get this job, Jim?*
40 *What did the notice say?*

Example 37 implies that the purchase took place when the speaker was in Edinburgh, a completed state. In 38 the speaker is interested in what led to the person acquiring a good command of English and in 39 in how Jim got the job. In 40 the focus is on the content of the notice when the person saw it.

2.2 Past: Historical events

The Past is used for historical events because the event is seen as taking place during a completed period of time, whether this is specified or implied.

41 *Columbus discovered America in 1492.*
42 *Sir Christopher Wren built St. Paul's.*

Although both St. Paul's and America still exist, the actions of building and discovering were completed long ago.

2.3 Past with Type 2 stative verbs

intellectual states

The Past is used with verbs referring to intellectual states (see Chap. II, 3.3, Type 2) e.g. *expect, imagine, know, notice, realise, think,* when the context implies that the state described by the verb is completed:

43 *Your house is much bigger than I expected.*
44 *We didn't know you were expecting a baby.* (i.e. Now we know.)
45 *I didn't realise he was a Catholic.* (i.e. Now I know that he is.)
46 *I thought she'd left for New York!* (i.e. Now I know she hasn't.)

2.4 Past used for expressing attitude

attitudinal past

The attitudinal past is used with Type 2 and Type 3 stative verbs to reflect a tentative attitude on the part of the speaker, often to express politeness. It is often combined with the Progressive in this attitudinal function (see Chap. II, 3.4, examples 98 and 99).

47 *We wondered if you could help us to find an exchange partner.*
48 *Did you want to speak to me?*
49 *Were you intending to buy this car, sir?*

Notice that a similar phenomenon occurs in German:

50 *Wollten Sie mich sprechen?*

2.5 Perfect with since/for (= German *seit*)

The tense used depends on the syntactic function of *since*, which can be a preposition, adverb or temporal conjunction. In the first two cases we normally only use the Perfect (but see below, 3.1, for exceptions). The German preposition *seit* translates as *since* when it refers to a point in time and *for* when it denotes a period of time: see 51 and 52 below. In 53 *since* is an adverb.

51 *They've lived here since the war.* (preposition *since* = point in time) — *since* (prep.)
52 *We've known them for ages.* (preposition *for* = period of time) — *for* (prep.)
53 *Tom left a week ago and we haven't heard from him since.* (adverb) — *since* (adv.)

since (conj.)

When *since* is a conjunction introducing a subordinate clause, the main clause always takes the Perfect. The subordinate clause takes the Past when the situation described is seen as a point in time which is completed:

Perfect – Past

54 *We've had nothing but trouble since we bought this car.* (conj.)
55 *Ever since we got here I've been feeling cold.* (conj.)

When the situation described in the subordinate clause is seen as a period of time, the Perfect is used in both clauses. This normally implies that the situations in both clauses occur parallel to each other over the same period of time. In this type of sentence the compound conjunction *for as long as* often occurs as an alternative to *since*:

Perfect – Perfect

56 *Ever since I've known him he's been a chain smoker.* (conj.)
57 *You've drunk at least five whiskies since you've been here.* (conj.)
58 *She's been going out with Jason for as long as I've lived here.*

Note

> A peculiarity of this use of *since* in 56 and 57 is that it in fact refers to a period, not a point in time.

In all three functions, viz. as a preposition, adverb and temporal conjunction, *since* can also be used with the Past Perfect (see 2.7 below).

2.6 Progression from Perfect to Past

A common function of the Perfect is to announce something which the speaker assumes is not known. We therefore often find conversations and news items beginning in the Perfect. Once the announcement has been made, the speaker then switches to the Past:

59 *I've just been to the pictures. They were showing* The Washington Werewolf.
 – *Did you like it?*
 – *It was a bit gory.*

60 *News is just coming in that President Zog of Ruritania has been assassinated. He was being driven to an official reception when a member of the Ruritanian People's Liberation Front threw a bomb at his limousine. His chauffeur was also killed in the blast.*

This switch from Perfect to Past is also common in news items in German. American English often replaces the Perfect by the Past for this announcement function (see the use of *I finished* in the cartoon below).

BLONDIE

2.7 Past Perfect

In English the Past Perfect (also known as the 'Pluperfect') contrasts with the Past, with the Past Perfect referring to a situation taking place before the one denoted by the Past:

61 *Janet came to Germany in 1990. She had learnt German at school in Scotland, but soon discovered that it was only enough to get by on. She had not anticipated having such difficulties.*

Use of the Past Perfect is normally only obligatory if the order of events in the narration is different from the actual sequence of events in reality, as in the two examples in 61. When the sequence is the same in reality as in the narration, normally the Past is used, though the Past Perfect is still possible:

62 *Janet (had) learnt German at school in Scotland and did not anticipate having any difficulties. However, when she came to Germany in 1990 she soon discovered that her German was only enough to get by on.*

after, before, since

Similarly, the Past Perfect is optional, provided the sequence of events is clear from the context, e.g. with the conjunctions *after, before* or *since*:

63 *After Mary (had) fed the cat, she sat down to watch TV.*
64 *We (had) had no experience with estate agents before we bought this house.*
65 *I hadn't heard from Jenny since she (had) left school.*

Both as a preposition, adverb and conjunction, *since* can also be used with the Past Perfect. Compare:

66 *They had been close friends since childhood.* (preposition)
67 *I met him once in Monte Carlo but I hadn't seen him since. I was shocked when he died in 1997.* (adverb)
68 *We were very sad when they moved to New Zealand. We had known them since they first arrived in Leicester.* (conjunction)

III.3 Exceptions

3.1 Past with adverbs normally signalling Perfect

Some adverbs which in British English normally collocate with the Perfect (see above, III.1) can occur with the Past when the period of time involved is completed. Compare:

69 *We already discussed that proposal at our last meeting.*
70 *Did you ever manage to contact that old flame of yours in Cuba?*
71 *We never got mugged when we were living in New York.*
72 *He was still waiting for us at the airport despite the two-hour delay.*

3.2 Present with since

Sometimes usage is not totally consistent, and the Present or Past occurs with *since*:

73 *It's at least fifteen years since we last met.*
74 *It was ages since we had had a drink together.*

However, in types like 73 and 74, the Perfect or Past Perfect is also possible in the main clause. For similar examples, see Swan 1995, §499.

Exercises

1 Usage survey: Which tenses do you use?

- Circle the alternative which you would use in German. If you would use more than one, number them in order of preference (e.g. 1 for 'most natural', 2 for 'second best' etc.).
- Speculate on why you preferred these alternatives. Compare your results with those of other native speakers of German.
- Translate the German sentences into English.
- Compare the German sentences with your English translation. What differences do you notice?

1 ❐ a „Hast du in letzter Zeit Paul gesehen?"
„Ja, ich habe ihn gestern in der Stadt getroffen."
❐ b „Hast du in letzter Zeit Paul gesehen?"
„Ja, ich traf ihn gestern in der Stadt."
❐ c „Sahst du Paul in letzter Zeit?"
„Ja, ich traf ihn gestern in der Stadt."
English: __________

2 ❐ a „Als ich letzte Woche in Venedig angekommen bin, ist es sehr heiß gewesen."
❐ b „Als ich letzte Woche in Venedig angekommen bin, war es sehr heiß."
❐ c „Als ich letzte Woche in Venedig ankam, war es sehr heiß."
English: __________

3 ❐ a „Ich habe heute Morgen so einen Hunger gehabt, dass ich mir ein Spiegelei gebraten habe."
❐ b „Ich hatte heute Morgen so einen Hunger, dass ich mir ein Spiegelei gebraten habe."
❐ c „Ich hatte heute Morgen so einen Hunger, dass ich mir ein Spiegelei briet."
English: __________

Exercises

4 ❐ a Johnny hat sich ein Spiegelei gebraten, während er mit Jennifer gesprochen hat.
❐ b Johnny briet sich ein Spiegelei, während er mit Jennifer gesprochen hat.
❐ c Johnny hat sich ein Spiegelei gebraten, während er mit Jennifer sprach.
❐ d Johnny briet sich ein Spiegelei, während er mit Jennifer sprach.

English: __________

5 ❐ a Am Montag habe ich einen Kuchen gebacken, und dann bin ich in die Stadt gefahren.
❐ b Am Montag habe ich einen Kuchen gebacken, und dann fuhr ich in die Stadt.
❐ c Am Montag backte ich einen Kuchen, und dann fuhr ich in die Stadt.
❐ d Am Montag buk ich einen Kuchen, und dann fuhr ich in die Stadt.

English: __________

6 ❐ a Wir haben den alten Kühlschrank dagelassen, als wir ausgezogen sind.
❐ b Wir haben den alten Kühlschrank dagelassen, als wir auszogen.
❐ c Wir ließen den alten Kühlschrank da, als wir ausgezogen sind.
❐ d Wir ließen den alten Kühlschrank da, als wir auszogen.

English: __________

7 ❐ a Habt ihr auch den Herd dagelassen, als ihr ausgezogen seid?
❐ b Habt ihr auch den Herd dagelassen, als ihr auszogt?
❐ c Ließet ihr den Herd da, als ihr ausgezogen seid?
❐ d Ließet ihr den Herd da, als ihr auszogt?

English: __________

2 Linking past and present

Form a sentence using the Perfect which combines the ideas of the sentences given and includes the verb given in brackets.

Exercises

Example

My hands were dirty. Now they're clean. (wash)
→ *I've washed my hands.*

1 We used to own a caravan, but we sold it last month. (sell)
2 I did know the name of Jane's fiancé but I can't remember it now. (forget)
3 I dropped this vase and now it's broken. (break)
4 Marleen flew to Rome on Saturday. She's on holiday there now. (go)
5 Leonard went to Switzerland, but he's back now. (be)
6 Until yesterday I was perfectly healthy. Then I got a cold. (catch)

3 Focus on actions

Combine the sentences given by using the Perfect Progressive together with an adverbial phrase of time beginning with *since* or *for* (= *seit*).

Example

Gary is playing a computer game. He began at 4 o'clock.
→ *Gary has been playing a computer game since 4 o'clock.*

1 It's snowing hard. It started about 6 pm.
2 Ralph is playing football. He began three hours ago.
3 I'm reading this book. I started it this morning.
4 He's on the phone with his girlfriend. He rang her up an hour ago.
5 They're climbing Mount Everest. They set off up the mountain last Tuesday.

4 Witnessing a bank robbery

You have just seen a bank being robbed. You are telling the police what you saw. Use the Past Simple or Past Progressive, whichever is appropriate.

1 I / stand / in the bank / waiting to be served / when / two masked men / enter.
2 They / make / customers / stand on one side of the room.
3 While / one of the men / force / cashier / hand over / money,
4 the other / keep / customers / covered with a sawn-off shotgun.
5 The man / who / cover / us with the shotgun / wear / jeans / suede jacket.
6 I / not / have a chance / to see / what / the other man / wear.
7 The man in jeans / talk / to the other one / when / they / leave / the bank.

5 Cartoons

Choose the correct captions for the following pictures.

1 a When Dad has been to the pub I can smell his words!
  b When Dad went to the pub I can smell his words!
  c When Dad was in the pub I can smell his words!

2 a I know why you've married Dad. It's because he looks like me!
  b I know why you married Dad. It was because he looks like me!

3 Mum and Dad make me share everything with my sister.
  a I've just shared my measles!
  b I just shared my measles!

4 I don't understand food.
  a I eat it for years and I'm not full yet!
  b I'm eating it for years and I'm not full yet!
  c I've been eating it for years and I'm not full yet!

5 a Towels are for wiping off the dirt after you washed.
  b Towels are for wiping off the dirt after you've washed.

6 Teacher said they ring birds to find out where they fly to.
  a I haven't even known they have phones!
  b I didn't even know they had phones!

Exercises

6 Situations

Fill in the blanks with the most suitable forms of the verbs given in brackets. Do not use future or conditional forms.

1 '_____ (you; hear) the latest? Fiona _____ (have) a baby.'
'When _____ (that; happen)?'
'It _____ (not; happen) yet, silly.'
'No, I _____________ (mean), I _____ (not; know) she _____ (go) out with anybody.'
'Oh yes, she _____ (know) him for almost a year. They _____ (meet) when she _____ (work) as an au pair in Gloucester.'

2 I _____ (see) Mike the other day. He seems to _____ (go) through a bad patch recently. He _____ (be) out of work for six months now, his girlfriend _____ (just; leave) him, and he _____ (have) a nasty bout of flu over the past fortnight.'
'Yes, I _____ (see) him a couple of days ago. He _____ (look) pretty grotty, I must admit.'

3 'I _____ (look) for you all afternoon, Charles.
Don't you remember that we _____ (arrange) to meet in the Throne Room at 3.30? Where _____ (you; be)?'
'Sorry, mother. Camilla _____ (ring) me on my mobile while I _____ (talk) to the plants in the conservatory, and I _____ (just; forget) what we _____ (arrange; earlier).

4 'She _____ (never; be) the same since she _____ (fall) in love with the art master. When I _____ (first; come) to this school she _____ (be) only thirty, and she _____ (be) at the school now for 20 years, but she _____ (remain) very eccentric. At least, she _____ (always; seem) a bit weird to me for as long as I _____ (know) her. In fact, I think that over the past few years she _____ (get) more and more peculiar. Recently she _____ (even; ask) one girl if she _____ (fancy) being painted in the nude by the art teacher!'

7 Choosing verbs and aspects

Choose a suitable verb from the list below, completing the sentence with either *Have you ever* ... or *Did you ever* ...

be • climb • eat • meet • play • think • visit • work

Exercises

Example

→ *Have you ever visited* Naples before?

1 _____ a mountain?
2 _____ in a band as a teenager?
3 _____ about how difficult being a teacher is?
4 _____ with handicapped people?
5 _____ on a TV quiz show?
6 _____ haggis when you were in Scotland?
7 _____ David Dimbleby when you were working for the BBC?

8 Error spotting

You are an English teacher at a German school. Your students have just done a class test. Correct their mistakes.

1 *The Romans, who have ruled Britain for almost four centuries, have built many roads during that time.*
2 *Marcus told his sister, "I didn't visit my uncle in Eburacum lately."*
3 *Serenas father asked, "Have you seen Serena earlier this week?"*
4 *Marcus said to Serena, "So far we had luck, but I'm sure, that Otho and Rautio are soon back."*
5 *The soldier says that the british king Cassivelaunus already told the Britains to fight against the Romans*
6 *"How has Nipius Ascanius found out, that Marcus knows about the mine?"*
7 *He said, "Since Britain has become part of the Roman Empire for 50 years, life is becoming easier for many Britains."*

9 Don't be too tense, for your sins will be forgiven you.

Translate the following sentences, taking particular care with tense and the use of *for* and *since*. To help with the correct translation, first write down in the space provided what part of speech *seit* and its compounds are. Remember:

- *seit* = preposition or conjuction
- *seitdem* = conjunction or adverb

1 Seit dem 1. Januar rauche ich nicht mehr. (seit = _____)
2 Er trifft sich heimlich seit einem halben Jahr mit der Freundin seines besten Freundes. (seit = _____)

sich treffen mit = *to meet*

3 Jemand hat ihr neulich Pralinen aus Belgien mitgebracht. Seitdem stopft sie sich mit belgischen Pralinen voll. (seitdem = _____)

sich vollstopfen = *to stuff*

wie ein Loch = *like a fish*

preisgeben = *to disclose*
Herkunft der Gelder = *where the money (come from)*

4 Seit er den neuen Porsche hat, fährt er viel zu schnell. (seit = ____)
5 Oliver trinkt wie ein Loch, seit Sarah ihn verlassen hat. (seit = ____)
6 Seit Jahren weigert er sich, die Herkunft der Gelder preiszugeben. (seit = ____)
7 Seit Boris aufgehört hat, so viel Wodka zu trinken, geht es ihm viel besser. (seitdem = ____)
8 Seit er in sie verliebt ist, sieht er die Welt mit anderen Augen. (seit = ____)

10 Tourist guide

Some friends from the US are on a visit to Germany. You are showing them round Berlin and visit the Emperor William Memorial Church. You go to the exhibition there and see a photo of the church taken shortly after it was built.

a In sentences 1 to 6, use the facts below to tell your visitors something about the main events in the church's history.
b In 7 to 12, use the photos below to point out to your visitors how the church and its immediate vicinity have changed.

1 built 1891-1895 in honour of Emperor William I
2 badly damaged 1943 during Second World War in an air raid

Archiv für Kunst und Geschichte, Berlin

3 after the war plans to demolish the church
4 public opinion in favour of keeping the original church
5 architect Egon Eiermann's solution: integrate the ruined church and the new church
6 new church completed 1961 (same year as Berlin Wall)
7 since that time one of Berlin's major landmarks
8 most of the original church demolished
9 only part of the church steeple remained intact
10 the square surrounding the church (Breitscheid Square) enlarged
11 trams (AmE: streetcars) superseded by buses
12 the Romanisches Café (east of the church) replaced by the 22-storey Europa-Center

11 No news is good news

Your American visitors have been scanning the headlines of your newspaper to find out the latest news. You offer to translate the articles they show interest in. Difficult vocabulary has been given to help you.

1 BRITISCHE POLIZISTEN BEI STRASSENSCHLACHTEN VERLETZT
Bei Zusammenstößen zwischen der Polizei und asiatischen Jugendlichen sind zwei Polizisten verletzt und 25 Fahrzeuge in Brand gesteckt worden. Vier Demonstranten wurden festgenommen. Eine Sprecherin der Polizei bestätigte, dass die beiden Polizisten nur leichte Verletzungen hätten.

street fighting • clashes • Asian teenagers • be hurt • vehicles • set on fire • demonstrator • arrest • spokeswoman • confirm • minor injury

2 ISRAEL SCHIESST LIBANESISCHES FLUGZEUG AB
Die israelische Luftwaffe hat eine libanesische Cessna abgeschossen, die in den Luftraum Israels eingedrungen war. Nach Angaben der israelischen Armee reagierte der Pilot des Flugzeugs nicht auf mehrere Kontaktversuche von israelischen Hubschraubern. Die Maschine wurde vor der Küste nördlich von Tel Aviv abgeschossen, der Pilot kam ums Leben.

shoot down • Israeli air force • Lebanese • enter Israeli air space • according to • army report • aircraft • react to • attempt by helicopter to make contact • off the coast • be killed

3 ANTHONY QUINN IST TOT

Der US-Schauspieler Anthony Quinn ist am Sonntag im Alter von 86 Jahren in einem Krankenhaus in Boston gestorben. Er war vor allem für seine Titelrolle im 1964 gedrehten Film *Alexis Sorbas* bekannt.

US actor • best known • leading role • Zorba the Greek • shot in 1964

4 SIEBEN MILLIARDEN MARK GELDSTRAFE GEGEN TABAKKONZERN

Der amerikanische Tabakkonzern Philip Morris ist nach der Klage eines krebskranken Rauchers zu einer Geldstrafe in Rekordhöhe verurteilt worden: Das Gericht in Los Angeles wies das Unternehmen an, dem 56 Jahre alten Richard Boeken mehr als drei Milliarden Dollar zu zahlen. Philip Morris kündigte Berufung an.

billion • fine for tobacco firm • record fine be imposed on • after it was sued by • a smoker • contract cancer • instruct • 3 billion dollars • announce • appeal

5 ETA: KEINE NEUE WAFFENRUHE

Die baskische Terrororganisation ETA hat gestern eine Fortsetzung ihrer Gewaltstrategie angekündigt. Eine neue „Waffenruhe" sei nicht vorgesehen, sagte ein ETA-Sprecher in einem Interview. Er fügte hinzu, dass ein Gewaltverzicht nur im Rahmen eines Friedensprozesses in Frage komme.

no new truce • Basque terrorist organisation • announce • continue • strategy of violence • spokesman • plan • renunciation of violence • be feasible • as part of • peace process

IV Future Time

IV.1 Overview

1.1 Future time reference

In contrast to the Romance languages, e.g. French, Spanish or Italian, English does not have a morphologically distinct future tense, i.e. a future tense which contrasts with other verb forms by means of different morphological endings. Compare French *je marche* (Present) with *je marcherai* (Future), whereas the corresponding English forms are *I am walking, I walk* and *I'll be walking, I'll walk*, where the future is expressed by the modal verb *will*. The use of the modal verbs *will* and *shall* as markers of the future results in some degree of overlap between future time reference and some functions of these modals (cf. Chap. VI).

For reference to future time English also employs alternative phrases such as *be going to* and *be about to* as well as the Present. In some respects English is similar to German, which uses the auxiliary *werden* or the Present. English differs, however, in making greater use of the *will/shall* future (compared with the German use of *werden*) and in frequently using *be going to* for future reference.

History

In this lack of a morphologically distinct future tense English conforms to the pattern in other Germanic languages. Originally, e.g. in Old English, the Present was used to denote future events. By using the modal verbs *will* and *shall*, English gradually acquired a specific marker for future reference, although both *will* and *shall* still retain their original modal functions (see Chap. VI). This use of modals to express future time is typical of other Germanic languages, e.g. Dutch, where *zullen* (related to *shall* and German *sollen*) can be used for future reference, and Danish, where *skal* and *vil* can be used as markers of the future, though less frequently than in English.

IV.2 Normal pattern

Part of the difference in meaning between competing types of reference to the future can be summarised as the distinction between internal and external factors. An example of internal factors is those cases where speakers express their intention to do something. External factors are involved when speakers predict the effects of external events, for example. See 2.1 to 2.4 for more detail.

2.1 Future Simple

shall vs. *will*

The Future Simple (also known as the Simple Future) consists of the modal auxiliaries *will* or *shall* linked up with the (Non-Progressive) Infinitive. Older schoolbooks quoted the 'rule' that *shall* is used for the first person singular and plural, *will* for the other persons, but this pattern was never common in North America, Ireland, Scotland or even the North of England. It seems to have been a rule concocted in the 18th century by prescriptive grammarians trying to impose order on a bewildering variety of usage (see Crystal 1995, p.224, and Rissanen, in Lass 1999, p.210ff.), spreading via the schools into usage, but it never managed to gain much currency outside the South of England. Modern usage favours *will* and, in informal register, the contracted form *'ll* in all persons, although in Southern British English *shall* is very frequent in the first person, and is still preferred for this function by many speakers in this region, especially in more formal register. Corpus grammars such as Biber 1999 (p.489) and Mindt 2000 (p.589), however, confirm the far greater frequency of *will* compared with *shall*.

A Internal factors: spontaneous decision

To express willingness to do something in the future, *will* is used. This is common when making a spontaneous decision, which will probably be carried out immediately or in the near future. It is particularly frequent when speakers offer to do something or when they agree or refuse to do something. The use of *shall* in these functions is unusual. Notice that in German the normal pattern is the Present:

The Sun, London, © News International Newspapers Ltd
Found in David Crystal, The Cambridge Encyclopedia of the English Language, Cambridge 1995

1 *'This suitcase is terribly heavy.' 'Just a minute. I'll give you a hand with it.'* (cf. *„Ich helfe dir dabei."*)
2 *'I desperately need a new hoover.' 'Okay, I'll buy you one.'* (cf. *„Alles klar. Ich kaufe dir einen."*)
3 *'Could I borrow that video we watched in class?' 'Sure. I'll bring it to class tomorrow.'*
4 *I've asked Angus to lend me some money, but he won't.*

Similarly, *will* or *shall* is used for promises or threats, which by definition have a strong link with the future:

5 *We promise that we won't forget to take the dog for a walk.*
6 *I'll sue you!*

Since these types of usage often imply that some condition may be attached to the statement, use of *will* is similar to *will* used in conjunction with conditional and temporal clauses (see also Chap. V):

conditionals, temporal clauses

7 *I'll sue you if you don't fulfil all the terms of your contract.*

B External factors: prediction

An important function of *will/shall* is to predict future events. In these cases the modal verbs come closest to being pure markers of the future:

8 *The earth's temperature will rise by up to 6°C as a result of global warming.*
9 *The literature workshop will be held at the University's English Department.*
10 *We shall be out all day on Friday. Why don't you pop in tomorrow?*

detailed plans

In formal style *will* is often used to refer to events that have been planned in detail:

11 *The keynote speech by the Environment Secretary will be held at 10 a.m. in the main lecture theatre. Refreshments will be served afterwards in the University refectory.*

In cases like 11 the Present Progressive (i.e. *is being held ... are being served ...*)is normally preferred in informal language.

permanent situations

When we predict permanent situations, we use *will* or *be going to*:

12 *Thanks to medical progress, people will live longer in the future.*

Predictions, like decisions, promises and threats, are often made more precise by referring to the conditions attached, resulting in a conditional sentence or temporal clause:

13 *You'll never pass your exams if you don't get down to work soon.*
14 *When we get home we'll have a nice cup of tea.*

Similarly, the prediction is often accompanied by words or phrases modifying the prediction or making it more precise, e.g. *I'm sure, I expect, I think, probably, likely*. In fact, we frequently use *will* to predict something based on our opinion or past experience:

15 *I think you'll find there are no tickets left for tonight's concert.*
16 *Why don't you come and stay with us over Christmas. The kids will be so glad to see you again after such a long time.*

Commands are frequently formulated as simple predictions, both in military contexts and as a way of emphasising the speaker's authority:

17 *The platoon will attack the enemy position at 0500 hours.*

18 *You will meet your contact on Waterloo Bridge. His code name is Simon.*
19 *Applicants will check in at the enquiries desk in the foyer.*

This use of *will* is similar to the use of *be to* (cf. German *sollen*) in commands (see Chap. VI).

2.2 Future Progressive

The Future Progressive is formed by linking up the auxiliaries *will* or *shall* with the Progressive Infinitive. One function of the Future Progressive is simply to denote an ongoing activity or state in the future, combining the meaning of the Future with that of the Progressive. This type of use is often accompanied by the use of adverbials like *this time next week* or *in a month's time*.

future actions, states

20 *This time next week we'll be basking in the sun in the Canaries.*
21 *Don't worry, Mum. Ann's parents will be waiting for you at the airport.*

It is also used to predict what the speaker thinks is happening somewhere else:

22 *I wouldn't ring them now. They'll be having their afternoon nap.*

An important way in which the Future Progressive contrasts with the Future Simple is that it does not imply a decision, promise, threat etc. Compare:

neutral reference

23 *We'll discuss Scots law next week.*
24 *We'll be discussing Scots law next week.*

Sentence 23 implies that the speaker has decided to discuss the Scottish legal system the following week. Depending on the situation, this could either be a prediction or a decision made on the spur of the moment, e.g. because the lecturer has run out of time and therefore wants to deal with Scots law later. By contrast, 24 suggests that Scots law was going to be dealt with in the coming week anyway, as part of the normal course of events. A similar example is the typical formulation used by an airline pilot when announcing details of the flight:

25 *We shall be flying at a height of 35,000 feet.*

Here too the implication is that 35,000 feet is the normal altitude used by airliners flying this route, whereas the Future Simple would imply a spontaneous decision to fly at this altitude. Since airline pilots do not usually wish to give the impression that not everything is running according to plan, use of the Future Simple is rare.

planned actions

The Future Progressive is also used to denote actions which have already been planned or decided.

26 *I'll be going to the supermarket at around 11. Can I get you anything?*
27 *Will you be passing the chemist's on the way to the supermarket?*
28 *Will you be needing your car this evening?*

In such cases it is similar in meaning to the Present Progressive used with future reference, and can usually be replaced by the Present Progressive without change in meaning, as 29 and 30 illustrate:

29 *I'm going to the supermarket at around 11.*
30 *Are you passing the chemist's on the way to the supermarket?*

However, the Future Progressive can sometimes be used where the Present Progressive would not be possible, because the verb concerned is stative (see Chap. II). Hence the alternative to the Future Progressive in 28 is the Present Simple in 31, not a Progressive **Are you needing your car this evening?*

31 *Do you need your car this evening?*

polite use

In questions involving the second person, the effect of the use of the Progressive is to tone down the force of the verb.
Compare:

32 *When will you pay back the $300 you owe me?*
33 *When will you be paying back the $300 you owe me?*

The tone of 32 is quite brusque, roughly comparable to German *"Wann zahlen Sie mir endlich die $300, die Sie mir schulden?"* In contrast to this, 33 is more polite, because it implies that the speaker

assumes that the person owing the money plans to repay the debt and is simply giving the person a gentle reminder.
Similarly, compare:

34 *Will you pick us up from the station?*
35 *Will you be picking us up from the station?*

Sentence 34 is a request without frills, almost with the force of a suggestion, as would typically be used between good friends or close relatives, whereas 35 is more tentative and thus more appropriate for polite requests to people the speaker knows less well. This polite force of the Future Progressive is also evident in invitations:

36 *Will you stay for supper?*
37 *Will you be staying for supper?*

Example 37 is more courteous, suggesting that it is regarded as part of the normal course of events that the person addressed should stay for supper. This use of the Future Progressive is comparable with the attitudinal use of the Progressive with stative verbs (see Chap. II, 3.4, examples 97 and 98).

However, where the subject is not animate there is often little or no difference between Future Progressive and Future Simple.
Compare:

38 *The next flight to Manchester will be boarding at Gate 17.*
39 *The next flight to Manchester will board at Gate 17.*

The Future Progressive is more common in informal register, and, like the Progressive in general, seems to be on the increase (see Chap. II). informal

2.3 be going to

As with *will/shall*, two main types of future reference using *be going to* can be distinguished, depending on whether internal or external factors are involved. This construction is normally restricted to informal style, where it is often realised as a weak form /gənə/ (the corresponding strong forms are /ˈgɒnə/ in British, /ˈgɑːnə/ in American English). Reflecting this, it is sometimes spelt ‹gonna›. This spelling, however, is restricted to very informal texts such as comics or pop song lyrics, and should not be copied in general. informal

A INTERNAL FACTORS: INTENTION

animate subject

The construction *be going to* is used to express intention, usually implying that a decision has already been made. In this function it is of course restricted to contexts where the subject of the verb is a person or animate being.

40 *I've decided I'm going to take early retirement next year.*
41 *We're going to get married at Easter.*

It is not normally used for spontaneous decisions. Compare:

42 *I'm going to bake a chocolate cake for my grandchildren.*
43 *I think I'll bake a chocolate cake this afternoon for my grandchildren.*

Whereas 43 is used when a decision is made on the spur of the moment, 42 usually implies that the decision to bake the cake was made earlier.

B EXTERNAL FACTORS: PREDICTIONS BASED ON PRESENT EVIDENCE

The phrase *be going to* is also used when external factors are involved, i.e. for situations where predictions are made on the basis of evidence currently available to the speaker. In this type the subject can be either animate or inanimate:

44 *It looks like he's going to win the Grand Prix.*
45 *It's pouring down. You're going to get soaked.*
46 *I feel awful. I think I'm going to be sick.*

Often *will* is an alternative possibility:

47 *It looks like he'll win the Grand Prix.*
48 *It's pouring down. You'll get soaked.*

However, the two types of future reference are not always equivalent in meaning:

49 *I feel awful.*I think I'll be sick.*

Use of *will* is not possible, since it would imply a spontaneous decision, whereas vomiting is usually an involuntary act.

In conditional sentences *be going to* is less common, with *will/shall* usually being preferred.

2.4 Present Progressive

The Present Progressive is one of the main ways of referring to future time. There is usually a close link with the present, i.e. the verb denotes something that is already planned, arranged or decided. Like most uses of the Progressive (see Chap. II), it does not normally designate a state.

present link: planned, arranged, etc.

Use of the Present Progressive with future meaning is usually accompanied by an adverbial of future time, e.g. *on Monday, next week, in two years' time*, although this is not obligatory:

adverbials

50 *I'm starting at university in October.*
51 *We're going to Greece again for our holidays.*
52 *You'll never guess who's coming for dinner!*

It is used for actions over which we have some control, and is thus not normally chosen to express actions involving external factors (e.g. *It's going to snow soon*, but not **It's snowing soon*.).

The Present Progressive is also used for actions which are just beginning and are therefore on the borderline between present and future reference:

actions starting

53 *Robert, I'm leaving you.*
54 *I can't play with you now. We're going to my granny's.*

2.5 Present Simple

The Present Simple is used in main clauses to express the idea that an event in the future is definitely fixed. It is used, for example, for statements linked to the calendar:

calendar

55 *New Year's Eve falls on a Wednesday next year.*

It is typically used for timetables:

timetables

56 *Our flight's at 19.15 local time. We land at JFK five hours later.*
57 *What time does the film tonight start?*

It is not normally used to refer to an arrangement made in advance.

It occurs frequently in the subordinate clauses of conditional sentences and sentences containing a temporal clause (see also Chap. V), where the main clause involves future reference:

58 *If he mentions that again I'll scream.*
59 *When we arrive in Brussels we'll give you a ring.*

Here the verb in the main clause unambiguously marks the time reference, so that the subordinate clause remains unmarked.

2.6 Other verb phrases with future reference
The phrases *be about to* (followed by the Infinitive) and *be on the point of* (followed by the Gerund) refer to events which will happen very soon:

60 *We're just about to have lunch. Could you call back later?*
61 *I don't think I can help you. I'm on the point of leaving. I've got to meet an important client.*

The phrase *be due to* refers to things that are expected or arranged:

62 *The space shuttle is due to dock at the ISS in an hour's time.*
63 *British troops are due to arrive at Skopje airport shortly.*

IV.3 Exceptions

3.1 Present Simple used with personal plans
The 'timetable' use of the Present Simple is sometimes extended to related senses involving a personal subject:

64 *We leave for Prague tomorrow at the ungodly hour of 5.30 am.*
65 *We march at dawn.*

Exercises

1 Past, present and future
Write sentences to illustrate the use of the Progressive in the past, present and future based on the model sentence. The first sentence is done for you.

1 Kim always cycles to work. He sets off at 7.30 am and gets there at 8 am.
  a At 7.45 am yesterday Kim *was cycling to work*.

Exercises

b It's a quarter to eight. Kim _____.
c At 7.45 a.m. tomorrow Kim _____.

2 Every day, 85-year-old Mrs Mackintosh walks to the shops between 9.15 and 9.45, regular as clockwork.
a At 9.30 yesterday, Mrs Mackintosh _____.
b Look, it's half nine. Mrs Mackintosh _____.
c At 9.30 tomorrow Mrs Mackintosh _____ to buy her bottle of Guinness. 'It's what keeps me fit', she says.

2 Which future?

Fill in the gaps in the sentences below, choosing a suitable verb from the list. Use either the Present Progressive or Future Progressive. In some sentences both are possible. Where only one form is acceptable, explain why.

get • go • lie • live • play • take • widen

1 Have you heard? Robbie _____ engaged! I'm totally gobsmacked!
2 We _____ to Venice in a couple of weeks' time. We're both very excited – we've heard so much about the city.
3 I've just been offered a job in South Africa, so I _____ in Cape Town for the next couple of years.
4 I'd rather we didn't go to Aunt Jane's this evening. It's Friday – she _____ bridge with her friends.
5 You can expect delays in Sharples Road – they _____ the road during the next few weeks.
6 Mary can't come this afternoon. We _____ her to the zoo.
7 Just imagine! This time next week we _____ on one of those sunny beaches in the Seychelles in the shade of a coconut tree.

3 Being polite

Ask polite questions by using the Future Progressive.

Example

You want to use your father's car tonight.
→ *Dad, will you be using your car tonight?*

1 You want to invite your boyfriend/girlfriend around for a meal this evening. You'd rather be alone. Ask your flatmate if s/he is staying in tonight.

2 You've written a letter that needs posting. Your mother's going shopping. Ask her if she's passing a postbox.
3 Laura borrowed some of your CDs a month ago and hasn't returned them yet. Ask her how long she's going to need them.
4 Your editor is expecting the next chapter of your book, but you're a week past your deadline and you still haven't sent it to her. She needs to know when you'll send it. What does she say to you?
5 You've invited your professor to a party to celebrate your graduation on 17th July. He's a bit forgetful, and you'd like to remind him about it.
6 Some friends have told you that they would like to visit you in March, but you can't remember exactly when.

4 Plan or prediction?

Choose the most natural form of the verb in the sentences below. Cross out the incorrect verb and tick the box marked 'plan' or 'prediction', whichever is appropriate.

		plan	prediction
1	Don't worry about my piranhas. They aren't biting / won't bite you.	❒	❒
2	The weather forecast says it isn't raining /won't rain tomorrow.	❒	❒
3	I'm going / I'll go to London tomorrow. Do you fancy coming along?	❒	❒
4	I expect Jean is getting / will get the job. She's so well qualified, and terribly competent.	❒	❒
5	'Have you decided what to do about your car?' 'Yes, we're selling / we'll sell it.'	❒	❒
6	I'm looking after / I'll look after my neighbour's plants next week while she's away.	❒	❒
7	The doctor is seeing / will see you now.	❒	❒
8	She's having / She'll have an interview at C&A's the day after tomorrow.	❒	❒
9	We're staying / We'll stay at a posh hotel in Scotland for our honeymoon.	❒	❒

5 Future situations

Complete the following sentences, using either the Future Simple or *be going to*. In some cases, more than one answer may be possible.

1 'Why are you tidying up your room? That's not like you.'
'My girlfriend ____ stay with me over the weekend.'
2 'Have you any idea how this new photocopier works?'
'Hang on a minute. I _____ show you.'
3 This film is so sad. I think I _____ cry.
4 It's very sultry. There _____ be a thunderstorm soon. Look at all those black clouds.
5 The next generation _____ have to clean up the environmental mess this generation has caused.
6 'I _____ do some shopping in town.'
'Good! I _____ come with you.'
7 'Look! There's been an accident.'
'How awful! I _____ phone for an ambulance.'
8 'What are you taking the hoover outside for?'
'I _____ hoover the car.'

6 Intention, prediction or plan?

Supply the missing parts of the sentences below, using *be going to* or the Present Progressive. In some cases both verbs may be correct. Tick the boxes to show whether the verbs express intention, prediction (i.e. *be going to*) or a plan or arrangement (i.e. Present Progressive). Sometimes more than one form is possible.

		intention	plan	prediction
1	'What _____ (be) when you grow up?'	☐	☐	☐
	'I _____ (be) an astronaut.'	☐	☐	☐
	'And what _____ (do) tomorrow?'	☐	☐	☐
	'I _____ (go) hang gliding. I've got to start somewhere.'	☐	☐	☐
2	Before I apply for that job I _____ (find) out more about the company first.	☐	☐	☐
3	Gene technology _____ (have) an enormous impact on people's lives in the next few decades.	☐	☐	☐
4	Watch out! That car's booby-trapped. It _____ (explode) any minute!	☐	☐	☐
5	We _____ (move) to Berlin next year.	☐	☐	☐
6	'I can't come round tonight, I'm afraid.' 'That's a pity. Sharon _____ (be) disappointed. She was looking forward to seeing you.'	☐	☐	☐
7	Who _____ (come) for dinner, Martin?	☐	☐	☐

Exercises

8 We can operate, but it _____ (leave) an unsightly scar. ☐ ☐ ☐

7 Holiday plans

In a couple of days you're going on holiday to Switzerland and Austria. You are ringing a friend, giving details of your holiday. Your diary entries will help you to remember what places you'll be visiting. Give all the forms that are possible, using the verbs supplied in brackets.

'Hi Janet. I'm afraid we can't come to your birthday party after all. We've decided to go to Austria for a week. We need a short break.'

'Sorry to hear you can't come, Moira, but you certainly deserve a break. How long _____[1] (be) in Austria, and what places _____[2] (visit) there?'

'Well, on Monday the plane _____[3] (take off) from Gatwick at 6 pm. We _____[4] (land) at 9.20 pm, local time. Then on Tuesday the tour operator has organised a guided tour of Vienna. That _____[5] (start) at half nine. On Wednesday we _____[6] (go) on a boat trip up the Danube, staying the night at Melk. On Thursday we _____[7] (visit) Melk monastery. It looks very impressive, on a rock overlooking the Danube. Friday _____[8] (be) reserved for sightseeing and shopping. And on Saturday we _____[9] (leave) Vienna at 10.15 in the morning and we _____[10] (get) back in London just over two hours later.'

V Other Tense Uses (Indirect Speech, Conditional Sentences)

V.1 Overview

Although tenses usually refer to the time of an action or state (see definition of 'tense' in Chap. II, p.27), sometimes they are used for other purposes. One type already mentioned is the use of the attitudinal past (cf. Chap. III, 2.4), where the Past is used to express a tentative attitude by the speaker, although reference is to a present situation. Likewise, the Past is used as a marker of indirect speech and to denote hypothetical events, e.g. in conditional sentences.

History

In indirect speech and conditional sentences indicative forms have replaced an older subjunctive, which was still common in Old English. In modern English only a few relics of the subjunctive remain. In indirect commands a present subjunctive is still common in American English, and the subjunctives *be* and *were* still occur in many varieties of English. This replacement of the subjunctive by the indicative is typical of many other Germanic languages. Even in German, where the subjunctive is still very common, it is being increasingly replaced in indirect speech and conditional sentences by the auxiliary *würde* (see below).

V.2
Normal pattern
definition

2.1 Indirect speech

By indirect speech, also known as reported speech, we mean speech or thoughts that are reported by somebody, usually another person. It contrasts with direct speech in being less precise in reflecting the choice of words of the original speaker.

punctuation

In contrast to German, indirect speech is not introduced by a comma, since there is usually no speech pause. Compare:

1 *Oliver says that he doesn't like fish fingers.*
2 *Oliver sagt, dass er keine Fischstäbchen mag.*

Direct speech is normally marked by using quotation marks (also known in British English as inverted commas). In British English single quotation marks are used, whereas American English prefers double quotation marks:

3 *'I really like your new flat,' Jim said.* (British usage)
4 *"I sure like your new apartment," Jim said.* (US usage)

Note

> Notice that the comma ending the quotation comes before the quotation marks, not after it, as in German.

structure

Indirect speech, like direct speech, consists of a reporting clause and a reported clause. The reporting clause gives details about the act of reporting (e.g. saying, asking, ordering etc.), while the reported clause lists the content of the message. In the examples below in 2.1 and 3.1 the verb in the reporting clause is underlined, while the verb in the reported clause is in red.

types

There are three main sub-types of indirect speech: statements, questions, and commands. They differ from each other in meaning, which is reflected in the verb used in the reporting clause. They also differ in the constructions used to introduce the reported clause:

statements

1 Indirect statements contain words like *say, think, write*. Often the verb in the reporting clause gives more detail about the action of reporting, e.g. *add, answer, explain, reply, shout*. Some verbs have to be followed by the (indirect) object: *assure, inform, persuade, remind, tell*. The reported clause of indirect statements is frequently introduced by the conjunction *that*:

5 *We thought that Amy was living in Lisbon.*
6 *The airline assured them that their luggage was safe.*
7 *She told Brad that she was leaving him.*

Note: Notice that in 6 and 7 it is not possible to omit the indirect objects *them* and *Brad* respectively.

omission of *that*

The conjunction *that* is often left out in indirect statements, especially in informal English and after frequently used verbs such as *say, think*. In examples 5 to 7, for example, it can be dropped.

questions

2 Indirect questions have words like *ask, enquire, wonder* in the reporting clause. The reported clause is introduced by *whether, if* or a question word. The use of *if* to introduce an indirect question is particularly common in informal contexts.

8 *She asked the police if her bike had been found.*
9 *Desmond enquired when the next train to Bath was.*
10 *I wonder what Mary did with my pen.*

Indirect questions differ from direct questions in having normal word order, without use of inversion or the *do* auxiliary.
Compare the direct question equivalents to examples 8 to 10:

11 *'Has my bike been found?' she asked.*
12 *'When is the next train to Bath?' Desmond enquired.*
13 *'What did Mary do with my pen?' he wondered.*

commands

3 Indirect commands are characterised by verbs such as *command, insist, order, say, suggest, tell, urge* in the reporting clause. The reported clause is a *that*-clause. With some verbs the construction *to* followed by the infinitive is a possible alternative (see also Chap. VIII).

14 *Len's mother insisted that he tidy up his room.*
15 *He ordered that the troops' rations be halved.*
16 *We suggested that they should stay the night with us.*
17 *I told him that he should stop complaining.*
18 *I told him to stop complaining.*

Another feature of indirect commands is the use of the Present Subjunctive (as in 14 and 15) or the modal *should* with the infinitive (as in 16 and 17). The subjunctive is only distinguished from the indicative in the 3rd person singular, where there is no ending on the verb. It is particularly common in American English, which in many cases is more conservative grammatically than British English. In British English the *should* construction is preferred.

Indirect speech often involves a change in perspective. The person reporting what someone else has said is usually in a different situation (e.g. place, time, talking to a different person) than the original speaker. This different perspective is often reflected in changes in three main areas:

- pronouns
- adverbials
- verb tenses

Compare the examples below:

19 Sarah and David are walking along Canal Street. Sarah says:

'I don't like walking here late at night.'

20 David is walking along Canal Street later, telling Alison what Sarah said:

Sarah says she doesn't like walking here late at night.

21 David is telling Alison what Sarah said about Canal Street, which they can see in the distance:

Sarah says that she doesn't like walking there late at night.

22 David is telling Alison what Sarah said about Canal Street, which they can see in the distance. He is using the Past (i.e. *said*) to show that Sarah made this comment on a particular occasion in the past:

Sarah said that she didn't like walking there late at night.

These changes in pronouns and adverbials are similar to those in German and other languages, reflecting the change in time perspective which usually accompanies reported speech:

23 *'I passed my driving test last Thursday,' Ann said.*
24 *Ann said that she had passed her driving test the Thursday before.*

The phrase *the Thursday before* in 24 refers back to the Thursday before the day when the direct speech in 23 took place.

English differs from German in that it changes the tense in the reported clause if the tense in the reporting clause is in the Past or Past Perfect. This is known as backshift of tenses, because the tenses in the reported clause are shifted, i.e. moved, one tense further back in the past. A similar shift in tenses in indirect speech also occurs in other languages, e.g. French, Italian and Spanish. backshift

tense in reporting clause	tense in direct speech		tense in indirect speech (reported clause)
Past or Past Perfect	Present	→	Past
	Past	→	Past (or Past Perfect)
	Perfect	→	Past Perfect

The following examples illustrate tense use in direct speech compared with that in reported speech:

25 *'I'm sorry.'*
26 *She said that she was sorry.*
27 *'We're going home.'*
28 *They said they were going home.*
29 *'I saw you in the park on Monday.'*
30 *She claimed she had seen them in the park on Monday.*
31 *'I've just won $400!'*
32 *He said he had just won $400.*

As indicated in the table above, backshift is often optional where the verb in direct speech is in the Past, provided the time reference is clear from the context (see also 3.1 below). Thus, in 30 the Past would also be possible instead of the Past Perfect.

cf. German

German usage in indirect speech is markedly different from the pattern in English. In spoken informal German, the indicative is common, although subjunctive forms are also frequent, especially when there is no other marker of indirect speech (e.g. verbs of saying etc., or the conjunction *dass*). In formal speech and formal writing, e.g. newspaper reports or academic prose, extensive use is made of the subjunctive. To complicate matters, distinct forms of the subjunctive are restricted to forms of the verb *sein*, to the 3rd person singular of any verb in the Present Subjunctive and to the Past Subjunctive of strong verbs, as the forms in the extract below illustrate (verbs in the reporting clause are underlined, verbs in the reported clause are in red):

> Der Verteidiger bat, an den Zeugen Kirffel einige Fragen stellen zu dürfen; als ihm dies gewährt wurde, sagte er, bevor er die Fragen stelle, möchte er betonen, dass es ihm nicht darum ginge, Kirffel, den er verehre und als zuverlässigen Polizeibeamten und makellosen Zeugen schätze, eine Falle zu stellen, seinen Bildungsstand in Frage zu stellen oder ihn lächerlich zu machen; Hermes erhitzte und verhedderte sich ein wenig, als er hinzufügte, die Frage sei, obwohl wahrscheinlich nebensächlich erscheinend, für seinen Mandanten von entscheidender Wichtigkeit. Heinrich Böll, *Ende einer Dienstfahrt*. Munich, 1969, p.25.

In colloquial German the subjunctive is often replaced by the indicative or by forms involving *würde*, as in 33 below:

33 *Sie erklärte, dass sie in Nürnberg wohnen würde. Sie würde die Stadt deswegen gut kennen.*

Note

Notice that one possible English equivalent to this sentence has a Past resulting from backshift, but not *would*, which would be the backshifted equivalent of *will* in direct speech, and thus impossible in this context:

34 *She explained that she lived in Nuremberg, so she knew the city well.*

For an alternative possibility using the Present, see 3.1 below.
The subjunctive in German is a particularly useful marker of indirect speech in long passages where there is no reporting clause. Compare the German and English texts below:

> Nach seiner Meinung habe ihr Verfasser Längen- und Breitengrade der wichtigsten Orte von Georgien gesammelt und daraus eine Tabelle angefertigt, von der er, J.-N. Delisle, ein Georgisch geschriebenes Exemplar erhalten habe. Dieses habe die Namen von Provinzen und Städten nebst Längen- und Breitengraden der Städte unter dem lateinischen Kolumnentitel *Ex mathematico persico* enthalten. Mit dem ‚persischen Mathematiker' sei wahrscheinlich Uluġ Beg gemeint gewesen. Der georgische Geograph habe seinerseits aus (geographischen) Lexika ausgewählte Namen in zwei Kolumnen registriert und danach zwei weitere Kolumnen hinzugefügt ... (Fuat Sezgin, Geschichte des Arabischen Schrifttums, Vol. X. Frankfurt, 2000, p. 426)

> In his view its author had collected longitudes and latitudes of the most important places in Georgia and compiled a table of these, of which he, J.-N. Delisle, had obtained a copy written in Georgian. This had contained the names of provinces and cities together with longitudes and latitudes of the cities beneath a column with the Latin heading *Ex mathematico persico*. Delisle surmised that the 'Persian mathematician' was probably a reference to Uluġ Beg. The Georgian geographer, he claimed, had in turn recorded selected names from (geographical) reference works in two columns, then adding two columns ...

Note

Notice that in English it is often necessary in these cases to supply reporting clauses (e.g. *Delisle surmised, he claimed*) whenever the context does not make clear whether the verbs involved represent the view of the original speaker/writer or that of the person recording the message.

2.2 Conditional sentences

definition

Conditional sentences normally consist of a conditional clause, usually introduced by the conjunction *if*, followed by a main clause. In this section and part of section 3, the verb in the subordinate clause is underlined, while the verb in the main clause is in red. The conditional clause expresses what needs to occur so that something specified in the main clause can happen:

35 *If I <u>get</u> promoted, we can buy a new fitted kitchen.*

The subordinate clause introduced by *if* sets out the condition necessary for buying the new kitchen. Other introductory words which express the idea of a condition are: *as long as, on condition that, provided, providing, supposing, unless*. Notice that when *supposing* is used, the main clause consists of a question:

36 *Supposing your theory is correct, what repercussions will it have for us?*

types

Conditional sentences can be divided into two main types: those containing open and those with hypothetical conditions. The semantic difference between the two types of conditional sentence is reflected syntactically in the tenses of the verbs. In both types of conditional sentence, however, the verb in the subordinate clause tends to be syntactically simpler: we use Present Simple rather than Present Progressive, or Present rather than Future, or Past rather than Conditional. This may be due to the fact that the major focus in the sentence is on the time in the main clause.

A Open conditions

Open or real conditional sentences are those where the speaker regards it as possible that the condition may be fulfilled. The speaker's attitude remains open and neutral, as in 37:

37 *If you want to learn a language well, you need to work hard.*
38 *If you say that again, I'll scream!*
39 *She'll find it hard in this class if she hasn't had much experience with Year 9 kids at a comprehensive.*
40 *If that was Jessica, why didn't she say hello to us?*
41 *If they're interested in meeting us, why have they never got in touch?*
42 *If you're visiting London, come and stay with us.*

Although the commonest tense used in the *if* clause is the Present (as in 37, 38, 41 and 42), other tenses can also occur, e.g. the Perfect (as in 39) and Past (as in 40). In the main clause the most frequent tenses used are the Present for habits, generalisations or timeless statements (as in 37), and the Future for future reference (as in 38 and 39). However, the Past, Perfect and Imperative can also occur (cf. 40, 41 and 42 respectively).

Note

Notice that the equivalent German forms in these sentences use the indicative, not the subjunctive, which is reserved for hypothetical conditions.

Compare, for example:

43 *Sie wird es in dieser Klasse schwer haben, wenn sie noch nicht viel Erfahrung mit Kindern der 9. Klasse an einer Gesamtschule hat.*
44 *Wenn das Jessica war, warum hat sie uns nicht gegrüßt?*

In formal English the old subjunctive form *be* is sometimes used:

45 *If this be true, the situation will need to be reassessed.* (formal)

In sentences like 45, speakers normally prefer the indicative, i. e. *If this is true ...*

Sentences containing a temporal clause introduced by *when, as soon as, after* and similar temporal conjunctions have the same tenses as sentences containing open conditions:

46 *When you live abroad, you become more open-minded.*
47 *I'll give you a shout when she arrives.*
48 *As soon as he comes in, we'll all sing 'Happy birthday to you!'*

Note

The difference between *when* and *if* (both *wenn* in German) is that *when* is used for something that will happen, whereas *if* is used for something that may or may not happen (cf. the equivalent *falls* in German, which has this meaning exclusively).

B Hypothetical conditions

Unreal or hypothetical conditions are those which the speaker thinks will not be fulfilled in the future (49), are not fulfilled in the present (50) or were not fulfilled in the past (51):

49 *If he stopped being so fussy, he'd have more friends.*
50 *They would be staying with us if we had enough room.*
51 *If you'd listened to me, you wouldn't have got into this mess.*

In hypothetical conditions like 49 to 51, the verbs are backshifted as in indirect speech. Conditions with present or future reference take the

improbable conditions

impossible conditions

Past in the conditional clause (as in 49 and 50). These are often known as improbable conditions, since they are unlikely to be fulfilled. Conditions with past reference take the Past Perfect (as in 51). They are frequently referred to as impossible conditions, since they can no longer be fulfilled.

cf. German

In German both the subjunctive (often identical in form with the indicative) and *würde* followed by the infinitive can occur in either clause. Which form is used depends on the verb involved and whether the register is formal or informal. Past subjunctives are common with some verbs of high frequency such as *haben, sein, kommen* (viz. forms like *hätte, wäre, käme* etc.), but rarely used with most other verbs which have a distinct Past Subjunctive form, e.g. *befähle, genösse* from *befehlen, genießen*. Compare:

52 *Wenn er aufhören würde, so pingelig zu sein, hätte er mehr Freunde.*
53 *Wenn du auf mich gehört hättest, wärst du gar nicht in diesen Schlamassel geraten.*

Note

Notice that the functions of *würde* and *would* are different: whereas *würde* is a syntactic alternative to the Past Subjunctive, *would* marks the hypothetical nature of the utterance and is normally restricted to the main clause (for exceptions, see 3.2 below). In German there are often two forms possible, e.g. in 52 *aufhörte* and *würde er mehr Freunde haben* would also be possible, although they are less common.

In English, an old Past Subjunctive form of the verb to *be*, i.e. *were*, occurs quite frequently in *if* clauses:

54 *If this were a feasible proposition, we would prefer it.*

However, the normal Past tense form is also possible, and is in fact more common. Compare:

55 *If solar energy was cheaper we would use it.*

Only in the idiom *if I were you* (*an Ihrer/deiner Stelle*) is this relic of the subjunctive more common:

56 *If I were you, I wouldn't go to there – it's too risky.*

The regular alternative, i. e. *If I was you* ... is also possible in informal British English. Notice that American speakers usually regard it as non-standard.

For conditions referring to the future, two additional constructions are possible, *should* (cf. a similar German construction with *sollte*), and *was/were to*, both followed by the infinitive:

57 *If you should finish early tonight, we'll go for a drink.*
58 *If serious delays should occur, motoring organisations would set up a hotline to advise motorists of alternative routes.*
59 *If I was to tell you I'd won on the lottery, what would you say?*
60 *If she were to throw in the towel, would you take over?*

Both types occur in improbable conditions (cf. 58 to 60), but *should* can also be used in open conditions (cf. 57).

In formal register the conjunction *if* can be omitted and inversion used to mark the conditional clause. This is, however, only common with the forms *should, were, had*. It corresponds to a similar construction in German:

61 *Should you wish to reconsider our offer, we can be reached at any time on this number.* (= *If you should wish* ...)
62 *Were that to be true, I would resign. (= If that were ...)*
63 *Had we known that you were ill, we would have visited you. (= If we had known ...)*

Summary

Summary of tense use in English and German

In the table below, the German tenses are marked in red whenver German usage differs from English.

Types of conditional sentences	English		German	
	subordinate clause	main clause	subordinate clause	main clause
1 open condition (general reference)	PRESENT	PRESENT	PRESENT	PRESENT
2 open condition (future reference)	PRESENT	FUTURE	PRESENT	PRESENT or FUTURE
3 improbable condition	PAST	*would*	PAST SUBJNC. or *würde*	PAST SUBJUNCTIVE or *würde*
4 impossible condition	PAST PERFECT	*would have*	PAST PERFECT SUBJUNCTIVE	PAST PERFECT SUBJUNCTIVE or *würde*

Examples

Type 1 *If people don't pay, we take them to court.*
Type 2 *If it freezes this winter, the pipes will burst.*
Type 3 *If he swore at me, I would knock his block off.*
Type 4 *If she had gone on holiday earlier it would have been better.*

V.3 Exceptions

3.1 No backshift in indirect speech

Backshift only takes place when the verb in the reporting clause is in the Past or Past Perfect. When other tenses are used, i.e. those related to the Present, viz. the Present itself, the Future, the Present Perfect, there is no change in the tense used in the reported clause of indirect speech.

64 *'I've had enough – I'm resigning!'*
65 *She says she's had enough – she's resigning.*

The Past of the modal verbs *can, shall, will, i.e. could, should, would,* is not affected by backshift since these forms are no longer true past tenses, i.e. they are no longer the equivalents in the Past Tense of *can, shall* etc., having acquired different modal functions (see Chap. VI). Compare:

66 *'Could you give me a hand?'*

67 *He asked her if she could give him a hand.*

As was mentioned in 2.1 above, backshift is optional if the verb in direct speech is in the Past, providing the time of the action remains clear, as in example 68, which is just as acceptable as 30:

68 *She claimed she saw them in the park on Monday.*

Where there is no change of time reference in reported speech, e.g. where the statement is still valid when the action reported is being spoken or written, backshift is also optional:

69 *He asked his solicitor, 'What are your fees?'*
70 *He asked his solicitor what his fees are.*
71 *He asked his solicitor what his fees were.*

Both 70 and 71 mean the same and are equally acceptable. Similarly, an alternative to backshift in 34 is the non-backshifted 72:

72 *She explained that she lives in Nuremberg, so she knows the city well.*

Backshift is also less common when referring to timeless states:

73 *Galileo insisted that the Earth goes round the sun.*
74 *Barbara was claiming that Copenhagen is the capital of Norway.*

However, it is perfectly acceptable to use backshift in these cases, too, i.e. *went* in 73 and *was* in 74.

3.2 Use of will/would in conditional clauses

The modal verb forms *will* and *would* are not only used for the Future and Conditional. They can also be used in polite requests meaning 'be willing to': polite requests

75 *If you'll take a seat, I'll be with you in a minute.*
76 *I would be grateful if you would be so kind as to reply at your earliest convenience.*

A second and related use of the modal verb *will* is when it means an insistence on doing something, usually implying stubbornness (see insistence also Chap. VI). In these cases the modal verb is always stressed and the contracted form *'ll* is not possible:

77 *If you will keep teasing the dog, of course it'll snarl at you!*

would in both clauses

In spoken American English conditional forms of the verb can be used in both clauses, especially with improbable conditions. This usage is very informal, and is unacceptable in more formal registers, especially in writing. It is not used in British English.

78 *What would we say if our neighbors would do that?* (US usage)
79 *What would we say if our neighbours did that?* (British usage)

3.3 Use of should for would in British English

In British English, especially in English used by conservative speakers in the South of England, *would* can be replaced by *should* in the first person singular or plural:

80 *I should complain to the manager if that happened to me!*

This usage is parallel to the use of *shall* for the Future (see Chap. IV). It is optional and less common than the use of *would*.

3.4 'Mixed tenses' in conditional sentences

In the majority of cases the sequence of tenses in conditional sentences is as listed in the summary in 2.2 (on p.90). However, the tenses characteristic of improbable and impossible conditions can also co-occur in some contexts:

81 *If you'd listened to me, you wouldn't be in this mess.*

The tense of the subordinate clause reflects the fact that we are dealing here with an impossible condition – the person addressed obviously did not listen to the speaker. The result is expressed in the main clause, and is still apparent at the time of speaking. Compare this with the regular sequence of tenses in 51, where the main clause has *you wouldn't have got into this mess*, implying that the beginning of the process lies in the past. A similar pattern occurs in German.

Exercises

1 Court case

Underline the correct alternatives in the extract from a report on a rather strange court case set out below. In some cases, more than one alternative may be correct.

The judge informed Mr Randall that he is / was / has been / had been found[1] guilty of the murder of Arthur Reginald Webster, Charles Patrick Trumpington, John Malcolm Kerr, Felicity Jane Stone, Karl-Heinz Müller, Juan-Carlos Fernandez and the Right Honourable Nigel Warmsley Kimberley on or about the morning of 19th December 1972. He asked the defendant if he has / had / has had / had had[2] anything to say before sentence is / was passed[3]. Mr Randall replied that he is / was / has been / had been[4] very sorry and is / was / has been / had been[5] really ashamed of himself. He added that it is not happening / will not happen / would not happen / would not have happened[6] again. He said it is / was / has been / had been[7] really awful to have murdered so many people in such a short space of time. He continued, saying that he regretted that he has taken / took / had taken up[8] so much of the court's valuable time listening to the sordid details of these senseless killings of mine / those senseless killings of his[9]. He went on to say that he will like / would like / would have liked[10] to make a very sincere and personal apology to the judge for his appalling behaviour throughout the trial. He thanked the police, explaining that people shall realise / should realise / should have realised[11] how difficult the work of tracking down dangerous criminals like himself is / was / would be[12] and emphasised that he wishes / wished[13] to inform them that their fine work is / was / would be appreciated[14].

Source (adapted): Monty Python's Flying Circus, Just the Words. London, 1989, vol. 2, p.45f.

2 A naval incident

Read the following text.

In October 1995 the following radio messages were exchanged between a US naval vessel and the Canadian authorities off the coast of Newfoundland.
'Please change your course by 15 degrees north to avoid a collision.'
'I recommend that you change your course 15 degrees south to avoid a collision.'

'This is the captain of a ship of the US Navy. I repeat: you change your course.'
'No. I repeat: you change your course.'
'This is the aircraft carrier USS Lincoln, the second biggest ship in the Atlantic fleet of the United States. We are being accompanied by three destroyers, three cruisers and several ancillary vessels. I demand that you change your course by 15 degrees north, that is one five degrees north, or counter-measures will be taken to ensure the safety of this ship.'
'We're a lighthouse. Your move.'

You are the lighthouse keeper involved in the incident. You have been asked by the Canadian authorities to submit a report. Use the cues given below to formulate your report.

1 The US ship requested that ...
2 We replied ...
3 The captain of the US ship then repeated ...
4 and we repeated ...
5 They then pointed out that ... ... the second biggest ship in the US Atlantic fleet
6 and that they ... ... by three destroyers, three cruisers and several ancillary vessels.
7 They demanded that ...
8 We then informed them that ...

3 Dog talk

Complete the translation of the passage below written in indirect speech by filling in the gaps with the appropriate form.

Der alte Pfarrer Kolb aus Huskirchen unterhielt sich leise mit seinen
Old Father Kolb from Huskirchen was talking quietly to two of his

beiden Pfarrkindern ... über ein Thema, das keinen der Anwesenden
parishioners ... about a subject in which none of those present

außer ihnen so recht interessieren mochte: welcher Hund
apart from themselves could work up much interest, viz. which dog

bellen = *to bark*

in der vergangenen Nacht in Huskirchen gebellt habe; Frau
_____[1] *in Huskirchen* _____[2]; *Mrs Wermels-*

Exercises

Wermelskirchen meinte, es könne nur Grabels, des Gastwirts
kirchen said it _____[3] Grabel the landlord's Alsatian

Schäferhund Bello gewesen sein, während Frau Leuffen auf
Bello, while Mrs Leuffen guessed it _____[4]

Berghausens Pudel Nora tippte, der Pfarrer aber hartnäckig die
Berghausens' poodle Nora, and Father Kolb stubbornly

These vertrat, es sei Leuffens, des Stellmachers Collie Pitt
took the view that it _____[5] Leuffen the wheelwright's

gewesen; er wies gütig darauf hin, dass er in seinem Alter gar
collie Pitt; he intimated that at his age he _____[6] a lot

manche Nacht schlaflos verbringe, er erkenne alle Hunde von
of sleepless nights and _____[7] all the dogs in Hus-

eine Nacht schlaflos verbringen = *to have a sleepless night*
erkennen = *to recognise*

Huskirchen am Gebell, und Leuffens, des Stellmachers Collie Pitt
kirchen by their bark, and Leuffen the wheelwright's collie Pitt

sei ein besonders sensibles, sehr intelligentes, eifriges Tier, das bei
_____[8] a particularly sensitive, very intelligent, keen

dem geringsten Geräusch anschlage; er finge schon an zu bellen,
animal which _____[9] at the slightest noise; it even

anschlagen = *to start barking*

wenn er, der Pfarrer, manchmal mitten in der Nacht, um den
_____[10] when, sometimes in the middle of the night,

Pfeifenrauch auszulassen, sein Fenster öffne, Grabels Schäferhund
he _____[11] his window to let out the smoke from his pipe, whereas

Bello dagegen würde nicht einmal wach, wenn er, was oft geschehe,
Grabel's Alsatian Bello _____[12] when, as often _____[13], he _____[14]

geschehen = *to happen*

nachts noch, um frische Luft zu schöpfen, einen Spaziergang durch
a walk while it was still night through "his sleeping village"

einen Spaziergang machen = *to go for a walk*

„sein schlafendes Dorf" mache [...]; was Berghausens Pudel angehe,
to get a breath of fresh air [...]; as for Berghausens' poodle,

Exercises

wach werden = *to wake up*

so sei der einfach zu bange zu bellen, selbst wenn er wach würde.
it _____[15] simply too scared to bark, even if it _____[16].

Source: Heinrich Böll, *Ende einer Dienstfahrt*. Munich, 1969, p.50f.

4 Early Pennsylvania

The text below is an account by Richard Townsend, a Quaker who came to Pennsylvania with William Penn, its founder. Summarise the contents by using indirect speech in the ways indicated in the cues. Change tenses, pronouns and adverbials as necessary. The text was written in the 17th century. Use modern English in your summary, avoiding any archaic words in the original text.

At our arrival we found it a wilderness; the chief inhabitants were Indians, and some Swedes, who received us in a friendly manner.
Richard Townsend said that Pennsylvania ...
And though there was a great number of us, the good hand of Providence was seen in a particular manner; in that provisions were found for us, by the Swedes, and the Indians, at very reasonable rates.
He stressed that ...
explaining that provisions ...
Our first concern was to keep up and maintain our *religious worship* [...] and, as we had nothing but love and goodwill in our hearts, one to another, we had very comfortable meetings; and after our meeting was over, we assisted each other in building little houses for our shelter.
He explained that ...
adding that as ...
Furthermore, he said, after ...
And as our worthy Proprietor treated the Indians with extraordinary humanity, they became very civil and loving to us, and brought in abundance of venison. As, in other countries, the Indians were exasperated by hard treatment, which hath been the foundation of much bloodshed, so the contrary treatment here hath produced their love and affection.
He described how William Penn ...
with the result that they ...
He concluded that just as, in other countries, the Indians ...
so the opposite kind of treatment ...

5 What if?

Exercises

Speculate on what will, would or would have happened in the situations described below. Form conditional sentences.

1 This is the situation: Jordan is walking along a street in central Melbourne. He sees a cyclist frantically trying to get his bike out of the tram track in which it is stuck. A tram is fast approaching. Jordan shouts a warning.
   a What will happen to the bike if the tram hits it?
   b What would happen to the cyclist if the tram ran into him?
   c What would have happened if Jordan hadn't shouted to him?

2 It is a dark and stormy night. Paul and his girlfriend Alison are having a cuddle on the couch in a little cottage on the Yorkshire Moors. Suddenly there is a knock at the door. Speculate what they would do if it was
   a a hiker who's got lost on the moors
   b a sinister looking man who says he's come to check the electricity meter
   c Betty Formby from the next farm, who wants to borrow a packet of sugar

3 Speculate how history would have been different if the following events hadn't taken place:
   a Jesus Christ was born.
   b Russia joined the First World War in 1914.
   c Adolf Hitler survived an assassination attempt in 1939.
   d Two atomic bombs were dropped on Japan in 1945.

6 Expanding sentences

Supply a subject and the appropriate form of the verb *to be* in the conditional clauses below.

Example

If in doubt, ask for help.
→ *If you are in doubt, ask for help.*

1 If deprived of insulin, Anne would die.
2 If about to drive a long distance by car, make sure you have plenty of sleep.
3 The hospital could have saved his life if contacted in time.
4 If depressed, worried or just bored, phone 0124-763921.

5 If diagnosed at an early stage, this type of cancer might have been cured.
6 The brain would die if starved of oxygen for such a long time.
7 If asked politely, she would probably have agreed to help.

7 The state of the world

Use the notes below to form complete sentences involving conditionals. In some cases you will need to or can use the Progressive Infinitive.

If the world's population could be reduced to a village consisting of 100 people which reflected the ratios of all the peoples to each other, this is what it would be like:

1 It / contain / 57 Asians, 21 Europeans, 14 Americans (from North, Central and South America), and 8 Africans.
2 There / be / 52 women and 48 men, 30 whites and 70 non-whites, 30 Christians and 70 non-Christians, 89 straights and 11 gays.
3 Six persons / own / 59% of the village's entire wealth and all 6 / be / from the US.
4 Eighty / live / in dilapidated housing, 70 / be / illiterate, 50 / suffer / from malnutrition, one / die, one / be born, one / possess / a computer, and one / have graduated / from university.

8 SOS – Save Our Subjunctive

a Where possible, replace the verb forms in the German sentences below by a subjunctive.
b Then decide whether you yourself would normally use this subjunctive.
c Translate the gaps in the sentences below into English, using the vocabulary given. Take special care with tenses.

verbraunchen = (here) *to use*

1 Wenn ich vernünftig fahren würde, würde ich weniger Sprit verbrauchen.
If I _____ more sensibly, I _____ less fuel.

2 Selbst wenn der korrigierende Lehrer das als halben Fehler rechnen würde, so wäre das immer noch besser, als eine Lücke zu lassen.
Even if the teacher correcting it _____ it as half a mistake, that _____ better than leaving a gap.

3 So einer wie er wäre vermieden worden, wenn man damals die Gentechnik erfunden hätte.
Someone like him _____ if gene technology _____ at that time.

4 Wer diese Steuerreform vorziehen würde, würde einen katastrophalen Fehler machen.
Anyone who _____ this tax reform _____ a catastrophic error.

5 Wenn mich der Taxifahrer fragen würde, ob er den doppelten Betrag auf die Quittung schreiben soll, dann würde ich selbstverständlich nein sagen.
If the taxi-driver _____ me if he should write out twice the amount on the receipt, of course I _____ 'no'.

6 Wenn Gott nicht vergeben würde, wäre sein Paradies leer.
If God _____, His Paradise _____ empty.

Exercises

erfinden = *to invent*

9 Making choices

Underline the correct forms in the sentences below. In some cases more than one form is correct.

1 If a fly didn't have / wouldn't have wings, would it be called a 'walk'?
2 If you try / are trying to fail, and succeed / are succeeding, which did you do / have you done / would you have done?
3 We hadn't got / wouldn't have so many international research projects if we didn't have / wouldn't have the students from abroad, and my life was / were / would be less interesting.

Exercises

4

My little brother gave me a big colouring book for my birthday. It had been / would have been / were nicer if he hadn't filled / wouldn't have filled it in first.

5

The Independent, 25 April 1998

I just want you to know that I'm not the kind of guy who tries to pick up strange women in bars, but if I was / were / would be that kind of guy, you were / would be exactly the kind of woman I pick / picked / would pick up.

6 If bananas are grown / are being grown / be grown in the laboratory under sterile conditions, they are / are being / be / will be much more susceptible to attack by parasites.

7 If a turtle doesn't have / will not have a shell, be it / is it / would it be homeless or naked?

8

The Spectator, 27 September 1997

If James were / had been alive, that's just how he had wanted / would have wanted it.

9

The Spectator, 19/26 December 1998

If it wasn't / weren't / wouldn't be for my confounded job, I were / would be in the Costa del Sol for Christmas.

10 Q: Do you know what had happened / would have happened if it had been / were / would have been Three Wise Women instead of Three Wise Men?

A: They had / would have asked for directions, arrived on time, helped deliver the baby, cleaned the stable, made a casserole, and brought useful gifts.

VI Modal Verbs

VI.1 Overview

definition

Modal verbs, also known as modal auxiliary verbs, are used together with other verbs to show the speaker's attitude towards the factual content of what is expressed in the main verb. The main meanings they express are PERMISSION, OBLIGATION, VOLITION, POSSIBILITY, PROBABILITY, PREDICTION. The core verbs in this class in English are *can/could, may/might, must, shall/should, will/would*, which show typical syntactic features of modal auxiliary verbs, e.g. they lack an infinitive or participle and are followed by the infinitive without *to* (see also below). There is some semantic overlap between modal verbs and future reference (see Chap. IV).

Some verbs or verb phrases like *be to, be able to, be allowed to, be supposed to, have to, ought to, would like to* share some of the semantic or, in the case of *dare* and *need*, the syntactic features of the core modals. They can therefore be called marginal modals.

cf. German

The German equivalents of both core and marginal modals are *dürfen, können, mögen, müssen, sollen, wollen*, which have a syntactic pattern similar, though not identical, to that of the English core modals. One striking difference between the two languages is that English makes greater use of marginal modals.

Text

> The central strategic fact with which we live, and with which our descendants must live for ever, is that of nuclear weapons. The development and use of nuclear weapons during the Second World War changed the way the world worked for good. Even before the First World War the international community may have been groping its way towards a system within which international agreement would control the characteristics of weapons that might legally be used in war and any conflict threatening war would be submitted to supranational arbitration. John Keegan, *War and Our World* (p.64f.)

The above sample illustrates some typical features of core modals:

- the Present has no *-s* ending in the 3rd person singular, cf. *may*.
- the Past forms of core modals do not have past meaning: *might* simply implies less probability than *may*.
- the core modals are followed by a simple infinitive without *to*.
- the modals can combine with complex infinitives such as the passive infinitive, e.g. *might be used, would be submitted*, or the perfect progressive infinitive, as in *may have been groping*.

History

The core modal verbs of Modern English have their origin in the preterite-present verbs of Old English, e.g. *cann* 'knows', *mōt* 'must' etc. These were still used as lexical verbs. For example, even in Middle English they could still be followed by an object:

She koude muchel of wandrynge by the waye.
'She knew a lot about travelling'.

Similarly, they could be used without a following infinitive, as is still possible in Early Modern English, cf. Shakespeare's:

Sister farewell, I must to Coventry. (Richard II, I, 2)

Notice that these patterns are still possible in German, as in sentences like *Er kann gut Englisch* and *Ich muss nach Hamburg*. From late Old English times onwards this class of verbs became more important, since it provided alternative ways of expressing concepts like obligation, doubt, desire etc., which had formerly been expressed by the subjunctive. Thus the increase in use of modal verbs was accompanied by the decrease in use of the subjunctive. These verbs have also undergone important semantic changes since Old English times: *can* is no longer used in the sense of 'know', as it was in Old and Middle English; since the 19th century it has been used more and more for permission (i.e.

corresponding to *dürfen*), where previously *may* was normal, for example in sentences like *Can I borrow your comb*? (see below, 2.1 A).

As in the case of verb forms used with future reference, we can distinguish between two main types of modal verb usage, according to whether internal or external factors are involved. By internal factors we mean factors implying some sort of human control over events, i.e. permission, obligation, volition. By external factors we mean events which involve assessment of a situation rather than human control of events, i.e. possibility, probability, prediction.

VI.2
Normal pattern
internal and external factors

2.1 Permission, possibility: can/could, may/might, etc.

A PERMISSION

Nowadays *can/could* is the most usual way of asking for or giving permission, especially in informal situations. Its German equivalents are *dürfen* and, in informal German, *können*.

can/could: permission

1 *'Dad, can I use your car tonight?'* (= *darf, kann*)
'Yes, you can.' (= *darfst, kannst*)
2 *Until 1918, only men could vote in British elections.* (= *durften, konnten*)

be allowed to

The marginal modal constructions *be allowed to* or, less commonly, the more formal *be permitted to*, can also be used instead of *can/could*. This is, however, only frequent where the use of *can* or *could* might be unclear or ambiguous, as in example 2 above:

3 *Until 1918, only men were allowed to vote in U.K. elections.* (= *durften*)

The past tense form *could* is more polite than can (cf. *kann* versus the more polite *könnte* in German). When the person who is asked for permission replies, they use *can*, not *could*:

4 *'Mr Mackay, I've got to pick Nicky up from kindergarten at 3.30. Could I finish work early today?'* (= *könnte*)
'Yes, you can.' (= *können*)

The modal *can/could* is also used for requests. Here, too, *could* is more polite and less direct than *can*:

5 *'Can you post this letter for me?'* (= *kannst*)
'No, sorry, I can't. I'm pushed for time.' (= *kann*)
6 *I need £5. Could you lend me a fiver?* (= *könntest*)

It is also used when offering to do things for people. Here, too, use of the past tense form makes the offer less direct.

7 *I can go to the shops for you, Mum.* (= *kann*)
8 *We could drop you off at the doctor's.* (= *könnten*)

may/might: permission (formal)

An alternative way of asking for permission is *may/might*. It is mainly restricted to formal situations, is more obviously polite than *can*, and far more common in written than in spoken English. Whereas *can* is the unmarked, neutral modal referring to permission, *may* is marked in that it often implies that the speaker or (in questions) the person addressed has the authority to give permission. The past tense variant *might* is not used to refer to past time. It is an even more polite alternative to *may*. The German equivalent is *dürfen*.

9 *May I see your driving licence, sir?* (= *darf*)
10 *Might I trouble you for a light?* (= *dürfte*)

Use of *may* is particularly frequent in polite, formal situations, as in 9, which is what the police might say when stopping a motorist. Both *may* and *might* are often used in polite formulas to make a comment or ask a question, as in 11 and 12 respectively:

11 *Your garden looks lovely, if I may say so.* (= *darf*)
12 *Ladies and gentlemen, might I draw your attention to the fact that our time is running out?* (= *dürfte*)

In official notices, *may* is often used to give or withhold permission:

13 *Students may not use the staff car park.*

B Possibility and ability
can/could: possibility (theoretical)

We use *can/could* for situations involving a theoretical possibility. The German equivalent is *können*.

14 *Even experts can be wrong, you know.* (= *können*)
15 *Could people survive in space without oxygen?* (= *könnten*)

This use of *can/could* is the equivalent of saying *it is possible* or *it would be possible*, i.e. *can* is a neutral way of showing that a possibility exists, whereas *could* implies that this possibility is less likely. A similar distinction occurs in German between *können* and its Past Subjunctive (i.e. *könnte* etc). Compare 16 and 17, which are alternatives to 14 and 15 respectively:

16 *It's possible even for experts to be wrong, you know.*
17 *Would it be possible for people to survive in space without oxygen?*

The idea of possibility or ability in the past is expressed by *could*. In this sense it corresponds to German *konnte*:

18 *Anything could happen in Shanghai in those days.* (= *konnte*)
19 *Even when he was four he could play the piano.* (= *konnte*)

However, *could* is also used for a hypothetical situation, where it is the equivalent of German *könnte*:

20 *They're crazy. They could be kidnapped!* (= *könnten*)

be able to

For complex tenses like the Future or Perfect, which need to be followed by an infinitive or past participle (which the core modals do not have), the suppletive form *be able to* is used:

21 *We'll be able to fill you in on this situation when we've heard from our correspondent in Moscow.*
22 *I've not been able to reach Miranda yet.*

Note

> It is unusual to find this construction being used in the Present, where only *can* is normal. The core modal *can* is also common in future reference:
>
> 23 *We can discuss this right now. I don't mind.*
> 24 *I can pop in tomorrow, if you prefer.*

be able to: past achievement (obligatory)

By contrast, the suppletive form *be able to* is obligatory when it refers to past ability on a specific occasion, i.e. what could be called 'past achievement' (see also 2.4). Note that in these cases it is wrong to use *could* as the past tense form (but see 3.1):

25 *He was just able to catch his plane in time.* (= *konnte*)
26 *Were you able to talk to him before he died?* (= *konnten*)

In this past achievement sense *be able to* means the same as *managed to* (i.e. *jemand hat es geschafft, etwas zu tun*).

may/might: possibility (specific)

Whereas *can/could* is used to express a theoretical possibility, *may/might* denotes the possibility of an event occurring at a specific place or time. It often corresponds to paraphrases like 'perhaps something will happen', 'it is possible that something will happen'. The German equivalent is *kann, könnte*.

27 *It may rain tomorrow.* (= *kann*)
28 *After last night's gales, the line may be blocked.* (= *kann es sein, dass die Gleise …*)

Notice that it would not be possible to use *can* in 27, since it would focus on the theoretical possibility of rain the next day, which is too obvious to need mentioning. In 28 the meaning is 'it is possible that the line will be blocked'. It contrasts with the use of *can* referring to a theoretical possibility in 29:

29 *The line can be blocked to prevent the hijacked train being taken to London.* (= *kann*)

Notice a further difference in the use of *can* and *may* when they are negated:

30 *He may not be there.* (= *Es kann sein, dass er nicht da ist.*)
31 *He can't be there.* (= *Es kann nicht sein, dass er da ist.*)

Sentence 30 means that it is possible that he is not there, whereas 31 means that it is not possible that he is there.

The difference between *may* and *might* is that *might* implies that the chances of an event occurring are less. Although *might* was originally a past tense form, and is still used as such in the backshift of tenses (see Chap. V), it nowadays does not normally have past time reference. Compare:

32 *We may deal with Romanticism. If we have time, we might touch upon Coleridge's contribution.'* (*may* = *Es kann sein, dass wir ...*; *might* = *wir könnten ...*)

The above statements would lead the listener to conclude that a discussion of Coleridge was less likely than that of Romanticism.

2.2 Obligation, probability: have to, must, need, should, ought to

A Obligation
have (got) to: strong obligation

The modal used for expressing strong obligation is the marginal modal *have to* and the informal alternative *have got to*, which means the same.
The verb *have* and the particle *to* nowadays form an indivisible unit, which is also reflected in the pronunciation /ˈhæftə/. This shows assimilation of the voiced /v/ of /hæv/ to voiceless /t/ in /tə/ . The same is true of the 3rd person singular of the Present / ˈhæstə/ (cf. the normal pronunciation of *has* as / ˈhæz/).

Note

Note that *have got to* is sometimes spelt *gotta* (with *have* deleted). This is, however, only normal in very colloquial texts, e.g. comics, cartoons, and is regarded as non-standard:

33 *When you gotta go, you gotta go.* (= *muss*)

AmE, BrE difference

In American English, especially in spoken and informal usage, *have to* is the normal modal used for strong obligation, with *must* being avoided. In British English the similarity in meaning has led to semantic specialisation, with the two modals no longer being exact synonyms. In British usage, *have to* occurs in situations where external authority is involved, e.g. orders by other people, laws, regulations, or the constraints of the situation itself.

34 *My doctor says I've got to take more exercise.* (= *muss*)
35 *The stop sign means you have to stop here.* (= *man muss*)
36 *Most UK schoolchildren have to wear uniform.* (= *müssen*)
37 *I've got to drive the children to school this morning. There are no buses running. They're on strike.* (= *muss*)

Note

Notice that we do not often use a contracted form of *have to*, e.g. *I've to*. Forms like *I have to* are far more frequent.

The distinction between *have to* and *must* is only normal in British English and only occurs in the Present (with present or future reference). For other tenses, only *have to* is available as a suppletive form:

38 *I had to change trains in Milan to get to Venice.* (= *musste*)
39 *They'll have to mortgage themselves to the hilt for their new house.* (= *werden ... müssen*)
40 *I've had to cancel my subscription to the Economist.* (= *musste* or *habe ... kündigen müssen*)

Note

Note that in these tenses we use forms of *have to*, not *have got to*.

In affirmative sentences, *have to* can be paraphrased as 'to be obliged to'. In negative sentences, *do(es)n't have to* means 'to be not obliged to'. The two correspond to German *müssen* and *nicht müssen* respectively:

41 *Do you have to apply for a visa for the US?* (= *Muss man ...*)
42 *You don't have to be stupid to work here, but it helps.* (= *Man muss nicht ...*)

An alternative form of the question, which is common in British English especially, is to use the question form of *have got*:

43 *Have you got to apply for a visa for the US?*

An alternative to *have to* in questions and negations is the marginal modal *need*. Compare 44 and 45 with 41 to 43:

44 *Do you need to apply for a visa?* (= *Braucht man ...*)
45 *You don't need to bring me flowers.* (= *Du brauchst mir keine Blumen zu bringen.*)

need: obligation

The verb *need* is classed as a marginal modal because it shows typical features of the modal, viz. non-use of the *do* auxiliary in questions and negations, no -*s* ending in the 3rd person singular of the Present:

46 *Need she take an umbrella, do you think?* (formal)
47 *You needn't worry about the exam – it'll be a doddle.*

However, it is important to realise that this modal verb pattern is restricted to the Present. It does not occur in other tenses, e.g. the Past, where *need* is used as an ordinary lexical verb:

48 *You see, you didn't need to worry about the exam.*

A second important point is that this modal verb pattern is only common in the English of the South of England. In American English and many other varieties the only normal pattern is that of the lexical verb, whatever tense is involved. Even in the English spoken in Southern England, the modal verb pattern is more common in negative statements (i.e. 47) than in other cases, e.g. 46. For example, in questions the lexical verb pattern is more common, with 49 being far more usual than 46:

49 *Does she need to take an umbrella, do you think?*

In fact, the lexical verb pattern is always a possible alternative in Southern British Standard, although many speakers prefer the modal verb pattern with *need* in negative statements.

Note that this alternation between lexical verb and modal verb use also occurs with German *brauchen*, which in colloquial and non-standard usage can be used either with a following *zu* and the infinitive, or without:

cf. German *brauchen*

50 *Ich brauche nicht (zu) kommen, oder?*

The core modal *must* is used when the obligation derives from the speaker or (in questions) from the person addressed. As was already mentioned on p. 108, this pattern is restricted to British English and to present and future time reference, with American English normally using *have to*:

BrE: *must* strong obligation

51 *Darling, you must take more exercise.* (= *du musst*)
52 *Must we go into that all over again?* (= *Müssen wir* ...)
53 *Tom, I must stop now – I've got to drive the children to school.* (= *ich muss* in both cases)

Compare usage in 51, where the speaker is the source of authority for the obligation, with the use of *have to* in 34, where the obligation is from an external authority, viz. the doctor. In 52 the speaker is asking for denial of a presumed obligation from the person addressed. The speaker in 53 uses *must* to express the idea of a compulsion which is self-imposed, i.e. not due to some external factor as in *I've got to drive* ... This is the normal implication with *must* in the 1st person. In 51 to 53, however, it is also possible to use *have to*, since in most contexts the obligation can also be regarded as involving some sort of external obligation. This is not always the case, however, as 54 and 55 illustrate:

54 *Oh, but you must stay for dinner!*
55 *People must realise how serious this crisis is.*

Here only *must* is possible in traditional British usage, since neither case can be regarded as due to external factors: in 54 the host or hostess is insisting on the guest staying, while in 55 the speaker is expressing her or his own opinion that the crisis is serious. However, this traditional British pattern seems to be being influenced by American usage, with *have to* being used in sentences like 55.

must not = nicht dürfen

The negated form of *must*, i.e. *must not*, does not occur in American English. Instead, *cannot* or an imperative is used. In British usage *cannot* is also possible, but is felt to be weaker than *must not*. Note that *must not* means 'you are obliged not to do something'. It therefore corresponds to German *nicht dürfen*:

56 *You mustn't park your car here. This is a no parking area. Go and put it in a car park.* (BrE)
57 *You can't park your car here. This is a no parking zone. Go put it in the parking lot.* (AmE)

The use of *mustn't* in British English in 56 is equivalent to saying *Sie dürfen hier nicht parken*. For American speakers, so is 57. For British speakers 57 would be similar to German *Sie können hier nicht parken*, where the type of compulsion is not specified.

should: weak obligation

The core modal *should* also denotes obligation, but the obligation is much weaker than with *have to* or *must*, and often simply implies that something is advisable or desirable. It is frequently used to suggest something. Its German equivalent is *sollte*:

58 *Look at all this litter! People should be more careful!*
59 *You shouldn't park your car here. There are a lot of traffic wardens patrolling in this area.* (= *Sie sollten*)

An alternative to the core modal *should* is the marginal modal *ought to*, which also denotes weak obligation. They are usually interchangeable in meaning, but *should* is more common than *ought to*, with the latter normally only occurring in affirmative or negative statements, not in questions. Note that although there is a contracted negation *oughtn't to*, it is less frequent.

ought to: weak obligation

60 *Going outside in this weather – you ought to have more sense!*

B PROBABILITY
have to, must, should, ought to

These modal constructions can also refer to external factors which affect the degree of certainty involved in an event. Just as, with reference to internal factors, *have to* and *must* imply strong obligation, so also, when referring to external factors, they denote strong probability. The German equivalent is *müssen*:

61 *That has got to be Florence in the distance!* (US usage)
62 *That must be Florence in the distance!* (traditional British usage)

Use of *have got to* in types like 62 seems to be on the increase in British English, probably due to US influence.

Similarly, just as *should* and *ought to* denote weak obligation with reference to internal factors, when referring to external factors they express weak probability. Notice that here the corresponding German modal forms are *dürfte* or *müsste*:

63 *That should be enough.* (= *Das dürfte/müsste reichen.*)
64 *Now that I've patched up the hoover it ought to last a bit longer.* (= ... *dürfte/müsste er eine Weile halten.*)

2.3 Volition and prediction: will/would, shall/should

A VOLITION
will/would, shall/should

The major functions of the core modals *will/would* and *shall* are to form the Future Simple or Progressive (see Chap. IV). In addition, *would* is used as a hypothetical tense marker in conditional sentences (see Chap. V). Apart from these functions, however, several minor uses of *will/would* and *shall/should* survive as relics of the original senses of volition and obligation respectively.

will: requests

The core modal *will* is used in requests and in tag questions after an imperative:

65 *Will you help me to carry these boxes?* (= *Hilfst du mir ...?*)
66 *Pass me the chutney, will you?*

We use *would* to tone down the directness of such requests and make them more polite:

67 *Would you give me a hand with this typing, please?*

will: strong volition, refusal

It can also be used to express strong volition, e.g. repetition of an action despite the negative consequences (see also Example 77 in Chap. V), or a refusal to do something. In these cases the modal is stressed:

68 *This PC will keep crashing. It drives me up the wall!*
69 *He would keep asking me the same old questions.*
70 *The twins have locked themselves in their room and won't open the door.*
71 *My car wouldn't start yesterday. I think the battery was flat.*

Notice that *would* in 69 and 71 implies past time reference, not greater politeness. Examples 68 and 71 are reminders that this strong volition sense is not restricted to animate beings. It can also be used for machines when we treat them as if they had a will of their own. There is no single German equivalent to the above uses, though *wollen* can be used for types like 70 and 71. In cases like 68 and 69, repetition can be expressed by the adverbial *immer wieder*.

want: volition

For the special kinds of volition set out above, *will/would* is used. In Modern English, however, volition is of course normally expressed by the lexical verb *want*, which is by far the commonest equivalent to German *wollen*. Originally meaning 'to lack' (a sense retained in the related noun), *want* has ousted *will/would* in this volition sense. The original meaning survives in the Selkirk Grace, a Scottish prayer traditionally said before meals, where *wad*, i.e. *would*, means 'want' or 'would like to', while *want* keeps its original meaning of 'lack':

Some hae meat and canna eat,	'Some have food and cannot eat,
And some *wad* eat that *want* it.	And some want to eat who lack it
But we hae meat, and we can eat,	But we have food, and we can eat,
And sae the Lord be thankit.	And so may the Lord be thanked'.

The core modal *shall/should* is used for offers meaning 'do you want me/us to do something?' Its German equivalent is *sollen*. In American English *shall* is not used, being replaced by *should* or alternative constructions such as *do you want me to*. In British English *should* is also possible, but contrasts with *shall* in expressing a more tentative attitude and is thus regarded as more polite. The same patterns occur in tag questions following *let's*:

shall: offers

72 *Shall I help you to carry these boxes?* (British usage)
73 *Should we take a look at the new apartment?* (US usage)
74 *Should we re-think our approach, perhaps?* (British, polite)
75 *Let's go to the seaside for the day, shall we?* (British usage)

B PREDICTION
will: prediction (present)

Apart from predictions with reference to future time, which account for the vast majority of uses of *will* and are dealt with in the chapter on the Future (Chap. IV), *will* can also be used to make a prediction or supposition about something happening somewhere else at the present time:

76 *That will be Rachel. She said she'd be popping in about 10.*

habit

Similarly, *will* is used to refer to a habit or tendency, either in the present or the past:

77 *Boys will be boys.*
78 *Jonathan will sit playing with lego for hours on end.*
79 *Even in winter Jessica would go for long walks in the forest.*

In 77 the meaning is that boys tend to behave in ways which we would expect of boys. The use of *would* in 79 to denote past habits is quite common in descriptions, e.g. in novels. It is fairly formal and is only used for completed habits (see also *used to* below).

2.4 Marginal modals: be to, be said to, be supposed to, dare, used to, would like to

Apart from the marginal modals already discussed *(be able to, be allowed to, need)*, whose patterning partly overlaps, either semantically or syntactically, with that of the core modals, there are also several other marginal modals which play an important role in the semantic field of the modal verbs. These are *be to, be said to, be supposed to, dare, used to, would like to*.

be to: plans

This construction denotes plans or arrangements for the future which are made in the present or past. It is common in official contexts. In a shortened form, with *be* deleted, it frequently occurs in newspaper headlines. In German, it corresponds to *soll* for the Present, *sollte* for the Past:

80 *Rumour has it that the Cabinet are to review defence spending.* (= *soll*)
81 *The concert is to begin at 8pm.* (= *soll*)
82 *The anti-globalisation demo was to be held in Trafalgar Square, but it's now been switched to Hyde Park.* (= *sollte*)
83 *We were to meet at a bookshop off Tottenham Court Road, but she never turned up.* (= *sollten*)
84 CABINET TO REVIEW DEFENCE SPENDING.

be to: orders

This marginal modal can also be used for orders and commands. These can either be direct orders (as in 85) or indirect orders via a third party (as in 86):

85 *Sergeant, you are to take these men on the assault course at the double!*
86 *Pat is to put this in a left-luggage locker at Victoria Station.*

be said to: reporting

This phrase is used to state what is generally reported about people or things. It only occurs in the Present and Past and corresponds to German *sollen*:

87 *She's said to be a very talented musician.* (= *Sie soll ...*)
88 *The food situation after the earthquake was said to be catastrophic.* (= *soll ... gewesen sein*)

be supposed to: reporting

One use of this marginal modal is synonymous with *be said to*. It too is restricted in use to the Present and Past:

89 *He's supposed to be one of the richest men alive.*

be supposed to: expectation

It is also used to denote expected behaviour, often implying that these expectations will be disappointed. In the latter case it is often the equivalent of *sollte eigentlich* in German:

90 *Brenda is supposed to be bringing the drinks for the party.*

91 *Mike was supposed to be meeting us here for lunch, but there's no sign of him, and it's now 2.30.* (= *sollte eigentlich*)

The marginal modal *dare* is comparable to *need* in only partly showing typical syntactic characteristics of a modal verb. It is also used as a lexical verb, which occurs in all tenses, whereas the modal verb construction only occurs in the Present. Compare: *dare*

92 *Some elderly people daren't go out at night.*
93 *Some elderly people don't dare to go out at night.*

In 92 *dare* is used like a core modal (cf. *can't*), i.e. without the *do* auxiliary and followed by an infinitive without *to*. In 93 it functions like an ordinary lexical verb. The meaning is the same in both constructions. In most contexts normal usage nowadays prefers the lexical verb construction, except in a few phrases:

94 *I daren't ask the boss for another pay increase.*
95 *How dare you?*
96 *I dare say you're right.*

In 94 the core modal construction is more frequent, while in 95 and 96 only the core modal type is possible. This is a typical example of an older grammatical pattern falling into disuse, with relics being preserved in isolated phrases.

The construction *used to* denotes habits and states in the past which are now finished. It implies that the situation referred to has changed. The construction derives from the verb *to use*, which in the past also had the meaning 'to do something as a habit'. In Early Modern English it occurred in this sense in the Past, Present and Infinitive. In Modern English, however, this construction is limited to the Past. Speakers nowadays normally treat it as an indivisible unit, as is evidenced by its pronunciation /ˈjuːsttə/, with its unusual assimilation of the voiced /d/ of *used* to the voiceless /t/ of *to* (for a similar phenomenon, see *have to*, p. 107). Compare: *used to*

97 *I used to live in Warsaw.* (= *Ich habe früher in Warschau gelebt*)

> Notice that *used to* is often a good idiomatic way of describing completed habits or states which in German would be expressed by the Perfect or Past combined with the adverb *früher*. In these cases it is normally wrong to translate *früher* by *in former times*.

In questions and negations, *used to* is problematic. It is still occasionally used with modal verb characteristics, i.e. without the *do* auxiliary, as in 98:

98 *I used not to like jazz, but now I do.*

The corresponding contracted form *usedn't* is nowadays rare. Because the phrase *used to* is treated as a unit, questions and negations are normally formed in informal spoken English by using the *do* auxiliary. When these forms are written, they are sometimes spelt as in 99 and 100:

99 *Did you used to live in St. Andrews Road?*
100 *I didn't used to like jazz, but now I do.*

However, since a combination of *do* auxiliary and Past is normally impossible (e.g. **I didn't liked it*), the following forms are usually preferred in written English:

101 *Did you use to live in St. Andrews Road?*
102 *I didn't use to like jazz, but now I do.*

would like to

The marginal modal construction *would like to* only occurs in this one tense. It is a more polite equivalent to *want*. It normally corresponds to *möchte* in German:

103 *'Mummy, mummy, I want an ice cream!'*
'Tim, it's rude to say "I want". "I'd like an ice cream, please" is what you're supposed to say.'

> Notice that there is a tendency in English-speaking countries to use more overtly polite forms such as *would like to*, where *wollen* would not always be regarded as impolite in German:

104 *Would you like to have another beer?*
105 *Willst du noch ein Bier?*

3.1 Use of could in past achievement sense

VI.3 Exceptions

In negative sentences it is possible to use *could* to denote past achievement:

106 *I'm afraid I couldn't reach you this morning. The line was engaged.*

Notice that it would not be wrong to use *be able to* here.

Exercises

1 The ideal partner

Write five sentences each on the personality and interests of your ideal partner (i.e. 10 sentences in all), selecting these from the personality traits and interests listed below. Arrange them in order of desirability as follows:

- essential: *must*
- preferable: *should*
- possible: *can*
- unnecessary: *doesn't have to*
- unacceptable: *mustn't*

Personality
adventurous • affectionate • arrogant • caring • considerate • conventional • fashion-conscious • fun-loving • have a sense of humour • intelligent • laid back • reliable • romantic • self-confident • serious • shy • untidy

Interests
children • countryside • cycling • dancing • films • folk music • gardening • going to pubs • jazz • motorcycling • opera • pop music • reading • sport • theatre • travel • watching TV • wining and dining

Example

My ideal partner must be affectionate.
→ *He/She should be intelligent, etc.*

2 Manners maketh man

Take your cue from this much-quoted 14th-century saying, which means that good manners and politeness are essential for a person, and make the following sentences more polite by changing or replacing the modal given by one which is more polite. Where possible, use the right degree of politeness for the situation.

Example

Can I use your mobile? → *Could I use your mobile?*

1 Can we meet at two rather than three, Marjorie?
2 Shall I carry that shopping bag for you, Mrs Rigby?
3 Will you pass me the salt, please?
4 We want to see the manager.
5 Can I ask you a favour, Sir James?
6 Shall we go over that again?
7 I realise that you're very busy, Your Majesty, but can I have your autograph? It's for our Bertie. He collects them.
8 I want half a pound of mincemeat and two lamb chops.

3 A protest letter

Fill in the blanks in the letter of protest below by using modal constructions which correspond to the German cues given in brackets.

Democracy can only flourish if each individual is involved in the decision-making process: we _____[1] (wollen nicht) and _____[2] (können nicht) stand idly by while war-mongering decisions are made with lightning speed, because we know that revenge begets revenge. Everyone _____[3] (sollte) be deeply perturbed by extremism and religious fanaticism. However, this _____[4] (darf nicht) lead to us seeking our sole salvation in military solutions. We are concerned that the climate of fear and uncertainty _____[5] (könnte) be misused in order to curtail our civil liberties. We _____[6] (möchten) warn against over-reacting to the threat of terrorism. EU governments _____[7] (müssen) exert pressure on the US administration to de-escalate the situation before many innocent lives are lost. Europe _____[8] (darf nicht) make the error of sliding into war at the beginning of the 21st century as it did at the beginning of the 20th century.

4 Which would you say?

Underline the correct alternative in the sentences below. If there is more than one possible answer, explain the difference in meaning.

1 It can't / may not rain this morning after all. All I can see out of my window is blue skies.
2 That footballer can't / may not be very bright, but he can certainly play football.
3 Did you say that Hong Kong was the capital of China? That can't be / may not be right. It's Beijing, isn't it?

Exercises

4 She can't / may not have been much to look at when she was young, but she was always the life and soul of the party.
5 I'll try to reach John at his office, but he can't / may not be there. He often goes for lunch round about now.
6 It can't / may not be true that the President is an alien in disguise. I've had sex with him lots of times – I'm sure I would have noticed!

5 Possibilities

Make the sentences below more exact, as shown in the examples. Use a modal construction expressing possibility or ability, putting it in the first space provided. Then put its German equivalent in the second space.

Example

We caught the train just before it left.
→ *were able to catch* *konnten*

Mozart played the piano like a virtuoso when he was six.
→ *could play* *konnte*

Jane's in the shower, I think.
→ *could be* *könnte*

1 Bertha, Queen of the Amazons, saved her handsome lover Gary Pratt from the jaws of the Giant Wombat.

_____ _____

2 It's possible that scientists are on the verge of discovering a method of prolonging human life.

_____ _____

3 Laura spoke five languages fluently at the age of 7.

_____ _____

4 I caught my glasses before they fell into Lake Constance.

_____ _____

5 This formulation will perhaps lead to misunderstandings.

_____ _____

6 Using this new method, a team of researchers reduced the cortisone dose by an average of 36%.

_____ _____

7 Even when Joe was a toddler he swam like a fish.

_____ _____

8 It's possible that Brian is going through a mid-life crisis.

_____ _____

9 The plants fended off the attacks of crop pests better than when conventional methods were used.

_____ _____

6 'Might' is right

A terrorist atrocity has taken place in Ruritania. The country's head of government, President P. Brehn, wishes to be re-elected at the forthcoming elections and is taking a very hawkish attitude. A critical journalist interviewing the president refuses to be fobbed off with vague answers: fill in the gaps using modal expressions.

'The car bomb that went off in Constitution Square was clearly the work of the Ruritanian People's Liberation Front.'
'No, surely, it _____ [1] the work of the RPLF, but it hasn't been proved yet.'
'We haven't found all the evidence yet, but it has their fingerprints all over it.'
'So you _____ [2] be sure, in other words?'
'On the contrary, we're certain that it was the RPLF.'
'What makes you think that it definitely _____ [3] be the RPLF?'
'Because they're the only group in Ruritania with the logistic capacity to carry out atrocities like this.'
'Are you claiming that in the whole of Ruritania there is nobody who _____ [4] build a car bomb? That _____ [5] be true, surely? The technology isn't exactly difficult. You're always emphasising how highly educated Ruritanians are – thanks to your government's policies – so surely they _____ [6] be able to build something as simple as a car bomb?'
'There is nobody so misguided and evil in Ruritania – apart from the RPLF – who would perpetrate such an atrocity.'
'They _____ [7] be misguided, but that doesn't rule out the possibility that they _____ [8] contemplate such a course of action.'
'Oh, "Might, might, might" – you are always talking about hypothetical possibilities!'
'On the contrary, I am questioning whether might is right – whether the country's leaders _____ [9] be allowed to uncritically assume that a group of people _____ [10] be guilty on the basis of flimsy evidence.'

7 Warning! Modals ahead

Complete the sentences by saying what the signs mean. Then speculate on what hazards they might involve. Use modal expressions and the vocabulary listed to help you.

40 m.p.h. • a radar trap • car in front • to get towed away • low-flying aircraft • major road • overhead • pedestrian • slippery • to crash into sth. • to fine sb. for sth. • to lose control of sth. • to park • to run into sb./sth. • to run over sb./sth. • to skid • to speed • to startle sb. • vehicle

Exercises

This sign means that you <u>mustn't stop</u>.
You might get fined by a traffic warden.

1 

This sign means that you _____

2 

This sign means that you _____

3 

This sign means that there _____

4 

This sign means that you _____

5 

This sign means that there ____

6 

This sign means that there _____

7 

This sign means that the road ahead _____

8 

This sign means that there _____

8 Error-spotting: equivalents of sollen

Correct any errors in the sentences below, using the first space provided. Give the German equivalent for the correct form of *sollen* in the second space. Take care: some sentences may be correct.

1 These chocolates shall be very good. That's what Linda says, at least.

_____ _____

2 You know, you are to be much more careful with these shoes – they were very expensive.

_____ _____

3 Ought I to lend you my mobile? Then you won't need to buy a phone card.

_____ _____

4 We should be meeting at the Irish Pub in Mowlam Street. I hope Pat hasn't forgotten.

_____ _____

5 Jane should be a very competent teacher. All the students like her.

_____ _____

6 Claire ought to ring this afternoon, but she hasn't so far.

_____ _____

7 Shall we treat ourselves to an Indian takeaway tonight?

_____ _____

8 We're not to be so arrogant towards developing countries, since the West is partly to blame for their poverty.

_____ _____

9 In for a penny, in for a pound

The British prime minister is to make a speech in favour of Britain joining the euro. As his ghostwriter you made a draft version of his speech. He likes it but wants it to be a bit snappier and less wordy. He has underlined the sections that he wants changing. Replace these by shorter modal constructions with the same meaning.

Ladies and gentlemen, over the past few months and years there has been much talk of the dangers to Britain of joining the European Monetary Union. It <u>is perhaps</u>[1] true that joining the euro is by no means a risk-free operation. Neither is life. We <u>are all required to</u>[2] take risks from time to time. In fact, if we <u>are not brave enough to</u>[3] take risks, it <u>is possible that we will</u>[4] later discover that we have missed the bus. Our European partners will <u>have no desire to</u>[5] take seriously a Britain which is forever standing timidly on the sidelines. If we are to be at the centre of the European project, it is vital that we[6] also share in the risks of that project. Of course it is not desirable that we[7] take unnecessary risks. That is why my Cabinet colleagues and I have insisted all along that it is essential that we[8] wait until the economic conditions are right. But neither is it advisable that we[9] be blind to the opportunities offered by the single currency. It is therefore necessary that we[10] remember that the bulk of our trade is conducted with Euroland. Using the same currency means that our exporters will be in a position to[11] cut costs, competing on a level playing field with other Europeans. In addition, it will perhaps[12] strengthen our position as an attractive location for inward investment from overseas. Many British people, of course, are reluctant to[13] give up the pound, which has served us well for over a thousand years. Yet we would do well to[14] remember that the pound itself derives originally from the Continent, and the system of pounds, shillings and pence which we used up to decimalisation in 1971 was an invention of the Frankish Empire. For the future of this country it is imperative that we[15] rediscover our European past so that we are able to[16] grasp the opportunities of our joint European future.

10 Situations

What would you say in the following situations? Use modal expressions in your answers. Choose the more polite alternatives in situations where you don't know somebody well.

1 A friend of yours is going on holiday to Sri Lanka. Tell her it's advisable to take anti-malaria tablets with her.
2 You are sitting in a crowded bus. A pregnant woman gets on the bus. You offer her your seat.
3 You're in a car with Ian. He is busy talking and doesn't notice that he is turning into a street with a no entry sign – it's a one-way street.
4 You recently saw a fantastic SF film, *Invasion of the Blob Monsters*. Tell your friend Steve that it's absolutely vital that he sees it.
5 Your elderly parents would like to visit you in New Zealand, but they are very nervous about changing planes in Singapore or Sydney. Tell them it's not necessary to change – there are through flights available.
6 The small but dynamic dot.com firm you work for has been awarded a lucrative contract. The staff have spontaneously

decided to go out and celebrate at an Indian restaurant. A new colleague, Yè Liú, is hesitant. You don't know him very well, but you want to encourage him to come along.

7 You are in a pub with Jimmy, your best friend. He is going to the bar to order the next round of drinks. You'd like a bag of salt and vinegar crisps and a packet of peanuts. What do you say to him?

8 You are Jimmy, getting the round of drinks. Ask the rest of the people you're buying the drinks for if they want you to get some crisps as well.

11 A macho's world

Fill in the gaps in the text below, taking particular care with modals.

Es gibt Männer, die nicht wollen, dass ihre Frauen arbeiten gehen.
There are men who _____[1] go out to work.

Mein Freund Herbert z. B. meint, seine Frau sollte zu Hause
My friend Herbert, for example, says his wife _____[2] stay at

bleiben, weil er als ehrlicher Grundstücksspekulant so viel Geld
home, because he earns so much money working as an honest

verdient, dass sie gar nicht arbeiten muss. Er hat ihr sogar gesagt,
property speculator that she _____[3] work at all. He even told her

sie muss zu Hause bleiben. Er sieht nämlich nicht ein, warum er
she_____[4] stay at home. After all, he doesn't see why he

sich ein eigenes Abendessen machen sollte. Und er kann es einfach
_____[5] make his own dinner. And he _____[6] stand it

nicht ausstehen, wenn er abends nach Hause kommt und sich
when he comes home at night and _____[7] get his slippers

selber seine Pantoffeln holen muss: Wer weiß – nach einem langen
himself: who knows – after a long day at work he _____[8] injure

Arbeitstag könnte er sich ja verletzen! Ich konnte ihn zwar über-
himself! *Admittedly, I _____[9]*

Exercises

zeugen, dass ein so kräftiger Kerl wie er das doch mit links schaffen
convince him that it _____[10] be a walkover for such a big strapping

müsste, aber er will trotzdem nicht, dass Jessica arbeiten geht. Jessica
guy as him, but he still _____[11] go out to work. However,

kann allerdings damit leben, den ganzen Tag zu Hause zu bleiben.
Jessica _____[12] live with staying at home all day.

Inzwischen kriegt sie regelmäßig Besuch von einem charmanten,
She now gets regular visits from a charming young insurance

jungen Versicherungsvertreter, und sie soll seine ausführlichen
salesman and _____[13] finding his detailed explanations on

Erläuterungen zu Herberts geplanter Lebensversicherung viel
Herbert's projected life insurance much more interesting than

interessanter finden als die Stelle als Lehrerin, die sie früher hatte ...
the job as a schoolteacher which she _____[14] have ...

VII The Participle

VII.1 Overview

definition
finite, non-finite

Participles, like the Infinitive, are a non-finite form of the verb, i. e. they can only occur on their own in a subordinate clause and are not limited by tense, number and mood, as finite forms of the verb are. For example, with a non-finite form like *being English* we do not know what time or how many people are involved until this is made clear by the finite verb in the main clause:

1 *Being English, I like a good joke.*
2 *Being English, they were hopeless at foreign languages.*

'present' and 'past' participles

There are two kinds of participle in English. One is traditionally known as the Present Participle, formed by adding *-ing* to the stem of the word, e. g. *living, crying, swimming, tearing, taking*. The conventional term used for the other is the Past Participle, which in regular verbs is formed by adding *-ed* to the stem, e. g. *lived, cried*. In the case of the irregular verbs known as strong verbs, the Past Participle is formed by a change in the vowel of the stem and/or the addition of the suffix *-(e)n*, e. g. *swum, torn, taken*. Other irregular verbs such as *cut, put*, have the same form in the Past Participle as the Infinitive. The Past

Participle has passive meaning if derived from a transitive verb, i.e. a verb taking an object, and active meaning if it is from an intransitive verb (see 3.1 for exceptions).

compound participles

There are also compound forms of the Past Participle: the Passive Participle *(being taken)*, the Perfect Active Participle to indicate one action or state occurring before another *(having taken)* and a combination of the two, the Perfect Passive Participle *(having been taken)*. The latter is rare, being restricted to formal register. The Perfect Active Participle tends to occur only when use of the Present Participle might lead to confusion about the time reference.

terminology

The terms Present Participle and Past Participle are not particularly accurate, since both the Present and the Past Participle can refer to past, present and future, as is illustrated by examples 1 to 5:

3 *That shirt was torn, but I've mended it.*
4 *Don't put these trousers on – they're torn.*
5 *If you climb over that barbed wire, your shorts will get torn.*

The meaning of the Present and Past Participle might be better described as imperfective and perfective respectively, since the Present Participle implies that the action or state is not necessarily completed, while the Past Participle denotes that the action or state is completed. Many modern grammars prefer to use the semantically neutral terms *-ing* form and *-en* form. However, the latter term is misleading, since most '*-en*' forms in fact end in *-ed*, and both terms are rather clumsy. We will, therefore, continue to use the traditional terms, despite their defects.

Both participles can either have adjectival or adverbial functions, as can be seen from examples 6 to 9:

6 *She caught a falling leaf in her hand.*
7 *The lost jewellery was discovered in a left-luggage locker.*

cf. German

The participles in 6 and 7 function like adjectives, cf. *a falling leaf, the lost jewellery* and their German equivalents *ein fallendes Blatt, der verlorene Schmuck*.

8 *Taking off her glasses, she wandered over to the window.*

9 *Used properly, this bike could last a lifetime.*

In 8 and 9 the participles behave like adverbials. They modify the verb of the main clause, giving more details in 8 on what was happening when the woman went to the window (viz. after removing her glasses) and how, in 9, the bike could last a lifetime (viz. if it is used properly). German does not use the Present Participle for this adverbial function, though there are comparable constructions in other languages, e.g. French (the *participe*), in Italian and Spanish (the *gerundio*) and in Russian.

cf. French, etc.

The Present Participle ends in *-ing* like the Gerund (see Chap. VIII). The difference between the two lies in their syntactic pattern. Whereas the Participle functions like a verb, the Gerund, though having verbal meaning, behaves like a noun. The Participle and Gerund, in fact, can be seen as elements in a continuum extending from a verb to a noun, with the deverbal noun being a fully-fledged noun which, however, began life as a verb:

Present Participle vs. Gerund

Type	Examples
Participle	*When building a house, construction firms need to take many factors into consideration.*
Gerund	*Building houses is expensive.*
Verbal noun	*The building of the Pyramids was a stupendous feat.*
Deverbal noun	*A lot of buildings were destroyed in the earthquake.*

In the above table, the participle clause has the same function as a subordinate clause *When they build a house ...* . The gerund *Building houses* is the subject of the sentence, i.e. it functions like a noun. The verbal noun (also referred to as the 'gerund' in some handbooks) contains more nominal, i.e. noun-like, features than the Gerund, e.g. it can be preceded by the definite article and followed by the preposition *of*, which are typical features of nouns. Finally, the deverbal noun, although it is derived from a verb, nowadays shows all the attributes of a noun, e.g. it can be used in the plural.

In actual usage it is not always easy to distinguish clearly between the Gerund and the Participle – there are sometimes fuzzy edges between different parts of the continuum (for a discussion of the problems, see

terminology

Quirk 1985, §17.54, note [a]). For this reason some grammars do not distinguish between the two, e.g. Quirk 1985 and Lamprecht 1989. Others do distinguish, but do not use the word *gerund*, preferring the term *-ing form*, e.g. Broughton 1990 and Hewings 1999. Since the Gerund and Participle in general show a spectrum of functions which can be distinguished fairly clearly, we will retain these two terms, as do the *Cornelsen English Grammar* and Ungerer 2000. Terms like *Present Participle, Past Participle*, and *Gerund* are at least in part unsatisfactory because they were originally terms taken from Latin grammar, which were then used to describe the different grammatical pattern of English (cf. Lamprecht 1989, §868 and Quirk 1985, §17.54, note [a]).

stylistic uses

Both the Present and Past Participle and the Gerund are very versatile constructions. They help to make a text more compact and concise. Participle constructions are very common in formal writing, not only in literature but also in technical and academic texts, providing a useful (and shorter) alternative to relative clauses. Compare:

10 *Chemical pesticides are of dubious value ecologically and almost always beyond the financial reach of small farmers producing for local markets.* (= ... *who produce* ...)

11 *Bananas modified genetically in this way were shown to be harmful to laboratory animals.* (= ... *which had been modified* ...)

History

The history of the Present Participle and Gerund is, to quote Lass in Blake 1992 (p.145), 'complex and somewhat murky'. The modern *-ing* form goes back to two clearly distinct Old English forms, a present participle ending in *-ende*, e.g. *helpende* (cf. German *helfend*) and a verbal noun with the suffix *-ing*, alternating with *-ung* (cf. German *Bewerbung*). In Middle English the participle ending *-and*, *-ende* or *-inde* (the exact form depending on the dialect) seems to have become confused with the verbal noun ending in *-ing*. Morphological confusion was then accompanied by syntactic confusion, with the verbal noun acquiring verbal features. This mixture of functions is still reflected in the pattern of usage in Modern English.

The development of the Past Participle is much more straightforward. In Old English it was usually marked by a prefix *ge-*, as in Modern German, and a suffix containing */d/* in weak verbs, e.g. *gelufod* 'loved', and /n/ in strong verbs, e.g. *geboren* 'born' or 'borne', i.e. 'carried'. In Middle English times the prefix was first weakened to ‹i›, as in the traditional song *Sumer is i-cumen in* ('Summer has come', literally 'Summer is come in'), and finally lost, while the suffix was retained, as illustrated by the modern forms *loved, born* and *borne*. There was no major change in the functions of the Past Participle comparable to those taking place in the *-ing* form.

VII.2 Normal pattern

Being verbal in function, participles cannot form the subject or object of a sentence (in contrast to the Gerund, see Chap. VIII).
They can either be used as attributes, i.e. they can modify the head of a noun phrase, act as a complement to the subject or object, or function as an adverbial modifier.

A ADJECTIVAL FUNCTION

2.1 Attribute

cf. German

Participles can be used like adjectives. Their meaning is similar to that of a relative clause. The German equivalent is usually a present or past participle with adjectival endings:

12 *Breaking news: Jumbo jet crashes off Cuba.*
13 *He died of a broken heart.* (= *an einem gebrochenen Herzen*)

level stress

In 12, *breaking news* is 'news which is breaking', i.e. news which is just arriving. In 13, a *broken heart* means 'a heart which has (been) broken'. The similarity to adjectives is also shared in the stress pattern: this type of structure uses level stress, i.e. (fairly) equal stress on the participle and noun. It contrasts with the stress pattern used when the *-ing* form is a gerund, where only the *-ing* form is stressed. Contrast the following pairs (NB: ['-] denotes a stressed syllable, [-] an unstressed syllable):

14 *A flying bird is a fascinating sight.*	['- - '-]	Participle
15 *He works as a flying instructor.*	['- - - - -]	Gerund
16 *A running engine is a pollutant.*	['- - '- -]	Participle
17 *These running shoes are great!*	['- - -]	Gerund

The participle constructions with level stress show parallels with adjectives preceding nouns, which also have level stress, cf. a *white* board (= 'a board which is white') with level stress, in contrast to the compound *whiteboard* (= a special board for writing on, used in teaching), which has stress on the first syllable. However, participles differ from adjectives in that they cannot be used in the comparative and superlative, nor can they be preceded by *very, rather, fairly* or similar modifiers (but see also 3.2).

The participle can also form part of compounds, particularly if it is derived from a transitive verb:

18 *English is the official language in most English-speaking countries.*
19 *Iran is a major oil-exporting country.*
20 *The theatre-going public will not stand for this sort of treatment.*

In these cases, too, level stress is used, with *English* and *countries* being stressed in 18, i.e. as ['- - - - '- -]. Notice that whereas *speaking* and *exporting* are formed from transitive verbs, *going* is derived from an intransitive verb. In general, past participles are only used before the noun if they are derived from transitive verbs and are thus passive in meaning (but see 3.1 for exceptions).

B RELATIVE CLAUSE FUNCTION
alternative to relative clauses

Participle clauses are often used as a stylistic alternative to relative clauses. They differ from relative clauses in only showing a basic distinction between unfinished versus finished action or state (i.e. the imperfective-perfective distinction mentioned above). More sophisticated distinctions of tense or aspect are not expressed:

21 *There's a man eating a doughnut over there.*
22 *Most of the topics discussed at the meeting involved security.*

The corresponding relative clauses would contain finite verbs:

23 *There's a man who is eating a doughnut over there.*
24 *Most of the topics which were discussed at the meeting involved security.*

cf. German

Two common equivalents in German are a relative clause and an extended adjectival complement preceding the noun:

25 *Drüben steht ein Mann, der einen Berliner isst.*
26 *Bei den meisten der auf der Sitzung besprochenen Themen ging es um Sicherheit.*

Like relative clauses, they can be used with a restrictive, i.e. defining, function, or a non-defining function (see Chap. XV). The latter type is far more common in formal contexts.

27 *The train standing at platform 9 is the 14.35 to Slough.*
28 *The person addressed by the journalist refused to reply.*
29 *Half an hour later Pendlebury, wearing a dirty trench-coat, emerged from the building.*
30 *The bouncer, angered by the teenager's remarks, thumped him hard in the face.*

The only indication of whether the participle clause is defining (as in 27 and 28) or non-defining (as in 29 and 30) is the non-use or use of commas (cf. Chap. XV).

2.2 Complement

A Subject complement

The Present Participle can be used as a subject complement i.e. to give more information about the subject of the sentence. This structure occurs with intransitive verbs of rest, e.g. *lie, remain, sit, stand, stay*, and verbs of movement, e.g. *come, go*.

verbs of rest, movement

31 *The two lovebirds stood gazing into each other's eyes.*
32 *The cat sat watching the mouse.*
33 *She came running when she heard Peter's howl of pain.*

German normally uses two main clauses linked by *und*:

cf. German

34 *Die Katze saß da und beobachtete die Maus.*

However, after *kommen* the Past Participle is used:

35 *Sie kam gelaufen, als sie Peters Schmerzensschrei hörte.*

The subject complement construction is also possible with the Past Participle, though it is used less frequently:

36 *The mouse sat paralysed with fear.*

After stressed *here* or *there* at the beginning of a clause or sentence, when they are followed by an unstressed personal pronoun, the Present Participle is used to give more details about the subject:

37 *Here she is, sitting on her patio.*
38 *There they were, as bold as brass, helping themselves to food from my fridge!*

After the passive form of verbs of perception and some other verbs we use the Participle to give more details about the subject (see below, 2.2 B, for more details):

39 *A girl was heard shouting for help.*
40 *They were left waiting outside the hotel.*

B OBJECT COMPLEMENT

verbs of perception

cf. German

The Present Participle is also used to provide more information about the object of the sentence. This occurs after verbs of perception, i.e. *see, hear, smell, taste, feel* and similar verbs, e.g. *notice, observe*, when these are followed by an object. Notice that in these cases German uses the Infinitive and, in colloquial language, *wie* followed by a subordinate clause containing a finite verb:

41 *We heard people screaming for help. (= Wir hörten die Leute um Hilfe schreien* or *Wir haben gehört, wie die Leute um Hilfe schrien)*
42 *Passers-by observed several masked men running out of the bank.*

These verbs can also be followed by the Infinitive without *to*:

43 *We heard people scream for help.*

The Present Participle, with its imperfective connotations, focuses on the action and is thus comparable to the use of the Progressive Aspect:

44 *People were screaming for help.*

The Infinitive simply states that an action took place and is comparable in this example to the Past Simple:

45 *People screamed for help.*

These verbs can also be followed by the Past Participle:

46 *He heard his name announced on the loudspeaker system.*

After the verbs *get, have* the Past Participle is used in the causative sense of 'to see to it that something is done', corresponding to German *etwas machen lassen*:

get, have

47 *I got my car fixed at that new garage in Vale Road.*
48 *He had his car repaired at his local garage.*

The two constructions are not totally synonymous. The first is more common in informal register, as is *get* in general. However, it also covers a wider semantic range than *have*. Compare:

49 *Could you get this text typed, please?*
50 *Could you have this text typed, please?*

Example 49 leaves it open whether the person addressed or someone else is expected to type the text, whereas 50 means that the person addressed will not be typing the text.

The Present Participle construction is also possible after the verbs *catch, find, get, keep, leave, set, start*. It often corresponds to a German Infinitive. When *get* is used with a Present Participle, it means 'to start doing something':

catch, find, get, etc.

cf. German

51 *I caught him trying to pick the lock of my car!*
52 *We'll soon get things working again, now that the power's back on.*
53 *The doorman kept them waiting outside the hotel.*

Notice that the Infinitive cannot be used after these verbs. With some of them, viz. *find, keep, leave*, and with the verbs *like, want, wish* the Past Participle can occur:

54 *Keep your mouth shut, or you're a goner!*
55 *I want that son of a bitch eliminated by sunrise.*

2.3 Adverbial modifier

A participle clause can be used as the equivalent of an adverbial clause referring to the time, reason or circumstances associated with an action. This type of clause is known as a related or attached participle clause. It does not contain a subject. The subject of the main clause to which the participle is attached functions as the implied

A RELATED PARTICIPLE CLAUSE WITHOUT A CONJUNCTION

subject of the participle clause. Notice that these clauses are much more common in formal register, especially if they come before the main clause. In informal register adverbial clauses introduced by a conjunction and containing a finite verb are preferred for references to time or reason, with two main clauses linked by *and* being preferred for reference to circumstances. This agrees with the pattern in German in both formal and informal registers. These clauses are used without an introductory conjunction provided the meaning is clear.

cf. German

1 Time

Participle clauses of time usually come before the main clause:

56 *Travelling around, you come across some very weird people. (= When you travel around ...)*
57 *Looking out of the window, she saw a man approach. (= While she was looking out of the window ...)*
58 *Getting into the car, they gave chase. (= After getting into ...)*
59 *Confronted with the evidence, the suspect confessed at once. (= When he was confronted with the evidence ...)*

2 Reason

Participle clauses of reason also normally precede the main clause:

60 *Not finding anyone at home, I put my visiting card in the letter box. (= Because I did not find anyone at home ...)*
61 *Feeling thirsty and lonely, he decided to go to the pub. (= As he felt thirsty and lonely ...)*
62 *Being a vegetarian, I'm not worried about BSE. (= Since I'm a vegetarian ...)*
63 *I can't get around much, not having a car.*
64 *Not wishing to get involved in a family argument, I made my excuses and left.*

Participle clauses containing *be, have, know*, or *wish*, as in 62 to 64, are normally clauses of reason.

Note

Notice that it is not always clear whether a participle clause implies time or reason:

65 *Hearing a noise in the cellar, I went down to investigate. (= When I heard ...* or *Because I heard ...)*

66 *Living in India, you soon pick up a smattering of Hindi.* (= *When you are living* ... or *Because you are living* ...)

3 Accompanying circumstances

The participle clause is often used to denote the circumstances accompanying an action. It normally follows the main clause. The German equivalents vary. One possibility is to use a subordinate clause introduced by *wobei*. A second is to have two main clauses linked by *und* or as two separate sentences. A third possibility, for sentences containing a past participle, is the same pattern in German:

cf. German

67 *He ran out of the house, dropping the keys in his haste.* (= ..., *wobei er in der Eile seine Schlüssel fallen ließ.*)
68 *Vanessa came in out of the heat, wiping the perspiration off her face with a towel.* (= *und trocknete* ...)
69 *Accompanied by his minders, the President went walkabout among the crowd.* (= *Von seinen Aufpassern begleitet, nahm der Präsident ein Bad in der Menge.*)

B Related participle clause with conjunction

If a related participle clause of time is placed after a main clause containing an object, it usually needs to be introduced by a conjunction, in order to avoid ambiguity. Here German has a subordinate clause containing a finite verb:

70 *Paul saw one of his students while queueing at the cash dispenser.* (= ... *while he was queueing* ...) (= ... *während er in der Schlange stand* ...)
71 *I met Ann the other day when taking the dog for a walk.* (= ... *when I was taking* ...)

If the conjunctions *while* or *when* are omitted, the participle clauses refer to the object, thereby changing the meaning. Compare:

72 *Paul saw one of his students queueing at the cash dispenser.* (= ... *one of his students, who was queueing* ...)
73 *I met Ann the other day taking the dog for a walk.* (= ... *when she was taking the dog* ...)

conditional participle constructions

Clauses with a conditional meaning have to be introduced by conjunctions like *(as) if, (as) though, unless*:

74 *He hesitated, as if waiting for a signal.*
75 *If treated fairly, most people will reciprocate.*
76 *Though sorely tempted, I did not retaliate.*

C MISRELATED AND UNRELATED PARTICIPLES

Misrelated participles is the term used for sentences where the subject of the main clause is not the same as the implied subject of the participle phrase. They are also, more picturesquely, known as *dangling* participles. Because they may be misleading, they are usually regarded as incorrect and therefore avoided:

77 **Being in charge, the accusation that he was incompetent was particularly annoying for him.*
78 **If paid generously, we can expect them to work hard.*
79 **While sailing across the Caribbean, several sharks attacked us.*

Example 77 implies that the accusation is in charge, because it is the subject of the main clause. Sentence 78 means that if we are paid generously, we can expect them to work hard, which is not the intended meaning. In 79, sharks have suddenly learnt how to sail. These sentences could be corrected as follows:

80 *Being in charge, he was particularly annoyed by the accusation.*
81 *If they are paid generously, we can expect good work from them.*
82 *While sailing across the Caribbean, we were attacked by several sharks.*

Sometimes, as in 81, the only way to avoid ambiguity is to completely recast the sentence (but see also 3.3).

unrelated participles

Misrelated participles should not be confused with unrelated participles, which are participles used in a general sense. The implied subject of the participle clause does not then need to agree with the subject in the main clause:

83 *Strictly speaking, this is incorrect.*
84 *Taking everything into consideration, you're probably right.*
85 *Judging from the look she gave me, we're no longer on speaking terms.*
86 *Putting it another way, they were simply careless.*

These are all cases where the participle clause expresses a comment made by the speaker or writer. German often uses a construction involving *man* in these cases.

D ABSOLUTE PARTICIPLE

1 Without introductory *with*

By absolute participle construction we mean a participle clause which has its own subject. This construction is usually more typical of formal register:

87 *He sat there, his knees knocking with fear.*
88 *The fighters roared overhead, their wings glinting in the sun.*

2 With introductory preposition *with*

In informal and spoken English it is much more common to introduce the absolute participle by the preposition *with*:

89 *With house prices increasing at this rate, soon only the rich will be able to afford their own house.*
90 *The ghost of Anne Boleyn appeared in front of the Tower of London, with her head tucked underneath her arm.*

VII.3 Exceptions

3.1 Past Participles with active meaning

In 2.1 A it was stated that the past participles used before nouns are normally those formed from transitive verbs, which are therefore passive in meaning. It is, however, possible with some intransitive verbs to use the past participles before the noun. Examples of this type are: *a fallen angel, an escaped convict, advanced learners* (for more examples, see Swan 1995, §404.3).

3.2 Adjectival features of participles

As was explained in 2.1 A, although participles used adjectivally share some features with adjectives, they differ from adjectives in not collocating with *fairly, rather, very* and similar modifiers and do not have a comparative or superlative. This is not true in those cases where the participle has changed word class and become an adjective, whilst retaining its original participle ending:

91 *I think teaching is probably more satisfying as a career than banking – though it pays less.*
92 *The audience was rather shocked by this remark.*

93 *The students were very bored by the lecture.*

3.3 Tolerance of misrelated participles

Although misrelated participles are generally frowned upon and subject to ridicule, they do occur more often than is realised. They are particularly frequent when the main clause has *it* or *there* as its subject:

94 *Knowing your interest in modern art, it would be unforgivable if you went to London without visiting the new Tate Gallery of Modern Art on Bankside.*
95 *Being pushed for time, there was not much I could say to console her.*

In formal and technical language other structures occur. Usually the potential ambiguity is resolved by the context or common sense:

96 *When producing goods for a mass market, knowledge of the factors affecting fluctuations in popular demand is vital.*
97 *Using modern techniques, the stem cells were subjected to careful analysis.*

Knowledge does not of course produce goods in 99, nor do stem cells use modern techniques. Because common sense tells people this, they are prepared to tolerate a misrelated participle in this sort of context. This is a reminder that the advantage of the participle clause is its conciseness, which is sometimes offset by a tendency to lack precision. Speakers and writers usually resolve the problem pragmatically.

Exercises

1 Here and there

Complete the following sentences using the phrases given below.

Example

→ There he is, _eating an ice cream_.

eat an ice cream • work in the garden • have a relaxing bath • tinker with the car • lie on the beach • use my mobile • play on the computer

1 We were walking along, looking for Karen, and there she was, _____! She said she'd been weeding it.
2 Oh, here you are, ____! I thought you were writing your essay. Isn't the sun too hot for you?
3 I was rushing around, desperately trying to get ready so that we could get to the theatre on time, and there she was, coolly _____!
4 Here you are, _____! Weren't you supposed to be doing your homework?
5 There she was, cheeky as anything, _____. She hadn't even asked me!
6 There he is as usual, _____. He should have been a mechanic.

2 Combinations

Combine the sentences, using a participle.

1 We saw people in the smoke-filled building. They were standing at the windows, trying to attract attention.
2 Don Corleone sat outside the café. He was watching the people on the piazza.
3 They lay in bed. They were smoking.
4 He stood there. He was dazed by the impact of the explosion.
5 The guerrillas watched the soldiers. They were coming out of the barracks.
6 She heard her name. It was being called out by the man at the bar.
7 We could smell the food. It was burning.
8 They were standing at the corner. They were gossiping as usual.

3 Science with style

Improve the style and conciseness of the following sentences from scientific articles by using participle constructions.

1 The team, which was headed by the embryologist James Thomson, used human embryos which had been created by artificial insemination in order to treat childless couples.
2 Before they operate, the team has to localise the source of the epileptic attacks.
3 The data which we obtain while we are doing this can then be used for other purposes.
4 They removed the remaining internal cell mass and transferred it into special cultures.
5 The lectures which were held at the Physics Department were part

of an experiment which was aimed at trying out new teaching methods. One important tool which was used was an electronic whiteboard. Two video cameras filmed the lecturer, while the sound was recorded by using cordless microphones.

6 The researchers transplanted the oligodendrocytes which had been obtained in the laboratory into the spinal cord of rats which were suffering from a genetic defect in the formation of their myelin sheaths. The cells attached themselves to nerve cells and produced myelin there.

4 Proper proverbs

Use participles to replace the sentences (1–6) so that they form the correct text of some traditional English proverbs. Then match them up with the meanings (a–f). Two proverbs mean the same.

Example

Fruit that is stolen is sweet. →Stolen fruit is sweet. (e)

1 A dog which barks never bites.
2 A mouth that is shut catches no flies.
3 Men who are threatened live long.
4 A stone that rolls gathers no moss.
5 If nothing is ventured, nothing is gained.
6 The first person who comes is the first to be served.

a A person who does not take risks will not be successful.
b People who use threats often cannot back them up.
c Silence can keep you out of trouble.
d Someone who always tries out new things stays on the ball.
e Things acquired after taking risks often seem more valuable.
f Whoever is fastest will be rewarded.

5 Your participle's dangling ...

Correct the dangling, i.e. misrelated, participles in the sentences below by using a conjunction, changing the word order, or restructuring the sentence.

1 Crossing the street at a zebra crossing, a car nearly ran me over.
2 Lying in bed, my thoughts ranged back over my past life.
3 As a rule my kids won't touch apples, but dipped in chocolate they lap them up.

Exercises

4 When parking their cars it is advisable that hotel guests remove all their valuables.
5 A dog bit the postman while delivering letters.
6 Humans can teach dolphins some very clever tricks, if properly trained.

6 A frustrating bus journey

Fit the two halves of the text together so that they make sense, inserting the numbers on the right-hand side of the page at the correct point in the text on the left. The text on the right contains participles. Note down what type they are. Change the punctuation as appropriate. The text is a modified extract from Kingsley Amis's novel *Lucky Jim*. The hero, Dixon, is on a bus to a station. He is in a desperate hurry because he needs to talk to the woman he loves before she takes the London train, but is frustrated because the bus is so slow.

The bus driver brought the bus to a gradual halt by the bus-stop outside a row of thatched cottages.	1 two old women dressed in black	Example
waited until the bus was quenched of all motion		
in a moment he heard their voices	2 before clutching each other and edging cautiously towards it	
then activity seemed to cease	3 crying unintelligibly to the conductor	
at least five seconds passed Dixon looked out of the bus to see what the cause of the delay might be	4 was the driver slumped in his seat, the victim of a stroke, or had he suddenly got an idea for a poem	
then, at last, the picture of sleepy rustic calm was modified by the fairly sudden emergence from a cottage some yards further of a third woman in a lilac costume	5 then approached it with a kind of bowed shuffle	
she looked keenly towards the bus and identified it without obvious difficulty	6 nosing its careful way on to the crown of the road	
the bus now set off, and the gap	7 galvanised by the	

between it and the lorry in front began to narrow

Dixon found that his whole being had become centred on the matter of the bus's progress

he just sat there

suddenly the lorry moved off into a lay-by

now was the time, he thought, for the driver to start making up for lost time, but the driver seemed blissfully unaware of this

Dixon lit another cigarette

just then the bus rounded a corner and slowed abruptly, then stopped

a tractor was laboriously pulling, at right angles across the road, something that looked like the springs of a giant bed

Dixon thought he really would have to go downstairs and knife the drivers of both vehicles; what next? what next? a hold-up, a crash, floods, an electric storm, a diversion, a low-level attack by Communist aircraft, sheep

he'd choose the last of these

the bus crept on, while every few yards troupes of old men waited

pitchings of the bus into the appearance of seismic laughter

8 sweating stealthily in the heat and the apprehension

9 stretching his face in a fresh direction at each overtaking car

10 with a reviving hope

11 jabbing with the match at the sandpaper as if it were the driver's eye

12 making a lot of noise

13 caked in places with earth

14 and decked with ribbon-like grasses

15 masked

16 with falling trees and meteorites

17 the driver being stung by a hornet?

18 if consulted

19 grinding its gears

20 to make their quivering way aboard

VIII The Gerund

VIII.1 Overview

definition

The Gerund, like the Present Participle, is formed by adding *-ing* to the stem. However, its syntactic functions differ from those of the Participle. While the Participle behaves like a verb, the Gerund is a kind of half-way house between verb and noun, sharing some of the characteristics of both of these parts of speech. Like a noun, it can function as the subject or object of a sentence:

noun-like features

1 *Skiing is fun.* (= subject)
2 *I like surfing.* (= object)

In these functions it is similar to the German verbal noun, which is formed from the Infinitive:

cf. German

3 *Skifahren macht Spaß.*
4 *Ich mag Surfen.*

Like a noun, it can occur after prepositions:

5 *Thank you for not smoking.*
6 *You've done us all a great favour just by being here.*
7 *The art of writing spread slowly.*

It can be modified by a noun or pronoun in the genitive:

8 *Jo's reading isn't yet up to scratch.*

verb-like features

However, the Gerund also shows typical features of the verb, e.g. it can distinguish between active (as in 8) and passive (as in 9):

9 *Being operated on always involves a certain element of risk.*

It can distinguish, in a rudimentary way, between past (the Perfect Gerund) and non-past (the Present Gerund):

10 *I'm proud of having served my country.*

The Perfect Gerund contrasts here with the Present Gerund, which would imply that the speaker is still serving his or her country:

11 *I'm proud of serving my country.*

The Perfect Gerund, like the Perfect Participle (see Chap. VII), is normally only used if we need to indicate that the action or state is completed. It is the marked form, while the Present Gerund is the unmarked form, which does not specify the time referred to.

Like a verb, the Gerund can also be followed by an object:

12 *I enjoy reading a good thriller in bed.*

History

The Gerund shares features of the noun and verb partly because of its origin as a verbal noun which merged with the Present Participle, sharing the same ending. This blend of different functions led to the syntactic re-ordering of functions as reflected in the modern distinction between the Gerund and Present Participle (for more historical background, see Chap. VII.1 and Blake 1992, p.145f.).

VIII.2
Normal pattern

The Gerund can assume various functions in the sentence, acting as subject or object. It can combine with prepositions to form adverbial modifiers, can occur in apposition and have its own subject.

2.1 As subject

cf. German

The Gerund is frequently used as the subject of the sentence. In such cases German often uses a verbal noun, unless the Gerund is followed by its own object, as in 14, when the Infinitive is usually preferred:

13 *Windsurfing isn't difficult.* (= *Windsurfen ist nicht schwer.*)
14 *Writing thank-you letters can be such a drag.* (= *Dankesbriefe schreiben kann ganz schön langweilig sein.*)

After the copula *be* the Gerund occurs as a subject complement:

15 *My hobbies are rock-climbing, snowboarding and reading.*

2.2 As object

The Gerund can also occur as the object of the sentence:

16 *Gary loves zapping through the TV channels. I hate it.*

However, after some verbs it is the only possible verbal element which can be used as an object – the Infinitive is not possible.
Common verbs in this category are listed in the box:

admit • advocate • avoid • carry on • delay • deny • dislike • enjoy • finish • give up • imagine • include • involve • keep • mention • mind • miss • postpone • practise • put off • quit • recall • recollect • risk • suggest

17 *It's better to avoid going on the M1 at weekends.*
18 *The work involves travelling to other countries quite a lot.*
19 *They kept reminding me that I was basically a foreigner.*
20 *Would you mind closing the window? It's draughty.*
21 *Quit stalling, will you? Get to the point.*
22 *I wouldn't risk buying those shares if I were you.*

cf. German

When the Gerund occurs as the object of the sentence, German usually has an Infinitive or a clause introduced by *dass*.

need, require

The verbs *need, require* and, in informal British English, *want* are followed by the Active Gerund with a passive meaning:

23 *The cellar needs redecorating*. (= *needs to be redecorated*)
24 *Most types of lentils require soaking before being cooked.*
25 *Your brakes want fixing*. (= *need to be fixed*)

semantic contrasts, e.g. *consider*

Depending on meaning, the same verb can take different syntactic patterns, e.g. *consider* in the sense of 'think about' (as in 26) uses the Gerund, but when it means 'regard as' it is either followed by an object and complement (as in 27) or by an object and Infinitive (as in 28):

26 *We did consider suing him for damages.*
27 *The government considers this development desirable.*
28 *Experts consider the risks to be manageable.*

forget, etc.

Similarly, verbs like *forget, remember, go on, stop, try,* and *mean* differ semantically, depending on the construction they take:

Gerund construction	Infinitive construction
forget doing sth. = etw. vergessen	*forget to do sth.* = vergessen, etw. zu tun
remember doing sth. = sich an etw. erinnern	*remember to do sth.* = daran denken, etw. zu tun
go on doing sth. = etw. fortsetzen	*go on to do sth.* = dazu übergehen, etw. zu tun
stop doing sth. = mit etw. aufhören	*stop to do sth.* = etw. unterbrechen, um etw. Anderes zu tun
it means doing sth. = es hat zur Folge, dass	*mean to do sth.* = etw. beabsichtigen
try doing sth. = etw. versuchsweise machen	*try to do sth.* = versuchen, etw. zu tun

forget

29 *I'll never forget going abroad for the first time.*
30 *You didn't forget to put the cat out, did you, dear?*

31 *I don't remember switching off the cooker.* remember
32 *Remember to water the plants while we're away.*

The Gerund in 29 and 31 refers back to events in the past, whereas the Infinitive in 30 and 32 denotes processes taking place in the past or future.

33 *Joe went on repairing his motorbike as if nothing had happened.* go on
34 *The lecturer went on to talk about the impact of the Crusades.*
35 *We've stopped buying beef.* stop
36 *I stopped to chat to the vicar after church.*

In 34 and 36 the Infinitive implies a change in activity.

37 *My flight's at two, so that will mean leaving here at twelve.* mean
38 *I really didn't mean to offend you.*

In 37 the Gerund expresses the idea that a specific factor, here the time of the flight, will have certain consequences.

39 *Did you try oiling the lock? Sometimes that helps.* try
40 *I tried to force the door open, but without success.*

In 39 the Gerund refers to one possible way of solving a problem.

hate, like, love, prefer

With the verbs *hate, like, love, prefer* either Gerund or Infinitive are possible, with little difference in meaning. The tendency is to use the Gerund for general statements and the Infinitive for specific ones (but see also 3.1):

41 *I like seeing the latest films.*
42 *I didn't like to ask him such personal question.*
43 *I'd like to see Ken Loach's new film.*

attempt, begin, continue, etc.

In other verbs like *attempt, begin, start, continue, intend, plan* both constructions are completely interchangeable (but see also 3.2):

44 *We began working at the crack of dawn.*
45 *I began to work when I was 16, at a chip shop.*

Verbs from the same semantic field are not necessarily combined with the same constructions: whereas *like, stop, remember* can be used with the Gerund or *to* followed by the Infinitive (see above), similar verbs such as *dislike, finish, recollect* can only take the Gerund:

46 *I've always disliked being talked to by strangers on trains.*
47 *Have you finished washing up yet?*
48 *I don't recollect ever seeing her do a stroke of work.*

advise, allow, permit, etc.

The verbs *advise, allow, permit, encourage, recommend* take the Infinitive with a personal object, but the Gerund when there is no such object:

49 *I would advise you to change your holiday plans.*
50 *I would advise reconsidering your offer.*
51 *The firm won't allow people to eat food at their workplace.*
52 *It is company policy not to allow smoking on the premises.*
53 *We'd recommend them to consult a solicitor.*
54 *They recommended booking early for the popular musical.*

2.3 After a preposition

The Gerund can be used after a preposition on its own or after a preposition which is preceded by an adjective, noun or verb. After any preposition except *to*, the Gerund is used. After *to* the construction used is either the Infinitive or the Gerund, depending on which word or words precede the preposition.

A PREPOSITION + GERUND
cf. German

After a preposition on its own the verb can only be in the Gerund. The German equivalents vary from prepositional phrases containing a noun (or verbal noun) to an infinitive construction or a subordinate clause:

55 *I got where I am today by working hard.* (= *durch harte Arbeit*)
56 *On entering the room he heard a muffled noise coming from the cupboard.* (= *Beim Betreten des Zimmers ...*)
57 *Never cross the road without looking both ways.* (= *ohne in beide Richtungen zu gucken*)
58 *After watching a documentary on the endangered habitat of the Australian kangaroo we went to bed.* (= *Nachdem wir einen Dokumentarfilm über den gefährdeten Lebensraum des australischen Kängurus gesehen hatten ...*)

Notice that in 58 the only normal construction would be the Present Gerund. The Perfect Gerund *after having watched* is superfluous, since *after* unambiguously indicates the order of events.

B ADJECTIVE + PREPOSITION + GERUND
cf. German

After an adjective followed by any preposition except *to*, the verb has to be in the Gerund. The commonest German equivalents are the Infinitive and a *dass* clause:

59 *He's good at finding solutions to tricky problems.*
60 *I'm sick and tired of telling you to shut up.*

to + Gerund

After an adjective followed by *to*, either the Gerund or the Infinitive are possible, depending on the adjective involved and its meaning:

61 *We're used to having a long lie-in on Saturdays.*
62 *I'm accustomed to having at least nine hours' sleep.*

used to doing (= accustomed) versus *used to do* (= past habit)

Notice the difference between *used to* with the Gerund, meaning 'accustomed to' (i.e. *an etwas gewöhnt sein*), which follows a copula like *be* or *become*, and the marginal modal *used to* (see Chap. VI, 2.4) with the Infinitive, denoting habits or states in the past:

63 *We used to live in Athens.* (= *Wir haben früher in Athen gelebt*)

to + Infinitive

In the majority of cases, however, *to* is followed by an Infinitive:

64 *I'm inclined to agree with you that standards are too low.*
65 *Something's sure to go wrong.*

Use of *to* followed by an Infinitive often contrasts with the use of a different preposition followed by the Gerund:

66 *He was obsessively afraid of making a mistake.*
67 *All you ever wanted to know about sex, but were afraid to ask.*
68 *I'm very interested in travelling.*
69 *I'll be interested to see the results of your research.*
70 *I'm keen on collecting stamps.*
71 *She's keen to see my latest painting, she says.*

In these types, the construction involving the Gerund is often used for a general pattern, e.g. making mistakes, travelling, collecting stamps, whereas the construction with the Infinitive refers to specific occasions. However, the distinction is by no means clear-cut, as can be seen from examples 72 to 75:

72 *I'm sorry for not replying sooner to your e-mail.*
73 *I was sorry to hear about your father's death.*
74 *I'm proud of being a Northerner.*
75 *We're proud to be Irish.*

Examples 72 and 73 both refer to specific occasions. The Infinitive after *to* could be used in both (in 72 it would be the Perfect Infinitive *to have not replied*). In 74 and 75, which denote general situations, both constructions are interchangeable.

C NOUN + PREPOSITION + GERUND
cf. German

Similarly, where a noun is followed by a preposition, the preposition is followed automatically by a Gerund unless the preposition involved is *to*. The corresponding German constructions are the Infinitive and a *dass* clause.

76 *Swiss police say there is no hope of finding the climbers who got lost in a snowstorm on the Matterhorn last week.*
77 *We have no way of knowing what the enemy will do.*
78 *There is no realistic possibility of achieving these growth targets during the first quarter of next year.*

possibility
opportunity

Notice that *possibility* cannot be followed by *to* and the Infinitive. Nor is it synonymous with *opportunity*. Whereas *possibility* is used to refer to a general and theoretical concept, *opportunity* denotes a specific situation when something can be done (i. e. corresponding in meaning to German *Gelegenheit*). It can be followed by either *of* and the Gerund or *to* and the Infinitive, without any difference in meaning:

79 *The possibility of outlawing war is, at the moment, very slight.* (= *Möglichkeit*)
80 *When I was 17 I had the opportunity of staying with a family in Naples for six months.* (= *Gelegenheit, Möglichkeit*)
81 *I had the opportunity to spend a year in Florence in 2001.*

chance

The noun *chance*, from the same semantic field, can also take both constructions, but with a difference in meaning. Compare:

82 *She only has a slim chance of passing the exam.*
83 *Is there any chance of getting tickets for tonight's concert?*
84 *Why don't you give me a chance to explain?*
85 *I hope we get a chance to put our feet up this weekend.*

The construction with the Gerund is used in the general sense of a possibility of something happening. In fact, in both 82 and 83 *chance* could be replaced by *possibility* (note, not by *opportunity*).
In 84 and 85, *chance* denotes a time or situation which is suitable for providing the opportunity to do something.

there's no point in
what's the use of

The Gerund is also used after idiomatic phrases ending in the nouns *point* and *use* (e.g. in *it's no use*):

86 *There's no point in complaining to the manager.*
87 *What's the use of worrying?* (= *Was für einen Zweck hat es ...*)

aversion to

Notice that *aversion to* is followed by the Gerund:

88 *I have a distinct aversion to eating garlic.*

D VERB + PREPOSITION + GERUND

After any preposition except *to*, the Gerund is used:

89 *She apologised for forgetting my birthday.*
90 *The firm specialises in manufacturing gearboxes.*
91 *I'm thinking of handing in my notice.*

to + Gerund

The verbs *look forward to* and *object to* also take the Gerund:

92 *We're looking forward to meeting Peter's fiancée.*
93 *I object to being treated so rudely!*

to + Infinitive

However, in the vast majority of verbs followed by *to*, this *to* is simply a marker of the Infinitive:

94 *She threatened to walk out on him if he didn't stop gambling.*

2.4 In apposition

definition

By apposition we mean the use of a sentence element which has the same reference and grammatical role in the sentence as another element. For example, in *Mr Johnson, the butcher, sells good meat,* the phrase *the butcher* is in apposition to *Mr Johnson*, i.e. it refers to the same person and has the same grammatical role, both being the subject of the sentence. The Gerund, too, can be used in apposition to the subject of the sentence. Compare:

Adj. + Gerund

95 *It's so silly moping around like this. Go out and get a job.*
96 *It seems hard watching him lose faith in himself like that.*
97 *It really isn't worth taking the car into Central London.*

Noun + Gerund

As the above examples show, the Gerund follows an adjective which is preceded by a copula (usually *be* or *seem*). The copula can also be followed by a noun:

98 *It's been a pleasure meeting you.*
99 *It was fun going with you to the disco.*
100 *It was bad luck not getting that job.*
101 *It's no use crying over spilt milk.* (= *Es hat keinen Zweck ...*)
102 *It's no good worrying. That won't solve anything.*

it's no use + Gerund
it's no good + Gerund

In many of these cases *to* with the Infinitive is a possible alternative construction:

103 *It's silly to mope around like this.*
104 *It's been a pleasure to meet you.*

Notice, however, that the Gerund is obligatory after *it's no use* and *it's no good*, as in 101 and 102.

2.5 Gerund with its own subject

The Gerund can also have its own subject, which can take the common case in nouns or the objective case in pronouns (on Case, see Chap. X). An alternative construction is the use of the genitive.

A SUBJECT IN THE COMMON OR OBJECTIVE CASE

With pronouns this construction involves the use of the objective case. Nouns, which apart from the genitive only have one other case, take the common case. This construction is known in older grammars as the *half-gerund*. Nowadays it is the normal pattern in both informal and formal English whenever the Gerund takes a subject. Compare:

105 *I can't imagine Martin wanting to emigrate to the US.*
106 *I can't imagine him being prepared to leave Europe.*

Both *Martin* and *him* in 105 and 106 respectively are the object of the verb *imagine*, hence the use of the objective case in the pronoun. However, they are also the subject of the Gerund, corresponding to sentences like *I can't imagine that Martin wants to emigrate* and *I can't imagine that he's prepared to leave Europe*. Compare 107 to 110 with similar sentences without a subject in 86 and 83:

107 *There's no point in us complaining to the manager.*
108 *Is there any chance of me getting tickets for the concert?*
109 *Is there any chance of John and me getting tickets?*
110 *Is there any chance of John and I getting tickets?*

Just as the objective form is used after the verb *imagine* in 106, so it is after the prepositions *in* and *of* in 107 to 109. The use of the hypercorrect subjective form *I* in 110 is due to the traditionally confused attitudes to case (see Chap XI, 2.4, especially examples 40 and 41).

In many of the constructions described in 2.2 and 2.3 the Gerund can take a subject.

B SUBJECT IN THE GENITIVE CASE

A stylistic alternative to the type outlined in 2.5 A is to put the subject of the Gerund in the genitive. This is far more typical of formal register, and is normally restricted to use with pronouns. Compare:

111 *I can't imagine his being prepared to leave Europe.*
112 *We're so glad about his passing the exam with flying colours.*

The genitive *his* in 111 is an acceptable, though less frequent, alternative to 106. It would be unusual to use a noun genitive *Martin's* in 105, however. In all cases where the genitive can be used, the common case (in nouns) or objective case (in pronouns) can be used and is more normal.

VIII.3 Exceptions

3.1 No Gerund after would

In 2.2 it was stated that the verbs *hate, like, love, prefer* can take either Gerund or Infinitive, with little difference in meaning. However, after the conditional form *would*, only the Infinitive is used:

113 *I'd like to see Ken Loach's new film.*

114 *We would prefer not to have you coughing in our faces.*

3.2 No Gerund after the Progressive

Verbs like *attempt, begin, start, continue, intend, plan,* where both Gerund and Infinitive can normally be used without any difference in meaning, do not use the Gerund after a Progressive:

115 *We were just beginning to check the car's fan belt when the gaffer told us to take a tea break.*

116 *I was planning to go to Ghent on a business trip next week, but my boss is in hospital, so I'm standing in for him.*

Exercises

1 Improving your style

Make the sentences below more fluent by using a gerund. Remember that it is unusual in Modern English to use infinitive constructions in subject position. Similarly, the verbal noun normally sounds much less fluent than the Gerund.

Example

The writing of essays is something I hate.
→ *Writing essays is something I hate.*

1 The censoring of newspapers is typical of a dictatorship.
2 To collect beer mats is my hobby.
3 My view is that to smoke is a very dirty habit.
4 Actually, I'm against the banning of soft drugs.
5 To be operated on is not something I would relish.
6 I'm basically against the executing of murderers.
7 The publicising of the names of convicted paedophiles could have very unfortunate consequences.
8 To accuse somebody publicly of a crime without providing evidence of their guilt is itself a crime.
9 To be accused of cowardice must be very embarrassing for a soldier.

2 Guess the Gerund

Guess which hobby or leisure time activity is meant and put it into the slot provided, using a gerund. All the terms are from VIII.1 to 2.

1 ... Havana cigars is one of the few luxuries I permit myself.

Exercises

2 ... is a very instructive hobby. You learn lots about different countries, their history, and snippets of their languages.
3 Now that he's retired, he has plenty of time for ... letters to the editor.
4 I like the excitement of ..., though I'm not so keen on it when a freak wave hurls you onto the beach.
5 I'm a couch potato, so I just enjoy ... the TV channels with a can of beer and a packet of cheese and onion crisps.
6 ... is an exhilarating sport, especially when you get to the top, but it can be risky if you don't take the right precautions, e.g. proper use of ropes, hooks etc.
7 What I most dislike about ... is having to queue up at the lifts for such a long time, and all those idiots on the slopes.
8 I think that ... is one of the best ways of broadening your horizon – seeing different countries and cultures etc.

3 Getting it right

Check these sentences to see that they're correct. If they are, tick (✓) the box. If not, put a cross (✗) in the box and write the correct version.

1 ❒ I remember meeting Alison at a party.
2 ❒ You know, Jim, I really mean turning over a new leaf. I'm giving up drinking for good.
3 ❒ He went on to play computer games although I'd told him to stop.
4 ❒ Please try being home early, will you?
5 ❒ I'll never forget to go to the dentist's for the first time.
6 ❒ Being in love means looking after your partner through thick and thin.
7 ❒ Did you forget switching off the car lights last night? The battery's dead.
8 ❒ I'm sorry. I didn't mean to interrupt you.
9 ❒ Did you remember to cancel your appointment with the physiotherapist?
10 ❒ Have you ever stopped thinking about God? Most people usually don't take the time to think about these things.
11 ❒ 'This VCR's on the blink again.'
❒ 'Have you tried to read the instructions in the manual?'
❒ 'I did try to find the manual, but I couldn't. Perhaps it got thrown out.'
❒ 'Well, you could try checking if the plug's firmly in the socket.

❐ Failing that, you could try giving it a bash. That sometimes works, believe it or not.'

4 Completing the sentence

Complete the sentences below in any suitable way, using the Infinitive or Gerund of the verb in brackets. If both are possible, give both. Supply a preposition where necessary.

1	If there's a flu epidemic, it's best to avoid ...	(go)
2	I hate ...	(borrow)
3	I'm English and I've never been abroad before, so I'm not used ...	(drive)
4	Lenny was a bit nervous in the boss's office, but he plucked up courage and decided ...	(ask)
5	For your type of hair, shampoo manufacturers recommend ...	(use)
6	At Xmas we always used to ...	(buy)
7	To be quite frank, I wouldn't like ...	(own)
8	I really dislike ...	(listen)
9	Do you mind ...	(wait)
10	Our lawn desperately needs ...	(mow)
11	We consider this course of action ...	(be)
12	My CIA contact suggested ...	(meet)
13	The workmen were attempting ...	(repair)
14	I'm a big fan of hers. Is there any possibility ...	(get)
15	Your car's blocking my exit. Would you mind ...	(move)

5 A midlife crisis

The photocopier you're using is going through a midlife crisis. What would he say? Underline all the correct forms. In some cases both may be correct.

Being frank / To be frank (1), being / to be (2) a photocopier is not much fun when you're one of the older models like me. I began working / to work (3) five years ago – that's a long time for a photocopier: one of our years is like ten of yours. I remember clearly being / to be (4) switched on the very first time – the day of my birth. I was so proud of being / to be (5) a photocopier. And who wouldn't have been? On my side was a little metal plate stating my rank in the social hierarchy: RANK XEROX, it said, and I knew that being / to be (6) a Xerox was the highest any mere mortal copier could aspire to. The other photocopiers said I was a snob and threatened going / to go (7) on strike, but I couldn't help being / to be (8) in love with my gleaming machinery, my speed and my high resolution copies. Ah, the joys of youth!

Then, about six months ago, they brought in a brand-new machine, one of those upstart colour copiers, no less. Imagine my horror when they ignominiously trundled me off into a remote corridor in the basement! Of course I immediately protested that I most strongly objected to be / to being (9) treated in this fashion after so many years of faithful service, stressing that I was not accustomed to be / to being (10) humiliated like this, but no-one was listening except the new boy, and he just went on sniggering / to snigger (11). Naturally I had been noticing the depredations of age even before this traumatic event. I kept overheating / to overheat (12), I was beginning using up / to use up (13) toner at a prodigious rate, and I couldn't stop jamming up / to jam up (14) – typical symptoms of the advance of senility. I started singing / to sing (15) 'Nobody loves a Xerox when he's forty', but the ignoramuses just sent a mechanic to fix the noise.

I was so frustrated that I even considered committing / to commit (16) suicide, but it's a sin, even for a xerox machine. Gradually I'm getting over it. It's just old age – what's the use of fretting / to fret (17)? There's no point in getting / to get (18) worked up about it. So I told myself it was silly moping / to mope (19) around like that and started looking / to look (20) on the bright side – it's been a pleasure copying / to copy (21) for all those people over the years, and anyway, as we 'Xeroxers' say, 'It's no use crying / to cry (22) over spilt toner' – the spilt toner of youth, that is.

6 Correcting a letter

Jasmin, the girl you give private tuition in English to, has asked you to look through the letter she has written to her Welsh penfriend. Correct any mistakes, using a dictionary where necessary. Watch out for punctuation and spelling, too.

Dear Sue,

thanks for your letter. I apologise for taking such a long time for replying, but I have been revising hard for my exams. Thanks that you told me about the book on David Lodge. I'll try buying a copy at our local bookshop. I'm so scared to fail English in my exams that to have it will make me feel much more confidant. My teacher also suggested to get a PC programm for improving my English grammer. What would you advise me doing? Is it worth to get one? Do you know of a good one? I hope you don't mind that I ask you all these questions, but I know that you had similar problems preparing for your exams.

I'm not only worried to fail my exams. Do you remember me telling you about meeting Mario at that party?

My parents don't approve that I go out with him. They say he's on drugs. That's rubbish. I know he's not, and I enjoy to be with him. I just wish my parents would stop to treat me like a child. Unfortunately I forgot to tell Mario that my parents are against that I go out with him. He came to our house yesterday for taking me to a party at Sandras, and my parents found out that I hadn't stopped to see him. We had a big fight about it at home. So now they won't allow me going out at the weekends. I'm so angry. But there's no point to get too worked up. Anyway, I still manage to meet him at a friends house. But I do miss to go to discos with him. He's such a good dancer.

You asked me in your last letter if I felt like coming over in summer. Yes, I'd like that. I'm looking forward to go on holiday when I've finished doing my exams, and to see you again would be great.

Love,

Jasmin

7 Situations

What would you say in the situations described below? Use the verb in brackets, followed by a verb in the correct construction.

Example

You are discussing with your partner what birthday present to get your son Alex, who is 6 years old. (suggest)
→ *I suggest getting him some boxing gloves.*

1 Somebody asks you how they can improve their Spanish before a trip to Spain. (practise)
2 A leading member of your tennis club has just died suddenly. The club was supposed to be celebrating its 20th anniversary. What do you say? (postpone)
3 You want to take out special health insurance cover for travel overseas. Ask the insurance company whether you need to cover doctors' fees. (advise me)
4 The partner in your law firm is telling you about the outcome of a court case she was involved in. Ask about what her client said. (deny)
5 You are talking to a friend from Russia who has been here for

several years. You know that borshch is her favourite dish. What do you say? (miss)

6 Ask politely what country somebody you have just met comes from. (excuse my ...)

7 Pam and Jim told you that their son Ian wanted to go on holiday with some older friends. Ian's only 15, and they're not too keen on the idea. You ask them what happened. (allow Ian ...)

8 Your father asks you where you'd like to go for a meal when you visit your parents on Saturday. What do you reply? (would prefer ...)

9 You are describing to a friend the sorts of things you like doing on holiday. (enjoy)

8 Advice to tourists

You've got a holiday job working for a travel agent's in the South of England. Three customers want some advice on holidays in the North of England. You have information available on three areas, the Lake District, the Yorkshire Dales and Northumberland. Using the customer profiles and area profiles below, advise each customer about which area is most suitable.

In doing this, use the structures listed below, choosing two structures from each box for each customer (i.e. a total of 12 structures). Do not use the same structure more than twice. If you need more information about these areas, go to the websites listed.

Example

'If you're intending *to go hiking a lot*, I would suggest *going to the Yorkshire Dales. But remember*, it's no use *assuming that you'll have fine weather, so I would* advise you to *take raincoats and wellies*.'

Lake District (www.lake-district.gov.uk/lakes/qualities.html)
Location: North-West of England
Attractions: countryside, wildlife, mountainous landscape, lakes
Leisure activities: mountain-climbing, fell-walking, sailing, hiking, angling
History: literary links with the Romantic movement (Wordsworth)
Food: Grasmere gingerbread

Yorkshire Dales (www.yorkshirenet.co.uk/visinfo/ydales/recreate.htm)
Location: central North of England, north of Leeds
Attractions: countryside, hilly moorland landscape, wildlife (especially birds)
Leisure activities: cycling, pot-holing (limestone caves), climbing, hiking, angling
History: medieval abbeys - Fountains Abbey, Jervaulx Abbey, Bolton Abbey
Food: Wensleydale cheese

Exercises

Northumberland (www.northumberland.gov.uk/)
Location: North-East of England
Attractions: countryside, wildlife (deer, birds, seals), hilly landscape, seacoast
Leisure activities: cycling, hiking, angling, sailing, canoeing, water-skiing, golfing
History: Hadrian's Wall (Roman), castles (Newcastle, Bamburgh, Alnwick)
Food: Craster kippers, seafood

Ann Barker (32)
Occupation: management consultant
Interests: history, canoeing, cycling, potholing

Len Barlow (52)
Occupation: manager, department store
Interests: poetry, angling, hiking, fell-walking, mountaineering

Corel Library

Steve Carré (34)
Occupation: Latin teacher
history, cheese connoisseur, angling, golfing, hiking, sailing, water-skiing

Box 1
avoid
enjoy
interested in
involve
It's no good ...
It's no use ...
look forward to
practise
suggest
there's no point in ...
try

Box 2
advise you
if you are intending
if you are planning
maybe you would like
perhaps you would prefer
they don't allow you
they don't permit you

9 **Mind the gap!**

Translate the gaps in the sentences below into English, using a gerund.

1 Ich bin dagegen, dass Studierende solche Bücher kaufen.
I'm _____ books like that.

2 Unsere Organisation befürwortet die Abschaffung der Todesstrafe.
Our organisation _____ the death penalty.

3 Ich kann mich nicht entsinnen, je gesehen zu haben, dass diese
I can't _____ these children
Kinder sich waschen.
having a wash.

4 Er kommt ständig zu spät. Ich bin es leid, das dulden zu müssen.
He _____ late. I'm _____ tolerate that.

5 Hör auf zu jammern. Du hast das Rauchen doch noch gar nicht
_____. *You haven't even given up _____ yet!*
aufgegeben!

6 Die Chancen, dass so etwas passiert, sind gering.
The _____ are slight.

7 Nachdem wir 100 Kilometer im Jeep auf staubigen Feldwegen
After _____ 100 kilometres in the jeep on dusty tracks we
gefahren waren, hatten wir große Lust, einige Dosen Foster's zu
really felt like _____ a few cans of Foster's.
trinken.

IX Number

IX.1 Overview

definition

By number we mean, in Modern English, the distinction between singular and plural to denote one or more than one countable item respectively.

Number, i.e. the contrast between singular and plural as well as the possibility of using the indefinite article, only occurs with countable nouns. In the case of uncountable nouns no number contrast occurs. Compare 2.1 below.

History

In the noun category of number Modern English has changed radically since Old English times. It is also quite different from the more conservative Germanic languages such as German and Icelandic. Modern English has developed a much more regular system of marking the plural of nouns compared to Old English and many modern Germanic languages. This pattern was well established by the 15th century (see Lass 1999, p.140f.).

IX.2
Normal pattern

2.1 Countable and uncountable nouns

Syntactically, nouns can be divided into three major groups on the basis of the features set out in the table below. Proper nouns normally have no plural and are not preceded by any determiner. Countable nouns have a plural form and co-occur with the definite and indefinite articles, and with the quantifier *some* followed by the plural. Uncountable nouns can be used with no determiner, with the definite article, or with the quantifier *some*. When used as a quantifier, *some* is normally pronounced [səm]. In other functions *some*, pronounced [sʌm] (e.g. meaning 'a certain person or thing') has a different syntactic pattern.

	Features of noun classes		
feature	proper nouns	countable nouns	uncountable nouns
no determiner	*Christopher*		*music*
definite article		*the book*	*the music*
indefinite article		*a book*	
quantifier		*some books*	*some music*
plural		*books*	

Semantically, countable nouns (also known as 'count nouns') denote individual countable units, while uncountable nouns designate a mass or continuum and are therefore also known as 'mass nouns'. Compare the examples of count and mass nouns in the text about Karl Marx by Sir Isaiah Berlin below.

Text

"... He lives in one of the worst and cheapest neighbourhoods in London. He occupies two rooms. There is not one clean or decent piece of furniture in either room, everything is broken, tattered and torn, with thick dust over everything ... manuscripts, books and newspapers lie beside the children's toys, bits and pieces from his wife's sewing basket, cups with broken rims, dirty spoons, knives, forks, lamps, an inkpot, tumblers, pipes, tobacco ash – all piled up on the same table ..." (Berlin 1978, p.142)

In the sample text there are far more countable nouns (the nouns underlined) than uncountable nouns (in red). Nouns referring to substances such as dust, tobacco or ash are usually uncountable. The vast majority of countable nouns have a regular plural, spelt *-s* or *-es*. Compare this with the pattern for the corresponding nouns in German, which even in such a short text has five major plural types:

-(e)n	Gegenden, Zeitungen, Frauen, Tassen, Gabeln, Lampen, Pfeifen
ZERO	Zimmer, Möbel, Löffel, Messer
-e	Stücke, Manuskripte, Tische
umlaut + -e	Körbe
-er	Bücher, Kinder, Ränder, Tintenfässer, Gläser

Many nouns can be either countable or uncountable, often with different meanings. Examples of this type are *stone, cake, paper*.

1 *The ashes of the campfire were still glowing.*
2 *I wish you wouldn't leave your cigarette ash all over the place!*
3 *'Do you fancy a cake?' 'No thanks, I don't like cake.'*
4 *What are these blonde hairs doing on your jacket? My hair is brown!*
5 *Waitress, two teas, please!*
6 *Would you like some tea? I've just made some.*

Although the noun categories countable and uncountable occur in both German and English, this does not mean that words with comparable meaning in the two languages are necessarily in the same grammatical categories.
Compare:

Spielzeug : toy *Gemüse : vegetable*
Möbel : furniture *Information : information*

7 *Iss doch dein Gemüse auf. Es ist gesund.*
8 *Eat your vegetables. They're good for you.*
9 *Können Sie mir einige Informationen geben?*
10 *Can you give me some information?*

Common English nouns which are uncountable in contrast to their German equivalents, which are usually countable, are listed below.

uncountable	countable	uncountable	countable
advice	*Rat(schlag)*	homework	*Hausaufgabe(n)*
damage	*Schaden*	information	*Information, Auskunft*
evidence	*Beweis*	news	*Nachricht*
furniture	*Möbel*	progress	*Fortschritt*

Compare:

11 *She gave me some advice on which university to study at.* (= *Ratschläge*)
12 *The hurricane caused a great deal of damage.* (= *Schäden*)
13 *The evidence of his guilt was overwhelming.* (= *Beweise*)
14 *We're getting some new furniture tomorrow.* (= *neue Möbel*)
15 *I've got tons of homework to do!* (= *Hausaufgaben*)
16 *His information isn't always reliable.* (= *Information[en]*)
17 *There's no news of the missing pot-holers.* (= *Nachricht[en]*)
18 *Form 5A haven't made much progress in French.* (= *Fortschritte*)

Occasionally people feel the need to treat some of these uncountable nouns as if they referred to single units. In such cases they use special words for this purpose, e.g. *item, piece,* etc. Note that these words often only collocate with specific uncountable words:

19 *I'll give you a piece of advice.*
20 *The auctioneers assessed the value of each piece of furniture.*
21 *An item of information like this is invaluable.* (also: *a piece*)
22 *What a stroke of luck finding you here!*

However, it is important to realise that this usage is the exception, not the rule. English treats words like these as uncountables in the vast majority of cases.

The English words listed below are used both as mass nouns and countable nouns, though in different meanings:

uncountable		countable	
business	Geschäft	business(es)	Firma
experience	Erfahrung(en)	experience(s)	Erlebnis
interest	Zins(en)	interest(s)	Interesse
work	Arbeit	work(s)	Werk

23 *How's business?* (= *das Geschäft, die Geschäfte*)
24 *He's a millionaire who owns lots of businesses in Britain.* (= *Firmen*)
25 *You learn from experience.* (= *Erfahrung*)
26 *The speaker told us of a strange experience she had in Nepal.* (= *Erlebnis*)

27 *The interest on our mortgage is horrendous.* (= *Zinsen*)
28 *List your leisure time interests on the back of the form.* (= *Interessen*)
29 *Work like that is pretty back-breaking.* (= *Arbeit*)
30 *I've just bought the Complete Works of William Shakespeare.* (= *Werke*)

2.2 Regular noun plurals

English is similar to French, Spanish and Portuguese in having only one type of regular plural formation. In this it is unique among Germanic languages. The Modern English plural derives from an Old English *-as* plural of the *a*-stems (e.g. OE: *stānas* 'stones') which expanded to other noun classes, eventually replacing the nine plural endings of Old English by one. Only a few relics of the older patterns still survive (see below 3.2).

The regular plural morpheme {*-es*} has three allomorphs /ɪz/, /z/ and /s/: allomorphs

1 /ɪz/ is used after words ending in sibilants: /ɪz/

/-z/ *sizes, roses*
/-s/ *horses, faces, boxes*
/-ʒ/ *mirages*
/-ʃ/ *dishes*
/-dʒ/ *bridges, cages*
/-tʃ/ *churches.*

2 /z/ occurs after words ending in all other voiced sounds, i.e. vowels or voiced consonants: /z/
lies • *boys* • *dogs* • *beds.*

3 /s/ is used after words ending in voiceless (non-sibilant) consonants: /s/
cats • *months.*

This allomorphic pattern is identical to the one occurring in the genitive (see Chap. XI, 2.1) and in the third person singular of the Present Simple of verbs.

IX.3 Exceptions

3.1 Use of indefinite article with uncountable nouns

Although uncountable nouns cannot normally occur with the indefinite article, this is sometimes possible when their meaning is qualified. This is particularly common if the nouns concerned denote emotions or mental ability. Note that these nouns cannot be used in the plural:

31 *He has a profound distrust of foreigners.*
32 *We are looking for applicants with a good knowledge of Spanish.*

3.2 Irregular plurals in native words

Most of the irregular noun plurals in native words are leftovers of an earlier more complex pattern of noun classes. The majority are therefore closed classes, which are no longer having new words added to them. In some cases speakers have been unconsciously regularising the pattern in Modern English, particularly in informal English and with less common words. This is why there is frequently alternation between irregular and regular forms:

CONSONANT VOICING PLUS *-es*

singular /f/: plural /vz/ *calves • halves • knives • leaves • lives • loaves • shelves • thieves • wives • wolves*

Note

The following words have both irregular and regular plurals: *dwarf • hoof • scarf • wharf*

singular /θ/: plural /ðz/ *baths • oaths • paths • truths • youths*

All of these also have regular plurals in /θs/. In American English, only the regular plural is normal.

singular /s/: plural /zɪz/ *houses.*

History

These irregularities are the relic of an allophonic alternation in Old English: Old English had the phonemes /f/ /θ/ /s/ with the voiceless allophones [f] [θ] [s] initially and finally, and the voiced allophones [v] [ð] [z] in voiced environments, e.g. medially. Hence the alternation [f] - [v] (see also Faiß 1989, §2.9.8.5.), cf.:

OE	MnE
wulf /wʊlf/ [wʊlf]	wolf
wulfas /'wʊlfas/ ['wʊlvas]	wolves

Plurals formed by a change of vowel, cf. German *Fuß - Füße*, Swedish *fot - fötter* are a typical feature of Germanic, but nowadays they only form a small class in most Germanic languages, including English: foot – feet • goose – geese • louse – lice • man – men • mouse – mice • tooth – teeth • woman – women /'wʊmən/ - /'wɪmɪn/

UMLAUT PLURALS

33 *Lice are a big problem in many schools.*

This is a relic of the Germanic weak declension. In Dutch, Afrikaans and German it is one of the most common plural classes (cf. p.167). In English it is a very small class: *child – children* • *ox – oxen.*

PLURAL IN *-en*

34 *Many children today come from single-parent families.*

Notice that *children* contains three plural markers: *-en*, *-r* and the change in vowel (/ɪ/ for /aɪ/).

Note

1 Typical of neuter nouns in Old English (and still a large class in Scandinavian), this is also a very small class involving names of animals and fish: *cod* • *deer* • *salmon* • *sheep* • *trout.*

THE ZERO PLURAL

35 *The deer in the forest are very tame.*
36 *The giant salmon some fish farms produce are often genetically modified.*
37 *The trout we caught were enormous.*

However, some nouns referring to animals, birds or fish have acquired a zero plural in addition to the regular plural: *antelope(s)* • *crab(s)* • *duck(s)* • *fish(es)* • *herring(s)* • *rhino(s)* • *shrimp(s).*

Zero plurals tend to be restricted to hunting or fishing contexts:

38 *Look at those ducks on the pond!*
39 *The local landowner was shooting duck.*
40 *Look at all those fishes in the pond!*
41 *We caught loads of fish last weekend.*

The regular plural *fishes* is mainly used when the focus is on *fish* as individual items. In example 40 the zero plural *fish* is also common. Nowadays the zero plural *fish* is in fact the normal form.

Note

2 This class also includes nationality names ending in *-ese* and the noun *Swiss*: *Chinese* • *Japanese* • *Lebanese* • *Portuguese* • *Vietnamese* • *Swiss.*

42 *I know quite a lot of Japanese.*
43 *Most of the Swiss I know live near Lake Lucerne.*

3 The word craft meaning 'vessel' and the compounds *aircraft*, *hovercraft* also have zero plural. Compare:

44 *Several aircraft were grounded due to the bad weather.*

4 A fourth group with zero plural is quantity nouns. These nouns have zero plural when preceded by another quantity noun, usually a number. They have the regular plural when they refer to indefinite quantities: *dozen* • *hundred* • *thousand* • *million.*

45 *I'd like two dozen eggs next week, please, milkman.*
46 *Dozens of guardsmen fainted in the heat.*
47 *London's population is about seven million.*
48 *Millions of people will be affected if global warming continues.*

3.3 Irregular plurals in foreign words

variation in plural forms

There is a strong tendency for foreign plurals to be assimilated to the regular plural, especially in informal registers, whereas foreign plurals are more likely to be retained in technical and academic usage. Compare the regular plural *formulas*, used in general contexts, with the foreign plural *formulae*, used in mathematics, linguistics, etc. The semantic field of flowers is a good example of this. Since flowers are everyday items, their scientific names from Latin or Greek have become anglicised, with the result that only regular plurals occur, cf. *crocuses, geraniums, freesias, irises.*
In each group listed below there are potentially three possibilities:

a *The foreign plural is retained.*
b *The foreign plural and a new regular plural co-exist side by side.*
c *The word has acquired a regular plural.*

LATIN MASCULINE NOUNS IN *-us* (plural: *-i* /aɪ/ or /iː/)

a *alumnus – alumni* • *bacillus – bacilli* • *stimulus – stimuli*
b *cactus* • *focus* • *fungus* • *nucleus* • *radius* • *syllabus* • *terminus*

c *bonus* • *campus* • *census* • *chorus* • *circus* • *prospectus* • *status* • *virus*

Note

The variation in pronunciation of the Latin plural is due to two competing ways of pronouncing Latin words. The anglicised one is with /aɪ/, which was the type used in the traditional teaching of Latin at schools. When the pronunciation of Latin in schools was reformed in the early 20th century, the 'new' pronunciation with /iː/ spread to Latin plurals in English (see Allen 1970, p.102ff.). This is particularly striking with the plural *fungi*, which has four variant pronunciations, ranging from the most anglicised type /ˈfʌndʒaɪ/ via /ˈfʌŋgaɪ/ /ˈfʌndʒiː/ to /ˈfʌŋgiː/, the least anglicised variant. A similar alternation resulting from the difference between the traditional and reformed pronunciation of Latin in schools occurs in Germany in words like *Caesar*, *Cicero*, where the traditional pronunciation of ‹c› before a front vowel has [ts], while the reformed one has [k], as in Classical Latin.

LATIN FEMININE NOUNS ENDING IN *-a* (plural: *-ae* /iː/ or /aɪ/)

Here too, variation in the pronunciation is due to differences between the traditional and the reformed pronunciation of Latin, viz. /iː/ and /aɪ/ respectively.

a *alga – algae* *alumna – alumnae* *larva – larvae*
b *antenna* • *formula* • *nebula* • *vertebra*
c *area* • *arena* • *dilemma* • *diploma* • *drama* • *era*, etc.

LATIN NEUTER NOUNS ENDING IN *-um* (plural: *a* /ə/)

a *addendum – addenda* • *bacterium – bacteria* • *erratum – errata*
b *aquarium* • *curriculum* • *medium* • *memorandum* • *millennium* • *referendum* • *spectrum* • *stadium* • *stratum* • *symposium* • *ultimatum*
c *album* • *chrysanthemum* • *museum* • *premium*

An alternative form of assimilation to regular English noun patterns is illustrated by the words *agenda, data, media*, all originally the plurals of Latin singulars in *-um*: *agenda* has now been reinterpreted as a singular, acquiring a regular plural in the process:

49 *The agendas at these summit meetings are often very full.*

With *data* a different pattern has emerged. It is either used as a plural noun or as an uncountable singular. Both are equally common. Compare:

50 *Many of these data are inconclusive.*
51 *Much of this data is faulty or misleading.*

The loanword *media* is usually used as a plural noun, but is sometimes also reinterpreted as an uncountable noun. An alternative pattern, to treat it as a countable noun with a regular plural *medias* (cf. a similar tendency in French: *les médias*), is rejected by most speakers. The use as an uncountable noun (as in 53) is also frowned upon by many people:

52 *The media are often very intrusive.*
53 *The media tends to sensationalise this issue.*

LATIN NOUNS ENDING IN *-ex*, *-ix* (plural: *-ices* /ɪsiːz/)

The important nouns in this group have both plurals. Here the alternate plural forms have been functionalised semantically, acquiring different meanings:

appendix – appendices (= Anhang)
appendix – appendixes (= Blinddarm)

index – indices (= Indiz, Index, Messzahl)
index – indexes (= Register, Quellenverzeichnis)

GREEK FEMININE NOUNS ENDING IN *-is* (plural: *-es* /iːz/)

In this type, the *-is* of the stem is replaced by a plural ending *-es*, pronounced /iːz/, e.g. *analysis – analyses*:
analysis • basis • crisis • diagnosis • hypothesis • oasis • parenthesis • synopsis • synthesis • thesis

Note

The form *bases* can be either the plural of *basis* or *base*. Compare:

base	[beɪs]	–	*bases*	['beɪsɪz]	(= *Stützpunkt*)
basis	['beɪsɪs]	–	*bases*	['beɪsiːz]	(= *Grundlage*)

c *iris • metropolis* (regular plural only)

GREEK NEUTER NOUNS ENDING IN *-on* (plural: *-a*)

a *criterion – criteria • phenomenon – phenomena*
c *electron • neutron • proton* (regular plural only)

3.4 Nouns ending in -s taking a singular verb

These are uncountable nouns where *-s* is part of the stem, i.e. not a realisation of the plural morpheme. They therefore take a singular verb:

Noun: *-s*
Verb: singular

measles • *mumps* • *rabies* • *shingles*

DISEASES

54 *Measles is a typical children's disease. So is mumps.*

billiards • *darts* • *dominoes* • *draughts* (AmE: *checkers*) • *marbles*

GAMES

55 *Darts is very popular in British pubs.*

56 *The news of his tragic death has just reached us.*

news

3.5 Nouns ending in -ics normally taking a singular verb

These are uncountable nouns which refer to subjects, sciences or similar fields: *acoustics* • *athletics* • *economics* • *ethics* • *genetics* • *gymnastics* • *linguistics* • *mathematics* • *phonetics* • *physics* • *politics* • *statistics* • *tactics.*

Noun: *-ics*
Verb: singular

> Many of these words go back to Greek neuter plurals, e.g. *physics* derives from τὰ φυσικά, which became a neuter plural *physica* in Latin. This was often interpreted as a feminine singular in medieval Latin, with the result that most languages now treat the word as a singular, e.g. German *Physik*, French *physique*, Spanish *física*, whereas English retains the original plural form, though followed by a singular verb.

History

57 *Phonetics is useful in EFL teaching.*
58 *Politics is not everybody's cup of tea.*

Some of these nouns (viz. *acoustics, ethics, economics, mathematics, politics*) can also be used with a plural verb in special senses, usually denoting practical aspects of the related subject (see Lamprecht 1986, §140, and Biber 1999, §3.9.1.2). Compare:

59 *The acoustics in this room are terrible.* (= the room's acoustic qualities)
60 *His politics are pretty left-wing, I hear.* (= his political views)

Noun: *-ics*
Verb: plural

Corresponding to the subjects *statistics, tactics* there are also the countable nouns *statistic, tactic*. Compare:

61 *Quite frankly, I object to being treated as a statistic.*
62 *England's new coach wants to try out a new tactic.*

Noun: -*s*
Verb: plural

3.6 Nouns ending in -s taking a plural verb

These countable nouns ending in -*s* only occur in the plural and are followed by a plural verb. The first two categories refer to items consisting of two equal parts which are joined together, e.g. *glasses, scissors*. Compare a similar use of the plural in French – *les lunettes, les ciseaux* – and Russian – очки, ножницы Similarly Russian and Swedish, like English, use the plural to denote trousers: cf. брюки and *byxor*.

TOOLS, INSTRUMENTS

glasses • *spectacles* • *binoculars* • *scales* • *forceps* • *pliers* • *scissors* • *shears*

63 *These scissors aren't very sharp.*

CLOTHES

briefs • *jeans* • *knickers* • *pants* • *pyjamas* (AmE: *pajamas*) • *shorts* • *tights* • *trousers* • *(swimming) trunks*

64 *These jeans were only £20 at the January sales!*

If we need to talk about an individual item, we use the word *pair*:

65 *This is the second pair of scissors I've lost in a week!*
66 *Maria bought two pairs of jeans at C&A's.*

OTHER NOUNS

The use of the plural in other cases only reflects a plural entity in one or two cases, e.g. *clothes* (cf. German *Kleider*), *guts, stairs*. In many other cases the explanation for the plural form seems to be usage in the original language (often Latin). (For a more detailed list, see Quirk 1985, §5.77, and Lamprecht 1986, §137).

archives • *arms* • *ashes* • *clothes* • *contents* • *damages* • *earnings* • *funds* • *guts* • *minutes* • *premises* • *regards* • *relations* • *remains* • *stairs* • *surroundings* • *thanks* • *troops* • *valuables* • *wits*

67 *The archives contain all our records from 1934 to today.*
68 *The contents of this letter are top secret.*
69 *I'll sue you for damages. (damages = Schadensersatz)*
70 *The minutes of the meeting were taken by Mr Pettigrew.*
71 *The troops were billeted among the local population.*
72 *You've got to keep your wits about you when you're a lion-tamer.*

3.7 Nouns ending in -s taking singular and plural verbs

Noun: -s
Verb: singular/plural

These nouns have *-s* as part of the stem. They can refer to one or more than one item. When followed by a singular verb the word denotes one item, while a plural verb designates more than one item. There is no change in the ending of the noun: *means* • *series* • *species* • *works.*

73 *Television is an effective means of communication. (= ein Mittel)*
74 *All possible means have been implemented. (= alle Mittel)*
75 *This species will die out if we don't protect its habitat. (= diese Art)*
76 *Many species are threatened by agribusiness. (= viele Arten)*

With the following words a singular verb refers to one item, whereas a plural may refer to either one or more than one item: *barracks* • *headquarters.*

77 *The headquarters of London's police is at New Scotland Yard.*
78 *The Labour Party's headquarters are located in Millbank Tower.*
79 *The headquarters of several firms are in this area.*

3.8 Collective nouns taking a plural verb

Noun: collective
Verb: plural

In contrast to most collective nouns (see 3.9 below), these can only be followed by a plural verb: *cattle* • *clergy* • *people* • *police* • *poultry* • *vermin.*

80 *The cattle were grazing in the field.*
81 *Many people are sceptical about the alleged benefits of genetic engineering.*
82 *Anglican clergy are still divided on the issue of women priests.*
83 *The police are looking for a man in his mid-thirties.*
84 *Free-range poultry are usually healthier.*
85 *Vermin were a major source of disease in the Middle Ages.*

Note

When *people* means 'nation' (= *Volk*), it is an ordinary countable noun. However, it is usually followed even here by a plural verb. Compare:

86 *Churchill wrote A History of the English-Speaking Peoples.*
87 *Australians are a people who are crazy about sport.*

3.9 Notional concord

definition: concord

The term concord means number agreement between subject and verb.

grammatical concord

By grammatical concord we mean that the number of the subject of the sentence agrees with the number of the verb, i.e. if the subject of the sentence or clause is in the singular, the verb is also in the singular. This is the normal pattern in most languages, including English.

notional concord

However, in English an alternative pattern also occurs under certain conditions. Known as notional concord, it refers to a pattern where the semantic content of the subject determines what number the verb takes. Thus a subject whose form is plural but whose meaning is singular is followed by a singular verb, and vice versa. A typical example of this is the concord used with *the United States*. Compare the English version, using notional concord, with its German equivalent, which has grammatical concord:

88 *The United States wants to improve its relations with China.*
89 *Die Vereinigten Staaten wollen ihre Beziehungen zu China verbessern.*

The increasing use of notional concord, which is particularly frequent after collective nouns in British English, probably reflects the reduced importance of formal grammatical markers in the number system of nouns, and of the noun in general (cf. Leisi 1999, p.140ff.). This reduced importance is hardly surprising when we remember that a distinction between singular and plural is mainly made in the present tense of verbs, and even then only for the third person. The main areas where notional concord occurs are listed below (for more examples, see Swan 1995, §503f., and Quirk 1985, §10.35):

Noun: plural
Verb: singular

1 UNITS: Nouns in this category are plural in form, but refer to items regarded as single units. Hence the use of the singular verb:

United Nations • United States • fish and chips • R&D (= *research and development*)

90 *The UN is discussing the latest Middle East crisis.*
91 *The US has often criticised China's human rights record.*
92 *Fish and chips is my favourite dish.*
93 *We think that improved R&D is essential if we are to retain our market share.*

2 PHRASES OF QUANTITY OR MEASURE: These phrases referring to capacity, distance, money, time and weight are seen as units and as such are followed by a singular verb:

94 *Five litres of petrol isn't enough to get us home.* (capacity)
95 *Forty miles is a long way to walk.* (distance)
96 *That fifty dollars was all I had left.* (money)
97 *Four years is a long time to be away from your children.* (time)
98 *Three kilos is a lot to lose in a week.* (weight)

Noun: singular
Verb: plural

With names of sports teams, British English uses notional concord, i.e. the singular noun is followed by a plural verb.

99 *Have you heard? France have won the World Cup!*
100 *Wales, who have been doing well in rugby internationals recently, are due to meet New Zealand's All Blacks next month.*

QUANTIFIERS

After fractions and other quantifiers followed by a noun which semantically is plural, a plural verb is used:

101 *Half of the passengers were drowned when the ship sank.*
102 *Only a minority of people in Northern Ireland support violence.*
103 *Forty-five per cent of those interviewed favour lifting the ban on soft drugs.*
104 *A number of people have reported seeing UFOs.*

Note

The phrase *a number of* means 'several', and is therefore always followed by a plural noun and verb.

COLLECTIVE NOUNS

Collective nouns are singular in form, and thus take a singular verb. However, since they are also plural in content (i.e. they refer to a group of people), they can also take a plural verb. The latter construction is common (though usually optional) in British English, but rare in American English (see also Biber 1999, §3.9.2.3). Some examples of common collective nouns are listed below (see Quirk 1985, §5.108, for further examples).

army • audience • class • club • college • committee • company • council • couple • crew • crowd • enemy • family • gang • generation • government • group • majority • party • school • staff • team • university

105 *The family wants to move out of its council house soon.*
106 *My brother's family have decided to do without their holiday this year.*
107 *The government has decided to review its public spending priorities.*
108 *The government are publishing their White Paper next week.*

However, even in British English the collective noun has to take a singular verb when it is preceded by the following markers of the singular: *a(n)* • *every* • *each* • *this* • *that.*

109 *An army marches on its stomach.*
110 *Every family needs a proper roof over its head.*
111 *This government doesn't deserve to be re-elected.*

Names of companies and shops particularly, but also other institutions may conform to this pattern:

112 *ICI has been marketing more environment-friendly products recently.*
113 *ICI have decided to re-think their policy towards Greenpeace.*
114 *Fenwick's is starting its sale on winter clothes just after Xmas.*
115 *Woolworth's are reviewing their sales targets.*
116 *The BBC is re-thinking the format of its news programmes.*
117 *The BBC have been expanding their commercial operations.*

Exercises

1 Usage: What do you say?

- Tick the alternative which you would use in German. If you would use more than one, number them in order of preference (e.g. 1 for 'most natural', 2 for 'second best', etc.).

Exercises

- Speculate on why you preferred these alternatives. Compare your results with those of other native speakers.
- Translate the sentences into English, using the vocabulary given.
- Compare the German sentences with your English translation. Check in 3.6 and 3.9 that you have used the correct grammar. What differences emerge?

1 ❒ a Zehn Jahre sind viel Zeit.
❒ b Zehn Jahre ist viel Zeit.
English: _____

2 ❒ a Grünkohl mit Pinkel sind Dieters Leibgericht.
❒ b Grünkohl mit Pinkel ist Dieters Leibgericht.
English: _____

Grünkohl mit Pinkel = *curly kale with sausage*
Leibgericht = *favourite food*

3 ❒ a Diese Jeans sind mir zu eng. Ich habe nämlich zugenommen.
❒ b Diese Jeans ist mir zu eng. Ich habe nämlich zugenommen.
❒ c Diese Jeans-Hose ist mir zu eng. Ich habe nämlich zugenommen.
English: _____

eng = *tight*
nämlich = *you see*
zunehmen = *to put on weight*

4 ❒ a Die USA wollen gegen diese Maßnahme protestieren.
❒ b Die USA will gegen diese Maßnahme protestieren.
English: _____

5 ❒ a Die Hälfte der Befragten waren für die Todesstrafe.
❒ b Die Hälfte der Befragten war für die Todesstrafe.
English: _____

Befragte = *those interviewed*
Todesstrafe = *the death penalty*

6 ❒ a Ich finde, 50 Euro sind viel Geld. Für eine Eintrittskarte ist das zu teuer.
❒ b Ich finde, 50 Euro ist viel Geld. Für eine Eintrittskarte ist das zu teuer.
English: _____

Euro = *euro(s)*
Eintrittskarte = *entrance ticket*

7 ❒ a Wussten Sie, dass etwa 60 Prozent aller Iren in Städten wohnen?
❒ b Wussten Sie, dass etwa 60 Prozent aller Iren in Städten wohnt?
English: _____

8 ❒ a Mir gefallen diese Shorts. Ich nehme sie.
❒ b Mir gefällt diese Shorts. Ich nehme sie.
English: _____

gefallen = *to like*

2 Situations

What would you say in the following situations? Include one of the words below in each of your answers.

advice • evidence • experience • homework • information • luck • progress

1 You are interviewing an applicant for a job in your electronics firm. You want to find out how experienced the applicant is in the field of electronics. You ask:
'What _____?'
2 You're at a travel agent's. You want to know about cheap flights for students to Australia. What do you say?
'I'd like _____?'
3 You can't decide whether to take a module on post-war British history or one on the American Civil War at the British university where you are an Erasmus student. What would you ask your tutor?
'Can you give me _____?'
4 You'd like to take your son Billy to a football match, but you can't if he's got a lot of homework. What do you ask him?
'Billy, how _____?'
5 Jenny has been applying for jobs at local radio stations. You're curious to know how her applications have been going. You ask her:
'Have you made _____?'
6 You are investigating a murder. You think the proof you have that Mr Boothby killed his partner is not sufficient to persuade a jury. What do you say to your colleagues?
'I don't think the _____.'
7 Your friend has been trying to get a vacation job at a computer software firm so that he can buy a new motorbike. You ask:
'Angus, have you had _____?'

3 Breaking the bad news

Cruikshanks, a firm making toilet fittings, is in difficulties. Its director is giving a speech. Choose the correct alternative in his speech. In some cases more than one alternative may be correct.

1 'Ladies and gentlemen, the company ____ to close our factory in Scotland.
a decided b has decided c have decided
2 Due to the recession, the demand for toilet fittings ____ dramatically.
a slumped b has slumped c have slumped d are slumping

3 Cruikshanks ____ the view that the only way to cut our losses is to close one of our operations.
a take b takes c took d have been taking

4 Our Scottish factory ____ money hand over fist for five years now.
a lose b is losing c have lost d has been losing

5 In a nutshell, this company ___ prepared to keep a loss-making operation afloat.
a is no longer b no longer is c no longer are d are no longer

6 Over the past five years we have made losses totalling ___ in Inverlochy.
a two millions of pounds b two million pound
c two million pounds

7 Last year alone Inverlochy made a loss of £700,000. £700,000 ____ a lot of money for a medium-sized firm such as ours.
a is b are c are being d is being

8 A number of our Inverlochy staff ____ if we could avoid this drastic step by cost-cutting measures such as part-time work or shopping around for cheaper materials.
a has asked b have asked c asked d asks

9 Unfortunately this is not a practical proposition. The only way out is to sell the factory as soon as possible. Even a ____ delay would be disastrous.
a two month b two-month c two months' d two-months'

10 Ladies and gentlemen, I am very sorry that my news ____ so bad. I have every sympathy with the staff affected, but we feel that we have no other option. Are there any questions?'
a is b are c have been d has been

4 Statements

Form a statement about the objects illustrated below, using the adjective given in brackets.

Example

______________________________ (delicious)

→ *This cake looks delicious!*

______________________________ (beautiful)

→ *Those roses are beautiful.*

Exercises

1  ____________________ (graceful)

2 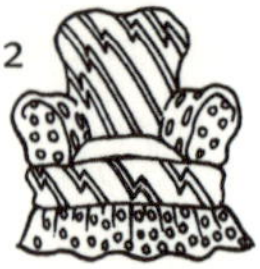 ____________________ (ugly)

3 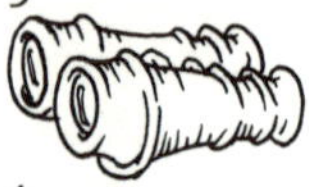 ____________________ (expensive)

4  ____________________ (cute)

5 

____________________ (happy)

6  ____________________ (cool)

7  ____________________ (greasy)

8  ____________________ (healthy)

9  ____________________ (silly)

5 Detecting number errors

Exercises

Cross out the incorrect plural forms of the nouns in the following sentences and write the correct version.

1 Most analysises of the censuses held in Britain since 1801 show that there is no correlation between the phenomenas of population size and prosperity.
2 The lifes of the larvas of the water boatman are a constant battle against predators.
3 Economic criterions alone are not always decisive in the successes of new products – ethics are also an important factor in some cases, e.g. in cosmetics which have not been tested on animals.
4 The hunters of the tribe used their knifes to cut up the carcasses of the two water buffalo before giving their wifes the meat.
5 Inaccurate diagnosis by doctors have been proved to be one factor in the excessive number of appendices which have been removed in hospital operations.
6 The data available on the curriculums of European universities confirm that there are enormous differences between universities in different parts of the EU, the disparity being partly due to the wide variation in syllabuses used.

6 Starting a newspaper report

Write the first sentence of a newspaper report to fit the headlines below. Remember the following typical features of headlines:

- grammatical words (e.g. *the*, auxiliaries) are usually omitted
- the Present Participle is often used instead of a Present Progressive
- the Past Participle is used for the Passive
- *to* + Infinitive is used instead of *to be* to when referring to future events
- headlines use specialist vocabulary (help is given in the vocabulary box)

Example

IRELAND TO MEET FRANCE IN JUNE RUGBY STAND-OFF
→ *Ireland are to play against France in an international match held in June, a spokesman for the Irish national team announced today.*

to axe sth.	= *to abolish sth.*	BT	= *British Telecom*
FT	= *Financial Times*	watchdog	= *regulatory body*
to back sth./sb.	= *to support sth./sb.*		

1 US TO BACK NEW PEACE INITIATIVE
2 HUNDREDS OF TOURISTS FEARED DEAD IN MID-AIR COLLISION
3 FIVE RARE SPECIES BECOMING EXTINCT EACH DAY, SCIENTIST CLAIMS
4 BT MAKING HUGE PROFITS, FT SAYS
5 SCISSORS NAMED AS MURDER WEAPON
6 R&D VITAL FOR EU'S FUTURE, COMMISSIONER WARNS
7 POULTRY NOT AT RISK IN SALMONELLA OUTBREAK, MINISTER CLAIMS
8 GOVERNMENT TO AXE EDUCATION WATCHDOG

7 Limericks

Fill in the blanks in the limericks below with the appropriate word.

1 There were once two alumni from Yale,
Who looked gloomy and ever so pale.
'There are no cute _____,
So let's go for a bungee,'
They said, and they jumped – what a tale!

2 There once was a pair of old _____,
Who said, 'It's not really nice:
When people wash hair,
It's really unfair.
It makes their hair lose all its spice!'

3 There once were two sceptical _____,
Who claimed, 'There isn't a God.'
An agnostic sailed by,
Saying, 'Pie in the sky,
What matters is simply my rod!'

8 Radio Gummersbach

One of the latest stars to hit the media scene is Radio Gummersbach, which has just launched a programme of news in English for its international audience. Their newsreader has asked you to check their English before they go on air. What changes would you make?

This is Radio Gummersbach, broadcasting on Long Wave in the 190 metres band and on Medium Wave in the 550 metres band. Here are the news.

Exercises

The United States have imposed punitive tariffs on european wines, cheeses and some other types of foods. The ban is in response to the European's refusal to accept the meat of genetic modified cows into EU countries. The EU commissioner for agriculture, Sean MacSlurry, stressed that EU are considering retaliatory action.

In Hungary, an estimated two millions of people were affected by severe flooding when the Danube burst its banks along a 50-miles stretch of the river north of the capital, Budapest. Half of the villages in the area has had to be evacuated. Two thirds of the cattle is feared drowned in the worst flooding to hit the region in living memory. The United Nations have offered Hungary emergency relief. Several EU countries have offered 6 million euro in immediate assistance. A spokesperson for the Hungarian government pointed out that while Hungary obviously welcomed this prompt assistance, 'Six million euro do not in fact go very far.'

The International Darts Federation are holding this years world darts championship in Heligoland, which is due to begin tomorrow. Darts have been gaining in popularity over the past years in several european countries. Ireland was the winner of last years championship, but the hot favourite this year are Denmark. Denmarks chances seemed to fade a fortnight ago when their star player, Jens Søndergård, caught measles from his six years old son. 'Luckily measles were only a minor setback, and now I'm fighting fit again,' Jens said today.

And now the local news. Householders living near the busy airport of Cologne/Bonn have been complaining of the noise due to the large number of aircrafts taking off from and landing at the airport. A spokeswoman for the Porz residents association said: 'The data we have on the health hazards posed by aircraft noise shows that many people suffer from considerable stress as a result.'

The police has arrested eight youth in connection with several stabbings after an argument at a Gummersbach disco ended in fighting. Ten people was injured, two of them serious. The police says that they confiscated a total of five flick-knifes, three knuckle-duster, two baseball bats and a bicycle chain.

An international group of experts on fish-breeding are currently visiting the Gummersbach area. They are on a fact-finding mission to study intensive methods of rearing and protecting freshwater fishes, particularly salmon, trouts, pikes and breams. The group consists of four French, three Danes, two Irish, four Nepaleses, a Czech, two Swiss and three Pakistani.

You have been listening to Radio Gummerbach's international service. Our next news in English are at 9 pm.

X Gender

X.1 Overview

definition

By gender we mean the 'grammatical classification of nouns, pronouns, or other words in the noun phrase, according to certain meaning-related distinctions, especially a distinction related to the sex of the referent.' (Quirk 1985, p.314) This grammatical classification is reflected, for example, in words such as articles (as in German, French, etc.), or personal pronouns (as in English, German, French, etc.), when these refer to the noun. The gender classes of most European languages have only a limited connection to sex. A good example of this is the German 'masculine' class of nouns, which includes *der Mann, der Junge*, but also *der Schuh, der Tisch*. Similarly, the 'feminine' class contains *die Frau, die Ärztin*, but also *die Burg, die Straße*. 'Neuter' nouns, on the other hand, can refer to females, e.g. *das Mädchen, das Weib*. This loose link between sex and noun/pronoun classes is usually known as grammatical gender, in contrast to the much closer link between sex and noun classes existing in English, which is known as natural gender.

grammatical gender

natural gender

Note

The traditional terminology connected with gender – the 'masculine', 'feminine' and 'neuter' classes – obscures the fact that the original meaning of *gender* and its Latin ancestor *genus* is simply 'kind', 'class', having nothing to do with sex (Corbett 1991, p.1).

History

Whereas German, Icelandic and Norwegian have kept the three grammatical gender classes of Germanic and Indo-European (masculine-feminine-neuter), Swedish, Danish and Dutch have reduced them to two (common versus neuter). English and Afrikaans have gone even further, with only one class. Afrikaans resembles English in having an invariable definite article *die* and an invariable indefinite article *'n*. (König 1994, p.486 and p.491). Compare:

German	Dutch	Afrikaans	English
der Schuh	de schoen	die skoen	the shoe
die Frau	de vrouw	die vrou	the woman
das Haus	het huis	die huis	the house

The collapse of grammatical gender took place in English during the Middle English period, when English developed an invariable definite article, *the*. (Faiß 1989, §2.16.6.)

X.2 Normal pattern

In Modern English gender is only expressed overtly in the personal pronouns of the third person singular, viz. *he, she, it, his, her, its* etc., which in the vast majority of cases correspond to the natural classes 'male', 'female' and 'without sexual differentiation'.

animate vs. inanimate

In addition to this three-term distinction there is a two-term distinction between animate and inanimate in the relative pronouns *who* and *which*. Nouns can be divided up into different categories according to the way they collocate with *he-she-it* and *who-which*.

2.1 Gender-marked class (masculine or feminine)

GENDER-MARKED CLASS
morphology

Most nouns in this class, which refer to persons, are not marked morphologically for gender, i.e. only the meaning shows which sex is involved, not the form:
boy – girl • *man – woman* • *nephew – niece* • *uncle – aunt* • *king – queen*.

Some pairs of words are marked morphologically for gender, e.g. they show gender by adding an ending, normally by adding the French suffix *-ess* to the masculine member of the pair:
emperor – empress • *duke – duchess* • *host – hostess* • *prince – princess* • *steward – stewardess* • *waiter – waitress.*

ending *-ess*

Other examples of morphologically marked pairs, including morphological marking using compounds with *-man* or *-woman*, are:
hero – heroine • *usher – usherette* • *bridegroom – bride* • *widower – widow* • *businessman – businesswoman* • *policeman – policewoman* • *spokesman – spokeswoman.*

ending *-man/-woman*

2.2 Gender-neutral class

Nouns in this class are neutral as to gender reference, i.e. they can be used to refer either to a female or a male, depending on the specific situation. Compare:

GENDER-NEUTRAL CLASS

1 *We've got a new teacher. She's awfully strict.*
(= Wir haben eine neue Lehrerin ...)
2 *We've got a new teacher. He seems very nice.*
(= Wir haben einen neuen Lehrer ...)

Notice that, in English, gender is not specified until the personal pronoun *he* or *she* is used. By contrast, in German the gender is often specified by using a suffix, e.g. *-in.*

Some examples of members of this large class which occur frequently: *artist* • *author* • *cook* • *doctor* • *enemy* • *friend* • *guest* • *lecturer* • *librarian* • *manager* • *novelist* • *parent* • *person* • *professor* • *servant* • *singer* • *speaker* • *student* • *teacher* • *teenager* • *typist* • *writer.*

Note

Unlike *friend*, the compounds *boyfriend* and *girlfriend* refer to males and females respectively in a romantic and/or sexual relationship. However, in American English *girlfriend* is widely used by females to denote a female friend without any romantic or sexual overtones.

German has a few nouns which can refer to either males or females, e.g. *Gast, Idiot* ("Du Idiot!" can be used to address a male or female.). However, most German equivalents to English nouns in this class are specifically marked for gender, which is usually compulsory: *doctor* = *Arzt, Ärztin* • *professor* = *Professor, Professorin* • *librarian* = *Bibliothekar, Bibliothekarin.*

gender-neutral: expanding class

The gender-neutral class in English has been expanding rapidly in recent decades as people try to avoid sexual bias in language. Compare this with a similar pattern in Germany, where the politically correct form of address *Frau* has largely replaced the old distinction between *Frau* (= married woman) and *Fräulein* (single woman), or the more recent phenomenon of using the gender-neutral form *die Studierenden* in the plural instead of the traditional *Studenten* (masculine form used to include males and females) or the clumsy and unpopular *die StudentInnen*. Similarly, in English-speaking countries opponents of sexual bias have criticised the traditional forms of address *Mrs* ['mɪsɪz] (for married women) and *Miss* (for unmarried women), since no similar distinction is made for men (*Mr* for both married men and bachelors). The form *Ms* [mɪz] or [məz] was therefore proposed and is very common, though it has not managed to supplant *Mrs* and *Miss*. Many other terms have been suggested to avoid sexist usage. Several examples are listed below (more examples in CIDE 1995, p.1305 and Quirk 1985, §5.105):

avoidance of sexist usage

supervisor	instead of	*foreman*
firefighter		*fireman*
spokesperson		*spokesman*
chair(person)		*chairman*

Member of Congress	instead of	*Congressman*
flight attendant		*stewardess*
mail carrier (AmE)		*mailman (AmE)*
ambulance officer		*ambulanceman*
executive		*businessman*
camera operator		*cameraman*
salesperson		*salesman*
humanity, humankind		*man(kind)*

unmarked forms

In other cases unmarked forms like *author, manager, poet*, which were originally restricted to males, have come to be used for both sexes, partly because terms like *authoress* and *poetess* were felt to be pejorative, and *manageress* (used in BrE) was only used to refer to the female head of a shop or restaurant. Similarly, Charlie Brown in the cartoon in section 2.1 uses *hero* to refer to a female person.

personal pronouns

A similar pattern of avoidance of sexual bias occurs in the personal pronouns, where *they* is frequently used to avoid sexist *he* or a clumsy *he or she*. After the indefinite pronouns *somebody, anybody, everybody, nobody* etc. the use of *they* is nowadays the only normal form:

3 *Somebody's left* their *bag here.*
4 *Has anybody lost* their *umbrella?*
5 *Everybody likes clowns, don't* they*?*
6 *No one would do that to* their *child, would* they*?*

This pattern is, however, not simply a case of avoiding sexual bias, since it has been recorded since the 15th century (see Faiß 1989, §3.1.13.9.). Shakespeare, for example, uses it:

7 *God send everyone* their *heart's desire*. (quoted in Swan 1995, §227)

Similarly, sentences like 8 below (quoted in Faiß 1989, §3.1.13.9), reveal that avoidance of sexual bias is not the only motivating factor. The pronoun *they* seems to be used sporadically as a gender-neutral third person pronoun (cf. Finnish *hän*), which is singular in meaning even though it is followed by a plural verb:

8 *If there is a Barbara Wassman on board, could they make themselves known to the cabin?*

Other constructions after which *they* is used (though less frequently than in those illustrated in examples 3 to 6) are:

- *a person*
- *every, each* + Noun
- *who, whoever.*

9 *When a person gets married, they are making a big commitment.*
10 *Tell each person to take what they want.*
11 *Whoever rings, tell them I'm out.*

2.3 Common gender

COMMON GENDER

These nouns can either occur with animate pronouns, i.e. *who – he/she*, or with inanimate pronouns, i.e. *which – it*. The class contains a small number of nouns referring to young humans and nouns denoting higher animals, where sex is not always of primary importance: *baby* • *child* • *toddler* • *cat* • *dog* • *monkey* • *rabbit* • *hamster* • *blackbird* • *eagle.*

animate pattern

inanimate pattern

The use of either pattern depends on context. The animate pattern is mainly used when emotional attachment is involved, e.g. a parent talking about their baby, or someone referring to their pet, or if an animal is being regarded as if it were human. In other cases the inanimate pattern with *which – it* is preferred.

12 *Our baby is only four months old, and she's teething already.*
13 *My budgie is yellow, and he can say at least ten words.*
14 *As we were watching, the eagle dived for his prey.*

Contrast these examples with the emotionally neutral examples below:

15 *A child learns to speak the language of its environment.*
16 *The eagle is a bird of prey which uses its very good sight and sharp curved beak to devastating effect.*

This class differs from the gender-neutral class (see 2.2) in using *it*, not *they*, as an alternative to *he/she*.

2.4 Neuter gender

NEUTER GENDER

Objects, including ships, vehicles, and countries, normally collocate with *which – it*.

17 *This book, which is about Nice, is good. I got it at a jumble sale.*
18 *The Titanic sank after it hit an iceberg.*
19 *Our new car's fantastic. It's really economical on petrol.*
20 *This is a map of France, which is one of the largest countries in Europe.*

Similarly, lower animals normally use *which – it*: *ant* • *bee* • *beetle* • *frog* • *snake* • *spider* • *snail* • *tadpole* • *toad* • *wasp*.

21 *I've just been stung by a wasp! I killed it, though.*

X.3 Exceptions

3.1 Neuter nouns used as gender-marked nouns

Some types of neuter nouns collocating with *which-it* are occasionally treated as if they were gender-marked nouns.

NEUTER NOUNS (lower animals)

1 These nouns are sometimes reinterpreted as if they referred to higher animals, especially if there is an emotional link involved. They then collocate with *he* or *she*.

22 *I've got a pet frog. He's called Albert.*
23 *The bees who are from the new hive seem to be thriving.*

NEUTER NOUNS (countries)

2 When names of countries refer to political units, they can be personified as females, and are therefore treated as feminine, collocating with *she*:

24 *France has improved her economic performance recently.*
25 *Ireland is proud of her ancient Celtic language.*

NEUTER NOUNS (ships, vehicles)

3 Ships, cars, motorbikes and similar vehicles are sometimes treated (by male speakers) as if they were female, particularly if the speaker feels close emotional attachment to them. Note that some speakers feel that this usage is sexist:

26 *The Titanic sank after she was holed by an iceberg.*
27 *I've just had the car repaired. She's a real beauty now.*
28 *Is that your Harley-Davidson? She looks fantastic!*

3.2 Specifying gender in gender-neutral nouns

male student etc.

If the gender needs to be specified, the noun is preceded by *man/woman* or *male/female*, e.g.

29 *The number of women professors at universities is growing.*
30 *There are only two male nurses working at the hospital.*
31 *Male students are normally in a minority at university departments of modern languages.*

Use of the terms *male/female* is more typical of factual texts, e.g. in scientific or other academic writing, although there is a good deal of overlap between the two types.

Exercises

1 Idiots at large

In the texts below, taken from a US internet source, underline the gender-neutral noun and the corresponding personal pronoun which reveals which sex is involved.

1 "My daughter went to a local Taco Bell and ordered a taco. She asked the person behind the counter for 'minimal lettuce'. He said he was sorry, but they only had iceberg lettuce."
2 "I live in a semi-rural area. We recently had a new neighbor call the local township administrative office to request the removal of the Deer Crossing sign on our road. The reason: too many deer were being hit by cars, and he didn't want them to cross there anymore."
3 "I was signing the receipt for my credit card purchase when the clerk noticed that I had never signed my name on the back of the credit card. She told me she could not complete the transaction unless the card was signed. When I asked why, she explained that she needed to compare the signature with the one I had just signed on the receipt. So I signed the credit card in front of her. She carefully compared the signature with the one I had just signed on the receipt. As luck would have it, they matched."
4 "The stoplight on the corner buzzes when it's safe to cross the street. I was crossing with an intellectually-challenged co-worker of mine when she asked if I knew what the buzzer was for. I explained that it tells blind people when the light is red. Appalled, she responded, 'What on earth are blind people doing driving?'"

Exercises

5 "At a good-bye luncheon for an old and dear co-worker who was leaving the company due to downsizing, our manager commented cheerfully, 'This is fun.' He then added, 'We should do this more often.' Not a word was spoken. We all just looked at each other with that deer-in-the-headlights stare."

6 "I was at the airport checking in at the gate, when an airport employee asked, 'Has anyone put anything in your baggage without your knowledge?' To which I replied, 'If it was without my knowledge, how would I know?' She smiled knowingly and nodded, 'That's why we ask.' "

7 "When I arrived at an automobile dealership to pick up our car, we were told the keys had been locked in it. We went to the service department and found a mechanic working feverishly to unlock the driver's side door. As I watched from the passenger side, I instinctively tried the door handle and discovered that it was unlocked. 'Hey,' I announced to the mechanic, 'It's open!' To which he replied, 'I know – I already got that side.' "

2 Fighting sexism in language

Re-phrase the sentences below so that they are no longer sexist. The details given in section 2.2 will help you with this.

1 Man is a tool-making animal.
2 Most businessmen prefer to fly business class so that they can catch up on work on the plane.
3 Jason and Kathy have been man and wife now for almost a decade.
4 In this shot the cameraman needs to come up to within about four feet of Miss Hurley to get a good close-up of her face.
5 During committee meetings the chairman should ensure that each member of the committee has a chance to air his views.
6 Most firemen in Britain are council employees.
7 Wow! Look at that new BMW Mark's got! Isn't she brilliant?
8 When a patient enters a GP's surgery, the doctor stands up, goes towards the patient and addresses him by name. As soon as the patient is sitting down, the doctor asks the patient to tell him why he has come to his surgery.

3 The best choice

Choose the best alternative in the following situations by circling the letter concerned. Sometimes more than one alternative is possible.

Exercises

1 You are talking to a young mother about her 3-month-old baby. What do you say?

a *How old is it?*

b *How old is he or she?*

c *How old is your baby?*

2 John says his pet spider Arabella has escaped. You ask for more details.

a *Where did you see it last?*

b *Where did you see her last?*

c *Where did you see them last?*

3 Your Economics lecturer has just said to you, The Czech Republic has managed to reduce unemployment by 2%. How would you react to this statement?

a *Oh, has it?*

b *Oh, has she?*

c *Oh, have they?*

4 You see that a white handbag has been left on a seat in the bus. What would you say to the driver?

a *Somebody's left his handbag on the back seat of the bus.*

b *Somebody's left her handbag on the back seat of the bus.*

c *Somebody's left their handbag on the back seat of the bus.*

5 A feminist colleague is showing you her new Lamborghini. What do you say?

a *He's beautiful, isn't he?*

b *She's beautiful, isn't she?*

c *It's beautiful, isn't it?*

6 A British friend tells you: In Britain the government have been trying to prevent racism by introducing legislation.
How could you continue?

a *Yes, and Germany's been trying to persuade her neo-Nazis to re-join mainstream society.*

b *Yes, and Germany's been trying to persuade its neo-Nazis to re-join mainstream society.*

c *Yes, and Germany's been trying to persuade their neo-Nazis to re-join mainstream society.*

7 You find a fountain pen on your desk. What do you say?
   a *Has anyone left his pen on my desk?*
   b *Has anyone left her pen on my desk?*
   c *Has anyone left their pen on my desk?*

4 Translating

Translate the sentences below into English, taking particular care with gender reference. Some vocabulary is given to help you.

1 Die Schülerin weinte, weil die Lehrerin sie kritisiert hatte.
2 Wenn jemand nach mir fragt, sagt ihm, dass ich in zwei Stunden wieder da bin.
3 Frank, frag deine Freundin, ob sie das Buch bestellen kann. Sie ist doch Bibliothekarin, oder?
4 Frankreich hat am Montag seine Botschafterin aus Neuseeland abberufen.

abberufen = *recall*

5 Wer hat seinen Pulli hier liegen lassen?
6 Das würde doch niemand absichtlich machen, oder?

absichtlich = *on purpose*

7 Freitags geht sie immer mit ihrer Freundin tanzen.
8 Wer an diesem Seminar teilnehmen möchte, muss sich bis zum 1. März anmelden.

sich anmelden = *to register*

9 Unter den Anglistik-Studierenden sind Studentinnen in der Überzahl.

Überzahl = majority

XI Case

XI.1 Overview

definition

Case is a grammatical category in nouns, adjectives and pronouns which expresses the syntactic relations between words in a sentence by making morphological changes to the shape of these words, e.g. by the addition of suffixes, as in *John's bike*.

In most modern Germanic languages, case is no longer an important feature (see table below) and has in part been replaced by other methods of marking syntactic relations such as prepositions, e.g. the use of *to* in English, instead of an earlier dative, or the use of the preposition *of* as an alternative to the case suffix *'s*. When *of* is used in this way, it is often called the *of* genitive.

History

The earliest recorded stages of the Germanic languages had a well developed case system in all three word classes. Old English, for example, had four main cases – nominative, accusative, genitive and dative – with some relics of the instrumental. The majority of modern Germanic languages have lost most of these cases (see table below). This is part of a general tendency in most Germanic languages to move from a synthetic to a largely analytic structure (cf. the loss of cases in French, Spanish, Italian etc compared with their ancestor, Latin).

Number of cases in Germanic languages by word class						
word class	Icelandic	German	English	Danish	Dutch	Afrikaans
pronoun	4	4	3	3	3	3
noun	4	4	2	2	0	0
adjective	4	4	0	0	0	0

In the noun, as can be seen from the above table, English, like Danish, has only two cases, the genitive and the common case. The genitive has both expanded and contracted its field in English and North Germanic languages such as Danish and Swedish. In Old English, as in Modern German, the -s genitive could only be used with masculine and neuter nouns in the singular, whereas in Modern English it is used with animate nouns in the singular and plural, but not usually with inanimates (see table below, for exceptions see 3.2):

	masculine		*neuter*		*feminine*	
NHG	*Wolfs*	*Tages*	*Kalbs*	*Wortes*	*Witwe*	*Hand*
OE	*wulfes*	dæges	*cealfes*	*wordes*	*wuduwan*	*handa*
MnE	*wolf's*	*[of the day]*	*calf's*	*[of the word]*	*widow's*	*[of the hand]*

Dutch and Afrikaans have gone even further than English and have lost all the cases in the noun and adjective, replacing the genitive by the equivalent of an *of* phrase in Dutch (e.g. *de auto van de man* 'the man's car') and a possessive particle *se* in Afrikaans (e.g. *die man se kar* 'the man's car'). The latter is comparable to the non-standard German construction *dem Mann sein Auto*.

XI.2
Normal pattern
GENITIVE PLURAL

2.1 Morphological patterning of the genitive of nouns

The form of the genitive is more complex than the spelling indicates. For the regular plural genitive English has a zero genitive (see Quirk 1985, §5.113), where there is no ending in the spoken form, although it is represented in the spelling by an apostrophe. It thus has the same sound as the ordinary (common case) plural.

Compare:

the boys [ðə bɔɪz] *the boys' bikes* [ðə bɔɪz baɪks]

Only in the genitive of some irregular plurals is there a real, i.e. spoken distinction between the common case and the genitive:

the children *the children's ball*
the women *the women's hats*

GENITIVE SINGULAR

Like the plural morpheme (see Chap. IX), the genitive singular morpheme has three allomorphs: /ɪz/, /z/ and /s/:

1 /ɪz/ occurs after sibilants, i.e. after the phonemes /z/, /s/, /ʒ/, /ʃ/, /dʒ/ and /tʃ/ (but see 3.1 below):

/z/	*the rose's thorns; Louise's hair*
/s/	*the boss's son; Mr Lucas's house; Alice's cat; Karl Marx's birthplace*
/ʒ/	*the mirage's effect*
/ʃ/	*the fish's eyes; President Bush's term in office*
/dʒ/	*a judge's wig; George's dog*
/tʃ/	*the Church's aims*

2 /z/ after voiced non-sibilants (i.e. after all vowels and voiced consonants): *the dog's bone; the boy's tennis racket; Doug's Arabic grammar*

3 /s/ after voiceless non-sibilant consonants: *the cat's kittens; Keith's job*

2.2 Semantic patterning of the genitive of nouns

The synthetic *-'s* genitive is mainly used with noun classes referring to animate beings, i.e. persons and animals. It also occurs with collective nouns denoting groups of people:

PERSONS

Leonard's book; the teenager's motorbike; my mother-in-law's house

ANIMALS

Rex's bone; the ostrich's feathers; the bird's nest; the fish's scales

COLLECTIVE NOUNS

the US Administration's policies; the Cabinet's decision; the committee's proposals; the parish council's recommendations

2.3 Syntactic patterning of the genitive of nouns

The *-'s* genitive forms part of several syntactic patterns which reveal a use of case that is strikingly different from the way case is used in languages with a more synthetic structure, e.g. German and Latin. These patterns show how much English has changed from its original pattern, which was much closer to the synthetic type.

LOCAL GENITIVE

The genitive is often used without a following noun to refer to homes, shops and businesses. It can be regarded as a contracted form of a longer phrase containing the genitive, e.g. *John's place, the optician's shop*, in examples 1 and 2 respectively:

1 *Let's go to John's.*
2 *I've just been to the optician's.* (cf. *Ich war gerade beim Optiker.*)
3 *I'm going to the doctor's this afternoon.* (cf. *Ich gehe zum Arzt ...*)
4 *When we were in New York we went shopping at Macy's.*

Compare the parallel construction with the possessive pronoun in British English:

5 *Shall we go to yours?* (= *to your place*)

APOSTROPHE CONFUSION

Native speakers are not always clear about the status of the *-s* ending and sometimes confuse it with the plural, especially with names of shops or firms. Hence spellings like *Harrods, Barclays, Selfridges*, which have now replaced the original forms *Harrod's, Barclay's, Selfridge's*, even among educated speakers. Less educated users of the language tend to confuse the plural *-s* and the genitive *-'s* in other contexts, as can be seen on signs like **We sell fresh pie's* in shops (see Crystal 1995, p.203).

DOUBLE GENITIVE

The double genitive, also known as the post-genitive, combines an *of* genitive with an *-s* genitive. It, too, can be seen as a contracted form of a longer (and repetitive) phrase, e.g. *some friends of Ken's (friends)*:

some friends of Ken's (= *some of Ken's friends*)
a cousin of Fiona's (= *one of Fiona's cousins*)

a colleague of my brother's (cf. *eine Kollegin/ein Kollege meines Bruders*)

Compare the similar construction with the possessive pronoun:
a colleague of mine (= *eine Kollegin/ein Kollege von mir*)

GROUP GENITIVE

The group genitive occurs when the genitive morpheme *-s* is added to the end of a noun phrase rather than a single noun. Note that it is not possible in English to add the morpheme to the head of the noun phrase (i.e. *Queen* in 6 below), as would be the case in German:

6 *The Queen of England's palaces are very expensive to run.*
(cf. *die Schlösser der Königin von England*)

The construction most often occurs in noun phrases consisting of two nouns linked by *of*, but is also found in other constructions, e.g. after other prepositions, following nouns linked by the conjunctions *and/or*, and after relative clauses:

7 *He's the University of Oxford's Vice-Chancellor.*
8 *I saw the girl from Bristol's room-mate in town this morning.*
9 *Most of Henry the Eighth's wives came to a sticky end.*
10 *Have you seen Paul and Rachel's new flat yet?*
11 *I've been redecorating my mother-in-law's kitchen.*
12 *That's someone else's briefcase, isn't it?*
13 *I'll give you a ring in a week or two's time.*

The longer the noun phrase is, the more likely it will be that the use of the group genitive is restricted to informal, spoken English, as in examples 14 to 16 below:

14 *The lady next door's cat has just had kittens.*
15 *The man in the grey suit's car was stolen the other day.*
16 *The man I was talking to's hat was blown away by a gust of wind.*

In more formal English the group genitives in 14 to 16 would be replaced by constructions with *of*, as in 17 and 18:

17 *The car of the man in the grey suit was stolen the other day.*
18 *The hat of the man I was talking to was blown away by a gust of wind.*

The group genitive also occurs in Danish (19) and Afrikaans (20). Compare:

19 *dronningen af Danmarks slotte* (= *the Queen of Denmark's palaces*)
20 *Dit was die vrou wat so pas hier was se kind.* (= *It was the woman that's just been here's child.*)

The phenomenon of the group genitive illustrates that the genitive in these languages has moved away from its original function of a case marker. In English and Danish it is a bound morpheme (i.e. it is attached to a word), whereas in Afrikaans it is a free morpheme, i.e. it is a separate word.

2.4 Case in the pronouns

three-case distinction

Whereas the noun only has two cases, most personal pronouns have a three-case distinction: subjective – objective – genitive. This is also true of the interrogative pronoun *who – whom – whose*. The subjective case (e.g. *I, they*) is used when the pronoun is the subject of the sentence. The objective case (e.g. *me, them*) is used for the object of the sentence and after a preposition. The genitive (e.g. *my/mine, their/theirs*) fulfils the same function as the genitive of nouns. In the pronoun, however, a distinction is made between attributive use, e.g. *my, their* (traditionally known as the possessive adjective), and independent use, e.g. *mine, theirs* (traditionally known as the possessive pronoun). The former is used before a noun, the latter when the pronoun stands on its own or is used predicatively. Notice that the independent genitive forms *ours, yours, his, hers, its, theirs* are never spelt with an apostrophe. Compare the following examples:

spelling: independent genitive

21 *This is the Johnsons' house, isn't it?* (genitive plural, noun)
22 *Are you sure this is their house?* (attributive genitive, pronoun)
23 *No, theirs is the big detached house.* (independent genitive, pronoun)

As with the genitive of nouns, at first sight the subjective and objective cases of the pronouns look like cases in synthetic languages such as German, Latin or Russian. Yet a closer look at the sentences below shows that this is inaccurate:

24 *'Who's that?' 'It's me – Patrick.'*
25 *'Who broke this window?' 'Not us! It was them!'*
26 *'She's taller than him.' 'No, he's at least as tall as her.'*
27 *Oh, silly me! I'd completely forgotten that you're a teetotaller.*

Usage is quite different from German, which has the nominative in these types:

28 *Ich bin's – Patrick.* (cf. 24)
29 *Wir nicht!* (cf. 25)
30 *Sie ist größer als er.* (cf. 26)

English usage is comparable here to the use in French of the disjunctive pronouns *moi, lui, eux,* etc. Compare:

31 *C'est moi – Patrick.* (cf. 24 and 28)
32 *Elle est plus grande que lui.* (cf. 26 and 30)

Danish also has similar constructions to English (see Diderichsen 1976, §47). Summarising English and German usage, we can say that whereas in German the nominative is the basic, unmarked form, in English it is the objective case which is the basic, unmarked form. English uses the subjective case when the pronoun is followed by a verb. The objective case is used not only for the object and after prepositions, but also when the pronoun stands alone, as in examples 24 to 27. It also occurs as part of a noun phrase which forms the subject of the sentence, as in 33.

nominative versus objective case

33 *Jessica and me are going camping next weekend.*

influence of prescriptive grammar

This fairly clear-cut pattern has been somewhat obscured by the attempts of prescriptive grammarians in the past to regard Latin grammar as a universal model of 'correct' usage, which they also applied to English. For example, because the nominative is used in Latin after the verb *to be*, they claimed that the 'nominative' (i.e. subjective) should also be used in English in these patterns, e.g. that the 'correct' form was *It is I*, not *It's me*. They also taught that it was correct to say:

34 *She's taller than he.*
35 *He's at least as tall as she.*
36 *Jessica and I are going camping next weekend.*

In fact, most English speakers have never felt comfortable with these forms, and constructions like these are largely felt to sound unnatural and affected. As a result, in informal speech and writing, the forms illustrated in examples 24 to 27 have remained normal usage. In more formal language, alternatives like 37 to 39 are preferred:

37 *'Who broke this window?' 'We didn't. They did.'*
38 *She is taller than he is.*
39 *He is at least as tall as she is.*

The speaker's linguistic intuition that the subjective case is only possible when the pronoun precedes the verb is satisfied by supplying the auxiliaries *do* or *be*, thereby providing an alternative to the informal types illustrated in 24 and 26. However, there is no alternative to the objective in example 27. The result of prescriptive grammarians' influence in this field has been merely to make native speakers feel unsure about a perfectly natural speech pattern. This uncertainty is also reflected in the hypercorrect forms illustrated in 40 and 41:

40 *Between you and I, Walt is getting past it, you know.*
41 *I am writing to invite you to join my students and I at a screening of the film 'The Insider'.*

Because traditional prescriptive grammarians have campaigned vigorously against forms like *It's me*, speakers have subconsciously felt that there was something wrong with *me*, and replaced it by *I* in contexts felt to be grammatically unclear, e.g. when combined with a noun or another pronoun after a preposition or as an object, as in 40 and 41 respectively. Ironically, therefore, the effect of this prescriptivism has been to encourage an alternative construction which does not fit in with the Latin grammatical pattern either.

cleft sentences

In cleft sentences (see Chap. I), both the objective and subjective forms of pronouns occur, with the former more common in informal contexts, while the latter are preferred in more formal contexts. Compare:

42 *It was me who phoned you last night, not John.*
43 *It was I who informed the Minister, not Mr Appleton.*

Similar attempts to press English into the Latin mould have been made by prescriptivists for the interrogative and relative pronouns

who – whom

who – whom. The natural pattern, which is the only normal one in informal English, is to use *who* for both the subjective and objective functions:

44 *Who is observing the spy?* (= *Wer beobachtet den Spion?*)
45 *Who is the spy observing?* (= *Wen beobachtet der Spion?*)

The contrast between objective (45) and subjective (44) function is shown by inversion of the auxiliary *is* and the subject in 45, and by non-inversion in 44. Where there is no auxiliary, as in 46, the auxiliary *do* is supplied for the objective function (see 47):

46 *Who shot the sheriff?*
47 *Who did the sheriff shoot?*

This difference in the syntactic pattern is obligatory, which means that the synthetic distinction between *who* and *whom* has become superfluous, since it is optional: it is in fact not possible to say **Whom shot the sheriff?* i.e. a parallel construction to German *Wen hat der Sheriff erschossen?*

Prescriptivists have long encouraged the use of *whom* for the objective case, with the result that in formal contexts, especially in formal English, *whom* is common when it is used as a relative pronoun (see 48 and 49). However, in informal register *whom* is much less common, with a zero relative, *who* or *that* being normally preferred (see 50 and 51 respectively). For the interrogative pronoun, which is far more frequently used in informal register anyway, use of *whom* is regarded by most users of the language as unnatural and/or affected (see 52). For usage after prepositions, see 3.3 below.

48 *The suspect, whom the police arrested yesterday, was a 25-year-old man.*
49 *The person to whom we wrote on behalf of our client has since decided to drop all charges.*
50 *The boy (that) I met at a party last week is coming with me to a jazz concert tonight.*
51 *The garage mechanic (that) we were talking to said the exhaust pipe and catalytic converter would need replacing. That'll cost us a packet!*
52 *Who did you ring up just now?* (*Whom* would sound affected)

XI.3
Exceptions

3.1 Genitive of nouns ending in consonant + /z/ or /s/

In names ending in a consonant followed by /z/ or /s/, both the genitive ending /ɪz/ and a zero genitive is used. In writing the commonest forms are with zero genitive (spelt with an apostrophe), whereas in speech the most frequent forms are the regular genitive with /ɪz/. Thus people usually write *Burns'* but say /ˈbɜːnzɪz/, preferring the clearer regular marker of the genitive in speech. In the examples below the normal form is in red.

Burns' (Burns's) life	/ˈbɜːnz/ /ˈbɜːnzɪz/
Keats' (Keats's) poems	/ˈkiːts/ /ˈkiːtsɪz/
Dickens' (Dickens's) novels	/ˈdɪkɪnz/ /ˈdɪkɪnzɪz/
St. James' (James's) Park	/ˈdʒeɪmz/ /ˈdʒeɪmzɪz/

3.2 Use of the -s genitive with inanimate nouns

The genitive frequently occurs with certain classes of inanimate nouns, especially if they are of special importance to human beings:

PLACE NAMES

1 Names of places or institutions:

Planets:	*Jupiter's atmosphere • the Earth's climate*
Continents:	*Asia's population • Antarctica's natural resources*
Countries:	*Britain's economy • the United States' enemies*
States:	*Colorado's state capital • Queensland's beaches*
Cities, towns:	*Dublin's Georgian buildings • Galway's streets*
Institutions:	*IBM's sales • Rover's car plant • the CBC's programmes • MIT's reputation • Yale's alumni.*

The genitive is also common with nouns in this group (i.e. 1) and in group 2 when they are followed by an adjective in the superlative or ordinals such as *first, last, only* (see also Chap. XII). Note that the equivalent prepositional phrase is introduced by *in*; an *of* genitive is usually not possible:

53 *Britain's highest mountain is Ben Nevis.*
Cf. *The highest mountain in Britain* ... (= *Der höchste Berg Großbritanniens* ...)

54 *Germany's first currywurst was invented in Berlin in 1949.*
Cf. *The first currywurst in Germany* ...(= *Die erste Currywurst Deutschlands* ...)

2 This category contains common nouns referring to places or institutions: *the world's population explosion* • *the city's transport problems* • *the school's facilities* • *the University's research programme* • *the airline's deficit.* PLACE NOUNS

3 Expressions referring to time often take the *-s* genitive: *this week's news* • *last year's best-sellers* • *a hard day's work.* TIME EXPRESSIONS

This construction is also extended to the adverbs *yesterday, today, tomorrow*. Use of the *of* phrase is often not possible:

55 *"Darling, have you seen today's paper anywhere?"*

The Spectator 3 October 1998

'Trouble is by the time he gets here with it, it's yesterday's.'

4 The *-s* genitive can be used with other inanimate nouns. It is common in newspaper headlines, where it is often used to save space. In most cases, however, the *of* genitive is more usual and frequently preferable: *the body's needs* • *the book's impact* • *television's role* • *the room's size* • *the English Novel's evolution* • *the bath's fittings.* NEUTER NOUNS

56 *The word's function in this sentence is not altogether clear.*

3.3 Use of whom after prepositions

After prepositions, the relative pronoun *whom* is common, especially in more formal register, since it occurs in analogy with the use of objective pronouns after prepositions. Compare:

57 *The executive for whom she was preparing a report had a heart attack.*
58 *My Canadian friends, most of whom live in Halifax, Nova Scotia, are very hospitable.*

However, here too the tendency is for speakers to avoid the use of *whom* where possible, e.g. by placing the preposition at the end of the clause, as in 59, or by using a paraphrase, as in 60:

59 *The boss she was preparing a report for had a heart attack.*
60 *My Canadian friends – most of them live in Halifax, Nova Scotia, by the way, – are very hospitable.*

Exercises

1 Which one's the right one?

Choose the forms of the genitive which are correct. In some cases, more than one form may be possible.

	a	b	c
1	Johns alligator	John's alligator	Johns' alligator
2	children's games	childrens' games	childrens games
3	Graces garden	Grace' garden	Grace's garden
4	the boss's car	the bosses car	the boss' car
5	Bridget Jones' diary	Bridget Jones's diary	Bridget Joneses diary
6	John Knox' house	John Knoxes house	John Knox's house
7	womens' issues	women's issues	womens issues
8	the princesses children	the princess' children	the princess's children
9	Caths PC	Cath's PC	Cath' PC
10	Sherlock Holmes's assistant	Sherlock Holme's assistant	Sherlock Holmes' assistant

2 Be more specific!

Make the genitive phrases in the sentences below more specific by turning them into group genitives, using the cue given in brackets.

Example

She's the City's new mayor. (City of London)
→ *She's the City of London's new mayor.*

1 She's that man's daughter. (the man from Chicago)
2 Have you met that girl's boyfriend? (that girl over there)

3 I'll see you in a month's time. (a month or so)
4 That's that guy's crash helmet. (that guy in the leather jacket)
5 She's the President's daughter. (the President of Peru)
6 That's the pop singer's partner. (the pop singer we met last night)
7 Those are Charles's coronation robes. (Charles II)
8 She's married to the Bank's governor. (the Bank of England)
9 Can I borrow somebody's pen, please? (somebody else)

3 Case in context

Which of the alternatives given is the most suitable in the following situations? Circle the most natural version. In some cases, more than one version may be acceptable.

1 Your friend says to you at the church bazaar:
  a 'Lucky I! I've won a two-week trip to Majorca!
  b 'Lucky me!' I've won a two-week trip to Majorca!
2 Joan's mother asks her:
  a 'To whom were you talking outside?'
  b 'Who were you talking to outside?'
3 In a letter to the authorities, you write:
  a It was us who decided to sue the Browns, as the number of all-night parties had become so frequent that we saw no other solution.
  b It was we who ...
4 You are talking to a friend about your drinking habits:
  a 'Gary and I always get smashed at the Red Lion on Fridays.'
  b 'Gary and me ...
5 In a letter to a relative, you write:
  Our Sean is now taller than
  a us both.
  b we both.
  c we both are.
6 In a letter to an eminent academic, you write:
  Dr. Jeremy Soames,
  a who you met at last year's conference, is also interested in contributing to the festschrift.
  b whom you met ...
7 In a speech to the German-Irish Chamber of Commerce you say:
  'Several ministers
  a who I discussed this matter with expressed their approval of this proposal.'
  b with whom I discussed this matter ...

8 At a history seminar at Edinburgh University, the lecturer asks, 'Who handed in this essay with no name on?' You say:
   a 'I'm afraid it was I.'
   b 'I'm afraid it was me.'

9 At a party, you say to the journalist from The Times:
'But surely, Rupert Murdoch is twice as old as
   a her?'
   b she?'
   c she is.'

4 Error spotting

A German friend working with you for a firm in England has written a letter and asks you to correct it because, she says, your English is so much better than hers. Make any changes necessary so that the letter sounds more natural, also correcting any spelling mistakes.

Dear Gerry,
thank's for your letter. It must have been delayed, because according to it's postmark it was posted on 3rd April.

Lots of things have been happening here. Jean Lennox' little girl, Doris, was badly hurt in a hit-and-run accident the other day. I visited her in St. Thomas' Hospital, and she looked a real mess – multiple lacerations to the face, both legs in plaster, bruises all over. Jean said that the specialist responsible for cases like Doris' had told her that she was making good progress and should be out of hospital in a couple of weeks time.

I'm in hot water with my boss again. You remember her, don't you? She's the one who's hair always looks like a birds nest. Anyway, she hauled me over the coal's for skiving off work last week. I went home early to go to Jim. He was having a cocktail party at 3.30, and I didn't want to miss all the fun. Unfortunately for me, the bosses husband was there too. He's a colleague of Jim, and he spilled the beans to my boss.

I'm under a lot of pressure at work at the moment. We're trying to publish two books. Ones a new edition of the history plays of Shakespeare. The others a book about symphonies of Beethoven. I'm run off my feet, and sometimes I'm at my wits end as to how we can meet our deadline. Roll on the holidays, I say. In four weeks' we're off to the Canary's with a few friends of Keith. That reminds me. I must go to C&A soon. They've got some good summer dresses on special offer.

Love,
Sandra

5 Making headlines

Exercises

You are a junior reporter at a newspaper. One of the editors is off sick, and you have been asked to help out. Make suitable headlines, which should be short and snappy, for the news stories outlined below. The important words are underlined, and some typical headline vocabulary has been given to help you. Remember the following characteristic features of headline language:

- frequent use of *-s* genitive
- grammatical words (e.g. *the*, auxiliaries) are usually omitted
- Present Simple is used for Present Progressive or Perfect
- *to* + Infinitive is used for the Future

be given → to get	co-operation → links	criticism → critics
decide to → to seek	departure → exit	postpone → to shelve
prime minister → PM	proposal → plan	

Example

The police have defused a car bomb in Oxford Street in London.
→ POLICE DEFUSE CAR BOMB IN LONDON'S OXFORD STREET

1 The fastest roller coaster in Germany was opened yesterday in the Ruhr.
2 Princes Street in Edinburgh is to be given a face-lift.
3 The foreign ministers of the EU have decided to co-operate more closely on policy issues.
4 A think-tank set up by the prime minister has warned that the proposals made by the government aimed at more private sector involvement in the public services will not solve the problems in health and education.
5 The City of Birmingham Symphony Orchestra is facing bankruptcy after the departure of Sir Simon Rattle.
6 The strike by teachers, due to start on May 2nd, has been postponed after last-minute negotiations with the government.

XII The Adjective

XII.1 Overview

adjectives, adverbs: similarity

Adjectives and adverbs in English are closely related in form and meaning. This is also true of German and many other languages. Most adverbs in English are formed from adjectives, e.g.

quick (adj.) – *quickly* (adv.)
strict (adj.) – *strictly* (adv.)

In a different field of morphology, comparison, English adjectives and adverbs share the same ways of forming comparatives and superlatives. This is also true of German and many other languages. Compare:

a faster car (adj.) – *This car goes faster* (adv.)
the most convincing argument (adj.) – *He argued the most convincingly* (adv.)

semantic similarities

Semantically, too, these word classes have a lot in common (cf. Quirk 1985, §7.71). Compare the sentences with equivalent meaning below:

1	*She gave a good reply.* (adj.)	*Her reply was good.* (adj.)
2	*He is a good worker.* (adj.)	*He works well.* (adv.)

formal differences

Most adjectives and adverbs are distinguished formally from each other in English and German. Compare:

3	*This is a cheap video.*	*Das ist ein billiges Video.*
4	*This video is cheap.*	*Dieses Video ist billig.*
5	*He sold it cheaply.*	*Er hat es billig verkauft.*

German marks the adjective by means of inflections, but it only does this attributively, i.e. when it is in front of a noun. By contrast, English only marks the adverb, using a derivational morpheme. Neither language marks the adjective in predicative position, i.e. after verbs like *be, become, remain, seem, appear.*

History

In the oldest recorded form of English, Old English, adjectives were inflected for number, gender, case and according to whether they were part of a definite or indefinite noun phrase (König 1994, p.122), cf. Modern German *das schnelle Auto*, contrasting with *ein schnelles Auto*. Adjectival inflection died out during the Middle English period. Other Germanic languages have retained it in varying degrees. It has survived best in Icelandic and German, but is weakest in Dutch and Afrikaans.

XII.2 Normal pattern

2.1 Position of adjectives

Most adjectives can occur in both attributive and predicative position. In attributive use they are almost exclusively placed in front of the noun, as in other Germanic languages (but see 3.1 below).

2.2 Comparison of adjectives

English has two ways of forming the comparative and superlative. The first is the synthetic (or inflectional) type, involving the addition to the stem of *-er* and *-est* respectively. This is the normal way of forming the comparison for adjectives of one syllable. Compare:

synthetic comparison

sad – sadder – saddest
pure – purer – purest
free – freer – freest

analytic comparison

The second pattern is the analytic (or periphrastic) type, involving the use of *more* and *most* with the basic form of the adjective. This is the only way of forming the comparison for adjectives of more than two syllables. Compare:

6 *It's getting more difficult nowadays to find unspoilt beaches.*
7 *Wanting your children to be successful is the most natural thing in the world.*

either type

Two-syllable adjectives can often use either type of comparison. However, depending on the kind of adjective involved, one type is more common than the other. Disyllabic adjectives ending in the unstressed syllables *-y, -ow, -le* are the group where this synthetic comparison most often occurs. Compare:

easy – easier – easiest
narrow – narrower – narrowest
subtle – subtler – subtlest

Other examples of common adjectives in this group are:

-y	-ow	-le
angry	*hollow*	*able*
busy	*shallow*	*gentle*
hungry		*noble*
likely		*simple*

adjectives in *un-*

Use of the negative prefix *un-* does not affect usage. Thus, although *untidy* is, strictly speaking, a three-syllable adjective, it can use the synthetic comparison *untidier, untidiest* because it derives ultimately from the disyllabic adjective *tidy*.

adjectives in *-ly*

The synthetic comparison is less usual within the group of adjectives ending in *-y* if the suffix involved is *-ly*. Thus, whereas *easier, easiest* is the normal comparison of *easy*, in the case of *likely* the forms *more, most likely* are more frequent than the synthetic types *likelier, likeliest*.

clever, mature, etc.

The synthetic comparison is also possible with a heterogeneous group of adjectives, some of which are stressed on the final syllable. In these words, however, the analytic comparison is often more common:

clever	*pleasant*	*mature*
common	*quiet*	*obscure*
cruel	*solid*	*polite*
handsome		*remote*

other disyllabic adjectives

Apart from the types listed above, disyllabic adjectives take the analytic comparison, e.g. *more, most frequent*, not **frequenter, *frequentest.*

participles

Although the form of the adjective is the main factor determining which type of comparison is used, other factors are also relevant. Grammatical function is one: participles used as adjectives, for example, always use the analytic comparison, however many syllables they contain. Compare:

8 *I don't think I've ever seen jeans that are more torn than these!*
9 *One of the most moving things I've experienced in my life was when I talked to the Dalai Lama.*

frequency

A third factor is the frequency of the adjective concerned. Rare adjectives tend to use the analytic form even if they are monosyllabic (König 1994, p.540). Compare:

10 *I don't think anybody could be more fey than he is. He's weird!*

Note

Notice that the double comparison, i.e. the use of synthetic and analytic comparison with the same adjective, e.g. **more larger*, is nowadays regarded as non-standard. In Shakespeare's day it was still acceptable. Compare: '*This was the most unkindest cut of all.*' (*Julius Caesar*, III, 1).

History

In other Germanic languages the synthetic comparison is used either exclusively (e.g. in German and Dutch) or overwhelmingly (e.g. Danish, Afrikaans) (cf. König 1994, pp.463, 331, 491). In Old English only the synthetic type occurred, with the analytic alternative emerging during the Middle English period; its spread was possibly encouraged by the analytic French comparison, e.g. *(le) plus intéressant* (cf. Faiß 1989, p.133). The present distribution of the two types of comparison is very recent – not only in Early Modern English but also in the 18th and 19th centuries much greater variation was possible in the choice of analytic and synthetic types, e.g. Shakespeare uses *perfectest* (Barber 1976, p.201f., Faiß 1989, p.130). English seems to be moving towards a pattern where the analytic type is the norm.

2.3 Adjectives used as nouns

In contrast to many other languages, in English it is not normally possible to nominalise an adjective, i.e. to use an adjective on its own without a following noun. Compare the following English examples with their German and French equivalents:

usually no nominalisation of adjectives

11 *Poor little boy! Poor little thing!* (but not **Poor little*!)
cf. *Armer Kleiner!* and *Le pauvre petit!*

12 *The most important thing is to keep calm.* (but not **The most important is ...*)
cf. *Das Wichtigste ist, Ruhe bewahren.*
Similarly, *Le plus important, c'est de garder son calme.*

13 *Do you want the big cup or the small one?* (but not **the small*)
cf. *Wollen Sie die große Tasse oder die kleine?*
Likewise, *Vous voulez la grande tasse ou la petite?*

English either uses a following noun or the prop word *one*, with its plural *ones*:

14 *Which peppers do you want? The green ones or the red ones?*

Adjectives which denote a class of people can be nominalised, i.e. made into nouns by preceding them with the definite article, e.g. *the deaf*. This pattern is used for making generalisations about the class of people involved. When we are referring to specific members of this class, we use the adjective followed by *person* (or *man* or *woman*) in the singular, *people* in the plural. In other words, generic reference in the plural is expressed by a nominalised adjective, whereas specific reference in plural or singular is expressed by a combination of adjective and noun, i.e. without nominalisation of the adjective. Compare:

exception: partial nominalisation

15 *When Mary and Jane help each other with their French homework, it's like the blind leading the blind – neither of them are any good at French.*

16 *Many blind people subconsciously acquire a better sense of hearing to compensate for their lack of sight.*

Other examples of this pattern are:

generic (nominalised)	specific (Adj + Noun)
the handicapped	*handicapped people*

the poor — *poor people*
the innocent — *innocent people*

(see also Quirk 1985, §7.24)

adjectives and nouns referring to nationality

For gender-neutral specific reference to people from a small number of nations (Britain, England, Wales, Ireland, Holland, France, Spain) only the adjective followed by a noun like *person* (in the singular) or *people* (in the plural) is possible:

17 *I met an English person in Prague last year who came from my village!*
18 *Most Irish people I know only have a smattering of Irish.*

Compare this with the pattern normal with most terms referring to nationalities, where the original adjective has been completely nominalised, behaving like any normal noun:

19 *I met a German in Saragossa last year, and we've been sending each other e-mails ever since.*
20 *Most Germans I know speak very fluent English.*

Whereas in 17 and 18 *English* and *Irish* have to be followed by nouns in the singular and plural (it is not possible to say **I met an English*), words like *German, American, Scot, Greek* can be preceded by an article and take the plural ending *-s*, as in 19 and 20.
If speakers wish to specify the sex of the person concerned, special nouns are used, e.g. *an Englishman, an Irishwoman.*

Note

The final syllable *-man* is weakened to /mən/, i.e. /ˈɪŋglɪʃmən/. The plural of Englishman, i.e. *Englishmen* /ˈɪŋglɪʃmən/, therefore sounds exactly the same as the singular.

When we want to make generalisations about the whole group in question, we use the generic plural (see Quirk 1985, §5.56f.), consisting of a nominalised adjective preceded by the definite article:

21 *The English have a reputation for being reserved.*

Compare the words in this class:

country:	Britain	England, Ireland, Wales, Holland, France	Spain
adjective:	British	English, Irish, Welsh, Dutch, French	Spanish
gender-neutral:	a British person	an English person, Irish person etc.	a Spaniard
male:	a British man	an Englishman, Irishman etc	a Spanish man
female:	a British woman	an Englishwoman, Irishwoman etc.	a Spanish woman
generic:	the British	the English, Irish, Welsh etc.	the Spanish

Note

The terms referring to Britain and Spain behave rather differently from the other members of this class. For gender-specific reference to a citizen of Britain there is no noun corresponding to the type *Welshman, Welshwoman* – we have to use a combination of adjective and noun. The word *Briton* for British person is normally only used in journalese, statistics and some other restricted contexts (see Swan 1995, §114). The informal word *Brit* is often pejorative, i.e. it has negative associations. The term used for gender-neutral reference to a citizen of Spain is *Spaniard*, though *Spanish person* is also possible. There is no corresponding noun for specific reference to males and females. Instead, we use a combination of adjective plus noun.

XII.3 Exceptions

3.1 Adjectives used after nouns

Although adjectives in English, as in other Germanic languages, are normally placed before the noun, i.e. as premodifiers, in some cases they may follow it, i.e. as postmodifiers. This postpositive position is common in the following cases:

ending in *-able, -ible*

Some adjectives ending in *-able, -ible* can be put after the noun when they are either preceded by adjectives in the superlative or by the following adjectives, which specify items in a series or group:

all
every
first
last
next
only
} + Noun + Adj

Compare:

22 *Our organisation needs the best resources possible if it is to thrive.*
23 *They stock every type of pasta imaginable.*
24 *He took the next train available.*
25 *She was the only candidate suitable.*

Usually the adjective can also be placed in front of the noun. Compare:

26 *Our organisation needs the best possible resources if it is to thrive.*
27 *They stock every imaginable type of pasta.*

In some cases there is a tendency for the attributive position before the noun to express the idea of a permanent quality, whereas the postpositive use implies that the feature described by the adjective is temporary. Compare:

28 *There are about 5,000 visible stars, many of which can be seen from Europe.*
29 *It was a misty night, and the few stars visible were rather disappointing.*

Example 28 refers to a class of stars in general, i.e. those that can be seen by human beings, whereas 29 implies that the stars could be seen on a specific occasion. The latter can be regarded as a contraction of a defining relative clause *which were visible*.

adjective and complement

However, if the adjective is followed by a complement, the entire adjectival phrase has to follow the noun, as in 30. Contrast this with the German pattern, where the adjectival phrase precedes the noun, as in 31:

30 *The information obtainable in the brochure can also be accessed on the Internet.*
31 *Die in der Broschüre erhältlichen Informationen sind auch im Internet abrufbar.*

participles used as adjectives

When past or present participles are used as adjectives, in English they normally follow the noun:

32 *The <u>people</u> interviewed were a cross-section of British society.*
Noun Past Participle

33 *Most of the <u>patients</u> waiting had been there for at least two hours.*
Noun Present Participle

Some participles used adjectivally can be used both before and after the noun, without any difference in meaning. Compare:

34 *This aspect was dealt with in more detail in the preceding <u>chapter</u>.*
Participle Noun

35 *In the <u>chapter</u> preceding, all the examples were authentic.*
Noun Participle

In other cases the attributive position tends to refer to permanent features, while the postpositive implies temporariness (cf. examples 28 and 29):

36 *The spoken <u>language</u> is often far more innovative than its written*
Participle Noun
equivalent.

37 *The <u>language</u> spoken often has an effect on people's attitudes to*
Noun Participle
the speaker.

Whereas 36 refers to the spoken language in general, 37 means the language which is spoken in specific situations.

An adjectival complement placed before a noun is extremely common in German, though it is normally restricted to formal (especially written) German. In English, the equivalent construction is almost exclusively placed after the noun. Compare the following German and English sentences: cf. German

38 *Die Karte hat er einem kleinen, um 1110 n.Chr. verfassten <u>Buch</u>*
beigefügt. Participle Noun

39 *He enclosed the map in a small <u>book</u> written around 1110 A.D.*
Noun Participle

However, the commonest English equivalent to the German construction is a following relative clause. Compare:

40 *Stark ist der 3,0-Liter-Motor vor allem [...] in den auf extreme Belastungen abgestimmten Fahrwerkskomponenten.*
41 *The power of the 3-litre engine lies mainly in the chassis components, which are specially made to withstand extreme stress.*
42 *Jenkinsons im Jahre 1557 begonnene Reise führte über Moskau die Wolga abwärts nach Astrachan.*
43 *Jenkinson's journey, which was begun in 1557, took him via Moscow down the Volga to Astrakhan.*

semantic differences dependent on position

With the following adjectives there is a difference in meaning, depending on whether the adjective is used before or after the noun:

Adjective	Meaning before Noun	Meaning after Noun
concerned	besorgt	zuständig, betroffen
involved	verwickelt, kompliziert	beteiligt
present	gegenwärtig, derzeitig	anwesend
proper	richtig, ordentlich	eigentlich (adj.)
responsible	verantwortungsvoll	zuständig

Compare:

44 *Concerned parents have approached the school about the amount of bullying taking place there.* (= the parents are worried)
45 *The head of the school has discussed the matter with the children concerned.* (= the children who are affected)
46 *You need to get a proper dictionary, not that little thing you've had since you started learning German in Year 7.* (= ein ordentliches Wörterbuch)
47 *It's a suburb of Manchester, not really part of Manchester proper.* (= des eigentlichen Manchester)

3.2 Adjectives only used before nouns

adjectives only used attributively

Some adjectives only occur attributively, i.e. before nouns. Restrictive adjectives such as *main, chief, sole* (= *einzig*), *very* (= *genau)*, which limit the reference of the noun, are typical examples:

48 *He was the KGB's main contact in Vienna.* (not: *Their contact was main.)
49 *You're the very person we need for the job!* (= genau die Person)

Many adjectives used with agentive nouns, i.e. nouns which refer to a person doing an action, can only be used attributively (cf. also Example 2 *a good worker*):

50 *Frank is a heavy smoker.*

Notice that a sentence like *Frank is heavy* has a completely different meaning from Example 50, which is equivalent to *Frank smokes heavily*.

3.3 Adjectives only occurring predicatively

adjectives only used predicatively

Just as some adjectives are only used attributively, so others only occur predicatively. An important group in this class is adjectives beginning with *a-*. Some of these were originally prepositional phrases beginning with unstressed *on*, which was later weakened to *a-* (e.g. *alive* from Old English: *on līfe*), hence the restriction to predicative position. Common adjectives of this type are: *alive, alone, ashamed, asleep, awake*.

51 *A beautiful sunny day like this makes you feel glad to be alive.*

3.4 Differences in attributive and predicative usage

Some adjectives occur in both positions, but with a difference in form according to their position. The meaning is not affected:

drunken versus *drunk*

attributive	predicative
drunken	*drunk*
sunken	*sunk*

The difference between *drunken* and *drunk* is becoming blurred, with the latter gaining ground. The traditional pattern is illustrated by examples 52 and 53:

52 *What shall we do with the drunken sailor?*
53 *Let's go out and get drunk!*

Many people, however, now use *drunk* attributively, as in 54, where both forms are possible:

54 *He was arrested for drunk(en) driving.*

And notice that the official title of the US pressure group MADD is *Mothers Against Drunk Driving.*

sick versus *ill*

The two synonyms for 'unwell', *sick* and *ill*, are restricted to attributive and predicative use respectively in British English and more formal American English.

55 *The sick children were taken to hospital after contracting salmonella at a birthday party.*
56 *If both parents go out to work, who looks after the children when the kids are ill?*

The difference illustrated in examples 55 and 56 is typical of standard British usage. In informal American English, however, *sick* is used both attributively and predicatively, with no distinction in meaning. When *sick* is used predicatively in standard British English, it usually implies 'to vomit', 'to throw up'. Compare:

57 *I was foolish enough to mix my drinks, so I was sick.*

However, actual usage is more complex. Even users of standard British English will say '*I was off sick last week*' (i.e. predicative use) to refer to absence due to illness.

There is also a tendency to use *ill* attributively, though this is not yet regarded as standard usage:

58 *There's a lot of very ill people in our street.* (non-standard)

3.5 Adjectives as uncountable nouns: the supernatural

the supernatural, etc.

Some adjectives referring to abstract concepts can be used as nouns. In contrast to adjectives which identify groups, i.e. *the blind* (cf. 2.3 partial nominalisation) and *the English* (cf. 2.3 adjectives and nouns referring to nationality), they are followed by a verb in the singular:

59 *The supernatural has always fascinated him.*
60 *It's a short step from the sublime to the ridiculous.*

This construction is mainly restricted to a few abstract adjectives. It is commonest with superlatives:

61 *The worst is yet to come.*

3.6 Adjectives as countable nouns: the Greens

the Greens, etc.

Adjectives referring to colours are often nominalised completely when used to refer to groups of people, e.g. political parties or movements *(the Greens, the reds)*, ethnic groups *(blacks, whites)*, or, in British English, members of Oxford or Cambridge sports teams *(a Cambridge blue)*. They show the typical features of countable nouns, viz. they can be preceded by the indefinite article and can be used in the plural. Compare:

62 *Some Greens want to boycott US goods if the US doesn't cut CO_2 emissions.*
63 *Many blacks complain of police harassment.*

Exercises

1 Comparisons

Put the adjectives given in brackets into the comparative form, using the synthetic form of the adjective where possible.

1 Arthur's _____ (heavy) than Gerald. Arthur weighs 10 stone, but Gerald's only 7 stone 11.
2 Lake Balaton in Hungary is _____ (shallow) than Lake Constance.
3 A computer is usually _____ (exact) than an abacus, but it's _____(likely) to break down.
4 The climate in the Sahara is of course much _____ (dry) than in the Congo.
5 Aunt Matilda is far _____ (spry) than she looks.
6 She's _____ (naive) than her sister.
7 The house they've moved into is a lot _____ (posh) than their old one.
8 Jim's room is much _____ (untidy) than mine.
9 "To be or not to be: that is the question:
Whether 'tis _____ (noble) in the mind to suffer
The slings and arrows of outrageous fortune,

Or to take arms against a sea of troubles,
And by opposing end them? (*Hamlet*, III, 1)

2 The handbag

You are the witness to a robbery in London. A German tourist has had her handbag stolen. She doesn't speak much English and is very distraught, so you accompany her to the police station and interpret for her. The policewoman interviewing her is very friendly, but doesn't speak any German.

P = Policewoman; T = Tourist.

P 'Well, Frau Ricke, can you describe the handbag for me?'
You „Können Sie ihr die Handtasche beschreiben?"
T „Ja, es war eine kleine schwarze aus Leder."
You 'It was a _____1.'
T „Sie war nicht teuer. Zum Glück habe ich meine teurere im Hotel gelassen."
You 'It wasn't expensive. Luckily she left her _____2 in the hotel.'
T „Das Ärgerliche an der ganzen Sache ist, dass mein Ausweis, die Kreditkarten und sehr wertvolle Ohrringe in der Handtasche waren."
You 'She says the _____3 about the whole affair is that her ID card, credit cards and some very valuable earrings were in it.'
T „Das sind die goldenen, die mein Mann mir zum 25. Hochzeitstag geschenkt hat."
You 'The earrings are the _____4 that her husband gave her for their 25th wedding anniversary.'
P 'You poor thing! That really is very annoying! Now, can you tell me something about the two men who attacked you?'
You „Sie sagt, ‚Sie Ärmste!' Sie meint, das wäre wirklich sehr ärgerlich. Könnten Sie ihr die beiden Männer beschreiben, die Sie überfallen haben?"
T „Ja gerne. Das waren ein großer und ein kleiner."
You 'It was a _____5 and _____6.'
T „Der kleinere war blond, etwas dick, um die zwanzig. Der andere war älter und hatte kurze dunkle Haare. Sie trugen beide Lederjacken und Jeans – sehr alte, schmutzige."
You 'The _____7 was fair, rather fat, in his twenties. The _____8 was older and had very short, dark hair. They were both wearing leather jackets and jeans – very _____9.'

T „Das Merkwürdige dabei ist, dass sie mir irgendwie bekannt vorkamen."

You 'She says the _____[10] is that somehow they seemed familiar.'

P 'I'm not surprised. We know them as *Little Joe* and *Dirty Harry*. They hang around Leicester Square waiting for tourists. You've probably seen one of our 'wanted' posters. The only thing that's surprising is that they're still not behind bars.'

You „Das überrascht sie nicht. Sie sind der Polizei unter den Namen Little Joe und Dirty Harry bekannt. Sie hängen am Leicester Square herum und warten auf Touristen. Wahrscheinlich haben Sie einen der Steckbriefe gesehen. Sie meint, dass _____[11], was dabei überraschend ist, ist, dass sie immer noch nicht hinter Schloss und Riegel sitzen."

3 Europe – heaven or hell?

Combine the two lists below to describe your dream or nightmare version of Europe, following the same format as in the example:

bank managers • comedians • cooks • lovers • mechanics • policemen
Italy • Ireland • Holland • France • Britain

1 Heaven is where Germans are the mechanics,
2 Italians are _____ .
3 Irish _____ .
4 Dutch _____ .
5 French _____ .
6 British _____ .

1 Hell is where the Germans are the policemen,
2 _____ are the mechanics,
3 _____ are the lovers,
4 _____ are the cooks,
5 _____ are the comedians,
6 _____ are the bank managers.

4 Generalising

The sentences below are not as precise as they could be, either because they contain sweeping generalisations or because they under-generalise. Rewrite them in the ways indicated to make them more accurate.

Exercises

Example

The rich give a lot of support to charities.
→ *Some rich people give a lot of support to charities.*

1 The elderly feel terribly alienated in our computerised society.
Many _____ .
2 The deaf can be helped much more effectively now by the latest hearing aids.
Most _____ .
3 The young think that they will never grow old, and the old have forgotten what it was like to be young.
A lot of _____ and many _____ .
4 We're collecting money for some homeless people in Africa.
We're collecting money for the _____ .
5 The unemployed just don't want to work.
A few _____ .
6 "Didn't Norman Mailer write some sort of novel about naked people?"
"Oh, you mean, The _____ and the _____!
But it's not really about naked people, or even dead people. It's about the Second World War."

5 New sentences for old

In the sentences below, which are modified slightly from authentic texts, you should first restructure the German sentence by using a relative clause, then translate this relative clause into English, as illustrated in the example.

In a underline the part of the German sentence which needs changing.
In b restructure this part of the German sentence.
In c translate this into English.
Watch the difference between defining and non-defining relative clauses (see Chapter XV).

Example

a Die hier abgebildeten Pullover sind in den Größen S, M, L und XL erhältlich.
b *Die Pullover, die hier abgebildet sind, ...*
c The pullovers *which are illustrated here* are available in sizes S, M, L and XL. (Or: The pullovers *illustrated here* ...)

1 a Der Ehemann der getöteten Missionarin und der Pilot überlebten den Absturz.

b _____ .

c The husband of the missionary _____ and the pilot survived the crash.

Exercises

2 a Nur an zehn der geprüften Seen ist das Baden im letzten Jahr verboten worden.

prüfen = *to test*

b _____ .

c Only at ten of the lakes _____ was bathing banned last year.

3 a Die Hamas-Bewegung rief zur Unterstützung des seit Ende September andauernden Palästinenser-Aufstandes auf.

andauern = *to continue*

b _____ .

c The Hamas Movement called for support for the Palestinian uprising _____ .

4 a Im Jahre 2000 verdunstete viel Wasser des schon zu normalen Zeiten sehr flachen Plattensees.

b _____ .

c In 2000 a lot of water evaporated from Lake Balaton _____ .

5 a Eine Gruppe von Abgeordneten befürwortet, dass spätestens bis 2010 auch die noch in Bonn verbliebenen Ministerien nach Berlin geholt werden sollten.

verbleiben = *to remain*

b _____ .

c A group of MPs is advocating that even _____ should be moved to Berlin by 2010 at the latest.

6 a Der von indischen Experten sorgfältig gewebte Stoff dieses Madras-Hemdes erhielt seine typischen Muster von den Briten, die Indien früher regierten.

weben = *to weave*
Stoff = *material*

b _____ .

c _____ derived its typical patterns from the British, who used to rule India.

7 a Die Prince's Foundation ist eine von Prinz Charles gegründete alternative Akademie für Architektur und Kunst.

b _____ .

c The Prince's Foundation is _____ .

Exercises

leiten = *to head*

8 a Das von Norbert Oellers geleitete Projekt analysiert das Verhältnis deutschsprachiger Autoren jüdischer Herkunft zum Zionismus.

b _____ .

c _____ analyses the relationship of German-speaking authors of Jewish origin to Zionism.

Klimaanlage = *air conditioning*
ausstatten = *to equip*
Benzin = *petrol* (BrE)/ *gas* (AmE)
Verbrauch = *consumption*

9 a Dieses mit Klimaanlage und Airbags ausgestattete Modell hat einen für Autos seiner Klasse äußerst niedrigen Benzinverbrauch.

b _____ .

c _____ .

6 A proper scandal

Put the words listed below in the correct space in each sentence. In some cases, more than one word may be possible.

concerned • involved • present • proper • responsible

At a press briefing dealing with the latest corruption scandal the government spokesperson claimed that the _____[1] people _____[1] had not yet been arrested. She stressed that the _____[2] government _____[2] were doing their best to find the _____[3] persons _____[3], but the complexity of such _____[4] processes _____[4] meant that the press should not expect quick results. The _____[5] government departments _____[5], she added, were very busy with their preparations for the annual budget, and in any case, the _____[6] procedures _____[6] had to be followed if the government were to maintain its reputation for _____[7] behaviour _____[7]. The statement was greeted at several points with ironic guffaws from the _____[8] journalists _____[8].

7 Record-breakers

Form sentences which fit the facts given in note form, choosing the correct alternative from the three possibilities given on the right. Use a superlative in each case. If both the analytic and synthetic superlative are possible, give both.

Example

long road (world) ...

a Route 66 (USA)
b the Transamazonica (Brazil)
c the Pan-American Highway

→ *The longest road in the world is the Pan-American Highway.* (NB: **of the world* is not possible in sentences like these, where the prepositional phrase follows a superlative.)

Exercises

1 rare disease (world) ...
a CJD (Creutzfeld Jacob disease)
b smallpox
c Marburg fever (Green Monkey disease)

2 common cause of sudden death ... (the developed countries)
a a stroke
b AIDS
c coronary heart disease

3 fatal epidemic (world) ...
a Ebola fever
b AIDS
c rabies

4 bloody battle (history) ..., with 1.22 million dead and wounded
a the Somme (1916)
b Stalingrad (1942-43)
c Gettysburg (1863)

5 The ... acute sense of smell (world), being able to smell a virgin female up to 11 kilometres away
a male wolf
b male emperor moth
c female elephant

6 heavy man (the US), Jon Minnoch, was ... when he died in 1983.
a 215 kg
b 362 kg
c 442 kg

7 ... extensive underground railway (Europe), with a total length of 408 km.
a London
b Moscow
c Berlin

8 complex motorway interchange (the U.K.) ..., with 18 routes at six levels
a M61-M62 at Spaghetti Junction at Worsley (near Manchester)
b the M6 at Spaghetti Junction at Gravelly Hill (near Birmingham)

c the M3-M25 at Virginia Water (near London)

9 narrow street (the EU) ..., at one part only 38 cm wide

a Elgin Street in Bacup (Britain)
b Trianglen in Store Heddinge (Denmark)
c Vicolo della Virilità (Italy)

10 big and famous department store (London) ..., with a total selling floor space of 10.5 hectares

a Harrods
b Marks & Spencers
c C&A's

XIII The Adverbial

XIII.1 Overview

The adverb in traditional grammar is a word class which has a large number of different functions, which are not necessarily shared by all members of this word class. Broughton 1990 calls it a 'rag-bag' class because it is so heterogeneous: adverbs like *soon, very, quickly* have little in common with each other apart from the fact that they are not nouns, adjectives, verbs, conjunctions or prepositions. For this reason linguists are redefining and reanalysing this class.

definition

An adverb is a word whose main function is to modify the verb, i.e. to give extra information about the verb:

1 *They were swimming quickly across the lake.*

terminology

Both *quickly* and *across the lake* tell us more about the action of the verb, stating how the swimming occurred *(quickly)* and where *(across the lake)*. Both have the same functions, but whereas *quickly* is a single word, *across the lake* is an adverbial phrase.
We often, rather loosely, use the term *adverb* to refer to both types, because they have the same function. Note that the adverbial phrase *across the lake* could be replaced with a single word, e.g. *there*, with no change in function. The term adverbial means any structure which

functions like an adverb. It is a general term which includes adverbs (i.e. single words), adverbial phrases, and adverbial clauses like *when I was a child*. In this chapter we will use the term *adverb* to refer to both single words and adverbial phrases.

Adverbs can also modify adjectives (as in 2), other adverbs (as in 3) and even whole sentences (as in 4):

2 *Jane gets terribly nervous before an exam.*
3 *My driving test went surprisingly well.*
4 *Luckily, no one was hurt in the car crash.*

position

Adverbs occur in three main positions in the sentence: in front position before the subject, in mid position before the main verb and in end position after the main verb (see 2.3 below for details).

Single-word adverbs are of two types. One type contains words which are not derived from other word-classes by means of a suffix, e.g. *abroad, here, just, only, somewhere, therefore, well.*

The second type consists of adverbs formed by adding a suffix, e.g. *-ly*, which changes an adjective into an adverb, or *-wise*, which turns a noun into an adverb. These are known as derivational adverbs, because they are derived from a different word-class:

5 *Drive carefully. This is an accident black spot.*
6 *He hurriedly put on his coat and ran out of the house.*
7 *You have to turn it anti-clockwise to unscrew it.*
8 *Weatherwise, we're in for a bad winter.*

adverb versus adjective

Example 6 reminds us that the adverbial ending can be added to participles like *hurried* when they are used as adjectives. In 8 we have a type often used in informal (especially American) speech, where the suffix *-wise* means 'as far as (the weather) is concerned'.
In English the adverb is marked, normally by the suffix *-ly*, while the adjective is unmarked.

9	*He bought the diamonds legally.*	Adverb
10	*It was a legal transaction.*	Adjective (attrib.)

In German it is the adjective which is marked, though only attributively, i. e. before a noun.

11 *Er hat die Diamanten legal gekauft.* Adverb
12 *Es war ein legales Geschäft.* Adjective (attrib.)

In both languages the adjective remains unmarked predicatively, i.e. after copulas like *be, become, get, remain, seem, appear* and the verbs of perception *feel, look, smell, sound, taste,* together with their German equivalents:

13 *The transaction was legal.* (= *Das Geschäft war legal*)
14 *The transaction sounded legal.* (= ... *hörte sich legal an*)

History English

To form an adverb in Old English, *-e* was normally added to an adjective. Hence the adjective *fæst* 'firm' contrasting with *fæste* 'firmly' (the original meaning still survives in *fast asleep*). In Middle English the *-e* ending was lost. This type survives in some adverbs, e. g. *fast* in *He walks fast* or *hard* in *She works hard.* In Old English the adjective suffix *-līc*, as in *līflīc* 'lively' could also take an adverbial *-e* suffix, e. g. *līflīce* 'in a lively way'. By the Middle English period this formation occurred so often that it became associated with the adverb, with the result that ME *-lich*, which later developed into *-ly*, became the normal suffix marking the adverb.

History German

The history of the adverb in German shows interesting parallels. In Middle High German the adverbial suffix was also *-e*, as is still reflected in the difference between adjectival *lang* in *Der Vortrag war lang* and adverbial *lange* in *Ich kenne ihn schon lange*. However, this distinction was later lost. In Middle High German adjectives ending in *-lich* added *-e* to form the adverb. This pattern was extended to other adjectives, and *-lich* was later interpreted as a mark of the adverb. Thus Luther forms an adverb *klerlich* from the adjective *klar* in *klerlich schreyben* (cf. *write clearly*). In later German this pattern died out, possibly due to the popularity of *-lich* as an adjectival ending.

XIII.2
Normal pattern
A ADVERBS ENDING IN *-ly*

2.1 Formation of adverbs

The formation of the large class of derivational adverbs taking *-ly* needs little comment, as it is largely regular.

pronunciation

One peculiarity in the pronunciation, however, is that all those adverbs formed from participles ending in *-ed* which are used as adjectives pronounce the participle ending in full, i.e. as /ɪd/. Contrast the following pairs:

15 *There has been a marked increase in drugs offences.* /mɑːkt/
16 *Imports to Euroland have markedly increased as a result of the strong euro.* /ˈmɑːkɪdli/
17 *The Cold War principle of mutual assured destruction was a macabre concept – no wonder its acronym was MAD.* /əˈʃʊəd/
18 *This problem might not be solved by money alone, but it will assuredly not be solved without it.* /əˈʃʊərɪdli/

comparison

Adverbs ending in *-ly* only use the analytical comparison with *more, most* (cf. adjectives, Chap. XII, 2.1). The vast majority are regular.

B ADVERBS WITHOUT *-ly*

A small number of adverbs like *fast* have the same form as adjectives. They are survivals of a type which used the old adverbial ending *-e*, which was later lost (see History box above). Other instances of this are *far, long*. Compare:

19 *It's a long haul from Australia to Europe.* (adjective)
20 *Have you been waiting here long?* (adverb)

> Notice that *long* in 20 functions like an adverb, not an adjective, although it does not have the typical adverbial ending *-ly*.

In informal register, especially in American English, this type is fairly common with other adverbs:

21 *Let's get out of here real quick!* (adverbs, AmE)
22 *He sure does act cool.* (adverbs, AmE)

Speakers of Standard British English would replace *sure* and *real* by *certainly, really,* etc., though they might use *quick* and *cool* as adverbs without an ending.

In the comparison of adverbs consisting of one syllable there is a similar tendency to prefer forms which are identical with adjectives instead of using the analytical comparison with *more, most*. This tendency, however, is restricted to informal register:

23 *Can you speak a bit slower, please?* (= *more slowly*)
24 *Which of you can do this crossword the quickest?* (= *most quickly*)

C Adverbs with *-ly* or without *-ly*

Some adverbs can take either ending, with no difference in meaning:

25 *His fists were clenched tight, his face a mask of hate.*
26 *His tightly clenched fists hit their target again and again.*

If the adverb follows the participle, as in 25, it has no ending, whereas it takes *-ly* if it precedes the participle, as in 26.

Some adverbs can have either ending, but have developed a semantic difference between the two types:

27 *They say still waters run deep.* (= *not shallow*)
28 *Public opinion is deeply divided on the issue.* (= *very*)
29 *You can fly direct from here to Warsaw.* (= *without changing planes*)
30 *She looked directly at the audience.* (= *in a direct manner*)
31 *You should work hard and play hard.* (= *intensively*)
32 *I hardly knew what to say to that.* (= *almost didn't*)
33 *Are you working late tonight, Gemma?* (= *longer*)
34 *I haven't seen Jason lately.* (= *recently*)
35 *Don't go too near that dog. It might bite.* (= *close to*)
36 *I nearly got bitten by a rattlesnake in Arizona.* (= *almost*)

In other cases the pattern is less clear:

37 *If you can't play fair, don't play at all.*
38 *I don't think my boss treats me fairly.*
39 *I was fairly tired last night.*

In some phrases *fair* is used as an adverb without an ending, e.g. *fight fair, play fair*, in the sense of 'according to the rules', as in 37. In a similar meaning with other verbs, as in 38, it usually takes the regular ending *-ly*. Finally, in a completely different meaning, as an intensifier in the sense of 'quite, rather', *fairly* is only used with the regular adverbial suffix (cf. 39). For more examples of adverbs distinguished in this way, see the list in Swan 1995, §21.2.

2.2 Semantic classes of adverbs

The position of adverbs in the sentence depends on various factors. The most important of these is the meaning of the adverb.
Examples of frequently used adverbs in these semantic classes are listed below:

connectors

Connectors are adverbs which link one sentence with the next: *after all, anyway, besides, by the way, consequently, firstly, however, in a nutshell, incidentally, in conclusion, in short, next, now, so, still* (= *however*), *then, therefore, thus, well*. For more examples, see Broughton 1990, §140. Connectors, not surprisingly, tend to occur in front position:

40 *She thinks it's a fantastic car. However, I don't agree.*

focus adverbs

Focus adverbs focus the listener's or reader's attention on a specific part of the sentence. Typical examples are: *absolutely, alone, also, either ... or, especially, even, just, mainly, mostly, neither ... nor, only, particularly, simply*. They usually occur in mid position or before the word or phrase they modify. One exception is *alone*, which always follows the word or phrase it modifies. Notice that *also* can occur in front position as a sentence adverbial (see below, p. 244).

41 *They also warned us not to go to Central Park at night.*
42 *We would especially like to thank the choir for being here tonight.*
43 *Reforming the universities alone will not be enough – we need to pump much more money into both research and teaching.*

Note: *also / auch*

Note that *also* is not used to modify a noun phrase, as *auch* is in German *(Auch die Engel essen Bohnen)*. Nor does it normally modify an adverbial phrase, as *auch* frequently does in German *(Es hat auch im letzten Winter viel geschneit.)*.
The main equivalents to German *auch* are:

- *also* (especially in more formal contexts; placed before main verb)
- *as well* (in informal register; at end of clause)
- *even* (if it is stressed and translates *sogar*)

- *not ... either* (in negative sentences, translating *auch ... nicht*)
- *too* (in informal register; after the word or clause it modifies)

Adverbs of frequency, e.g. *always, ever, frequently, never, normally, occasionally, often, rarely, seldom, sometimes, usually*, normally go in mid position. frequency adverbs

44 *We occasionally go skating at the local skating rink.*

However, frequency adverbs ending in *-ly* such as *daily, weekly, monthly* or adverbial phrases like *every day* usually go in end position:

45 *The Observer is published weekly.*
46 *We have lunch at one every day.*

Intensifiers, which are traditionally known as adverbs of degree, have to precede the word they modify unless this is a verb. When they modify verbs, they tend to occur in mid position, though they may occur elsewhere. There are two types of intensifiers. intensifiers

Upgraders or amplifiers intensify a word up the scale: *absolutely, awfully, completely, deeply, entirely, extremely, fully, highly, intensely, much, perfectly, profoundly, quite, really, simply, so, terribly, thoroughly, totally, utterly, well.* upgraders and downgraders

47 *She's awfully nice.* (upgrader modifying an adjective)
48 *I absolutely agree with your assessment of the situation.* (upgrader modifying a verb)
49 *Have you quite finished?* (upgrader meaning 'completely', modifying a verb)
50 *Your essay is quite excellent.* (upgrader meaning 'absolutely', modifying an adjective)

In British English *quite* is used as an upgrader with non-gradable words, i.e. words describing an extreme state (cf. 49 and 50). In American usage, *quite* is normally only used as an upgrader.
In British English *quite* also occurs as a downgrader when used with verbs and gradable adjectives, as in 53 and 54 below (cf. also German *ganz*).

Downgraders or downtoners scale down the meaning of the word: *almost, barely, enough, fairly, hardly, merely, nearly, only, partly, practically, pretty, quite, rather, scarcely*:

51 *This satellite dish is practically useless. It's always breaking down.* (downgrader modifying an adjective)
52 *We only had enough petrol for the next ten miles.* (downgrader *only* modifying a verb, downgrader *enough* modifying a noun)
53 *We quite enjoyed ourselves at that party.* (downgrader meaning 'quite a lot', modifying a verb)
54 *She's quite nice, isn't she?* (downgrader meaning 'fairly', modifying an adjective)

Note: *enough*

The adverb *enough* precedes a noun (as in 52) but follows an adjective (e.g. *big enough*).

manner

Adverbs of manner describe how actions and events occur. They usually go in end position. Examples: *badly, nicely, quickly, quietly, roughly, slowly, suddenly, well.*

55 *You've been progressing nicely with your English.*

place

Adverbs of place also normally take end position. Examples: *abroad, downstairs, here, home, in Bath, inside, in the street, outside.*

56 *Aunt Matilda lives in Singapore.*

sentence adverbs

Sentence adverbs refer to the whole sentence rather than individual elements in the sentence. Most of them occur in front or mid position. Examples: *actually, allegedly, also, certainly, clearly, definitely, frankly, foolishly, honestly, in fact, obviously, possibly, probably, seriously, surprisingly, understandably, unfortunately.*

57 *Actually, you'll find it far more convenient to fly to Spain.*
58 *Foolishly, despite all the warnings, we left the car unlocked.*
59 *Also, I'd like to renew my subscription to Private Eye.*

time

Adverbs of time such as *at 8 pm, for five days, in 2002, last year, now, recently, since 1972, soon, today* usually occur in end position:

60 *The doctor will see you now, Mrs Gould.*

If they are single-word adverbs, they often occur in mid position.

61 *I recently saw my former maths teacher in town.*

2.3 Position of adverbs

Meaning is the major factor which decides where the adverb should go in a sentence, but two more factors are also relevant, viz.:

- length
- stress

Length is important for the mid position, because normally only single-word adverbs are tolerated in this position (but see 3.2 below). Longer adverbial phrases would obscure the important relationship between subject, verb and object (see Chap. I). They therefore tend to be avoided.
Stress affects the adverb's position, too. If an adverb is stressed more than usual, it may take up a different position from its normal one. For example, adverbial phrases of time are placed in the prominent position at the beginning of the sentence, i. e. in front position, if they need to be given extra stress.

The diagram below illustrates the main positions taken up by adverbs in the sentence, according to semantic class (Aux = Auxiliary Verb):

Front		Mid			End
Adverb	Subject (+ Aux)	Adverb	(Aux +) Verb	Object	Adverb
• CONNECTORS • SENTENCE ADVERBS		• FOCUS • FREQUENCY • INTENSIFIERS			• MANNER • PLACE • TIME

One very important word order rule is that adverbs must not normally be placed between main verb and object, as is frequently the case in German (but see 3.2 for exceptions). Compare the English and German sentences:

62 *I often <u>get</u> <u>headaches</u> in the mornings.*
Verb Object

63 *Ich <u>bekomme</u> morgens oft <u>Kopfschmerzen</u>.*
Verb Object

64 *She speaks Greek very well.*
Verb Object

65 *Sie spricht sehr gut Griechisch.*
Verb Object

A Front position

Front or initial position is the normal position for connectors and sentence adverbs:

66 *By the way, that shipment of DVD players hasn't arrived yet.* (connector)
67 *Unfortunately there's no trace of your daughter in our records.* (sentence adverb)

When adverbs of frequency, manner, place and time need to be stressed, they can also be placed here. If negative adverbs such as *never, under no circumstances* or restrictive adverbs like *rarely, seldom* are placed in front position, inversion of the verb is necessary (see Chap. I).

68 *Sometimes we just go off into the hills.* (frequency)
69 *Rarely have I seen such courage and tenacity.* (frequency)
70 *Quietly they tiptoed along the corridor.* (manner)
71 *At university we never got up before 10 a.m.* (place)
72 *Eventually they decided to scrap the plan.* (time)
73 *For two hours I've been waiting here! What's the big idea?* (time)

B Mid position

Mid or medial position is the standard position for focus adverbs, adverbs of frequency, and intensifiers:

74 *They neither asked us for permission, nor did we give it.* (focus)
75 *I've rarely been asked such a stupid question.* (frequency)
76 *We thoroughly enjoyed your dinner party, Penny.* (intensifier)

Inversion after *nor* occurs in 74 because *nor* begins the clause (see Chap. I). Notice that 75 has normal word order when the restrictive adverb *rarely* is used in mid position, whereas in 69 inversion involving the auxiliary *have* was necessary. In 75 the adverb is put between the two auxiliaries *have* and *been*. This is the normal pattern (see also diagram on p. 245 above), although there are other possibilities (see 3.2 below).

However, in mid position it is also possible to use connectors, especially in formal register (cf. 77), adverbs of manner if unstressed (as in 78), and adverbs of time, provided these are short (cf. 79). This usually means that they are single-word adverbs:

77 *We thus determined to strike out for the nearest Alpine hut in a desperate attempt to survive the blizzard.* (connector)
78 *The tractor slowly negotiated the hill.* (manner, unstressed)
79 *Mr Barlow has handed in his notice, so we're now looking for a new sales rep.* (time, short)

Adverbs of manner often go in mid position when they modify a passive construction. They are unstressed in these cases, too:

80 *Nicky may have been badly hurt!* (manner, unstressed)

C End position

End or final position is the 'home' position for adverbs of manner, place and time:

81 *The line of pilgrims processed solemnly and with great dignity past their tormentors.* (manner)
82 *Pamela was still waiting patiently outside school.* (place)
83 *I saw Pete and Gloria in town yesterday.* (time)

When several adverbs occur in end position, the usual order is manner, place, time. Normally we avoid having three adverbs in end position by putting one adverb in mid or front position. It is, however, quite common to find two adverbs in end position. Notice the sequence of adverbs of manner and place in 81 and 82 (place = *past their tormentors* in 81, manner = *patiently* in 82), and place and time in 83 (place = *in town*). If several adverbs of time occur in end position, the more precise time references normally come first:

84 *Sheila was born at 11.45 pm on 2nd October in 1982.*
85 *Ronny got up at six yesterday morning.*

However, notice that both *at 11.45 p.m.* and *at six* can also be placed last in the sentence if we wish to emphasise them:

86 *She was born on 2nd October in 1982, at 11.45 pm!*

87 *Ronny got up yesterday morning at six! Normally we don't expect him to stir until 11.*

In end position we also find adverbs of frequency and some intensifiers:

88 *We don't go to the pictures often.* (frequency)
89 *I haven't seen her much in the last few weeks.* (intensifier)

XIII.3
Exceptions
A ADJECTIVES ENDING IN *-ic* formation

3.1 Formation of adverbs

One irregularity is that adjectives ending in *-ic* form their adverb by adding *-ally*. Compare the adjective in 90 with the adverb in 91:

90 *A characteristic feature of this novel is the use of flashback.*
91 *Characteristically, he paid for everyone's meal, being a very generous person.*

This also occurs with adjective pairs where there is a distinction in meaning according to whether the word ends in *-ic* or *-ical*:
92 *The economic problems of developing nations are partly due to the imbalance of power in the world.*
93 *Economically, developing countries have been doing rather better recently.*

There is one exception to this rule: the adjective *public* forms its adverb simply by adding *-ly*.

Pronunciation

> Notice that in all cases where the adverb ends in *-ically*, the three syllables of the spelling are reduced to two in the pronunciation. Thus *-ically* is pronounced /ɪkli/ in both *characteristically* and *economically*: /ˌkærɪktəˈrɪstɪkli/ and /iːkəˈnɒmɪkli/.

B ADJECTIVES ENDING IN *-ly*

There is no single-word adverb formed from adjectives ending in *-ly* such as *cowardly, friendly, lively, silly*. Instead, we use paraphrases:

94 *The band started playing in a lively manner.*
95 *Stop grinning at me in such a silly way!*

Adjectives ending in *-ly* which refer to frequency, e.g. *daily, weekly, monthly, yearly*, are also used as adverbs (see 2.2 above).

From among the words with irregular comparison, the forms of *little* are sometimes a source of error among learners. They are:

little (= *wenig*) – *less* (= *weniger*) – *least* (= *am wenigsten*)

96 *I slept very little last night.*
97 *We've got less time for partying now that we've got a toddler.*

The adverb *little* is far more common in formal contexts. In informal register it is normally replaced by the negation of its opposite, i.e. *not much*, or synonymous expressions such as *a lot of, a great deal of*, or the very informal *loads of.* Compare:

98 *We haven't got much time.* (= *wenig Zeit, nicht viel Zeit*)
99 *He's not got a lot of money.* (= *wenig Geld, nicht viel Geld*)

3.2 Position of adverbs

A Adverb between Verb and Object

Adverb Phrase

Although an adverb cannot normally be placed between the main verb and the object (see above, 2.3), there are two common exceptions to this important rule. An adverb can be put in this position if it is a fairly long adverbial phrase marked off by speech pauses, or by commas in written English:

100 *The hotel management introduced, at great expense to itself, a complex new security system.*
(introduced = Verb; at great expense to itself = Adverb; a complex new security system = Object)

Although this type of construction definitely does occur, learners would be well advised not to make a habit of using it.

Obj + Relative

A second common exception is when the object is followed by a relative clause. Since the normal pattern in English is to keep the relative clause as close as possible to its antecedent, i.e. the noun or noun phrase it refers to (see Chap. XV), in such cases the adverb is often placed before the object:

101 *Britain developed in the 18th century a society*
Verb Adverb Object
which differed strikingly from those on the Continent.
Relative Clause

102 *Please return by next week all the books you have borrowed.*
Verb Adverb Object Relative Clause

B THE ADVERB IN MID POSITION

be

The normal position for any adverb in mid position is before the main verb. With the unstressed copula *be* the adverb follows the verb:

103 *He's also a teetotaller, as well as a vegetarian.*
104 *The Joneses are often in Colorado on business.*

stressed *be* or auxiliary

However, when the copula *be* or an auxiliary is stressed, the adverb goes in front of them:

105 *They really are a nuisance, these people, aren't they?*
106 *He probably has annoyed her, you know.*
107 *You certainly do look stupid in those wraparounds.*

Aux + Aux

If two auxiliaries are present, the adverb normally goes between the two. However, it can sometimes occur after the second auxiliary, especially if the first auxiliary is a modal:

108 *You silly fool! You could have easily been injured!*

Notice that regular word order is also possible:

109 *You could easily have been injured!*

When sentence adverbs, intensifiers or adverbs of manner occur in mid position, the adverb is usually placed in front of the main verb:

110 *She says she'll have definitely finished her doctorate by May.* (sentence adverb)
111 *They've been thoroughly disappointed by his behaviour.* (intensifier)
112 *In a week's time Ann and Ray will be casually soaking up the sun on the deck of a luxury yacht somewhere in the Med.* (manner)

Because of the close semantic link between the intensifier and the main verb, the two cannot be separated, as is illustrated by 111. However, with sentence adverbs and adverbs of manner the adverb could also be placed between the two auxiliaries:

113 *She'll definitely have finished her PhD by May.* (sentence adverb)
114 *In a week's time they'll casually be soaking up the Mediterranean sun on the deck of a luxury yacht.* (manner)

Exercises

1 Conversions
Re-formulate the following sentences, converting the adjective and noun in each sentence to a verb and adverb or adjective, as appropriate.

Example

Your argument isn't very logical. → *You aren't arguing very logically.*

1 She gave me a shy look.
2 This guitar has a pleasant sound.
3 Janice's behaviour was terribly silly.
4 They held a public protest against the motorway.
5 They were involved in the illegal sale of designer drugs.
6 Genetic manipulation of humans opens up frightening possibilities.
7 Your actions were extremely cowardly.
8 The weekly publication of the casualty figures had a devastating effect on national morale.
9 The new professor gave a lively lecture.
10 'Cassius has a lean and hungry look.'
(*Julius Caesar*, I,2)

2 Interview at a posh school
Underline the correct alternatives in the following text about a working class boy's interview at a British grammar school.

The day I went for interview at grammar school I was *real/really* [1] scared. The school looked very *posh/poshly* [2]. I waited *patient/patiently* [3] for about ten minutes. Then the headmaster came along, looked at me *curious/curiously* [4] and asked me *polite/politely* [5] to come into his office. He seemed very *learned/learnedly* [6] in his black gown and dark-rimmed glasses, and I felt pretty *shy/shyly* [7] in these

Exercises

unfamiliar/unfamiliarly [8] surroundings. Nobody from our *local/locally* [9] primary school had ever been to grammar school. However, the headmaster looked at me *kindly/kind/in a kindly way* [10], and I answered his questions as *able/ably* [11] as I could. He said that on the whole my answers sounded pretty *sensible/sensibly* [12], and were *significant/significantly* [13] better than those of most of the boys he had interviewed that morning. I was surprised at how *simple/simply* [14] it had all been. So when I left the school after the interview I felt much *cheerfuller/more cheerful/more cheerfully* [15] than half an hour earlier.

3 Complete the sentence

Put the words and phrases in brackets in the most natural order.

1 They speak and write ... (fluently / Hungarian)
2 We waited ... (in the corridor / silently)
3 When Bolton's £2 million striker scored his third goal against Arsenal, Bolton supporters cheered ... (in Reebok Stadium / their team / wildly)
4 The submarine passed ... (just after midnight / quietly / through the Strait of Gibraltar)
5 Arthur and Kate are going ... (in the Czech Republic / next spring / on holiday)
6 The police arrested ... (last week / several members of the Heligoland Liberation Front)
7 He read ... (over breakfast / slowly / the newspaper)
8 We met ... (in Hungary / last October / Tony and Kate)

4 Commenting

Replace the phrases underlined by a sentence adverb, using those listed in 2.2.

Example

<u>It is obvious that</u> this problem cannot be solved overnight.
→ *Obviously, this problem cannot be solved overnight.*

1 <u>It is understandable that</u> raising taxes is unpopular.
2 <u>To be frank</u>, I prefer Marseilles to Lyons.
3 <u>It is unfortunate that</u> Tim's house was under-insured.
4 <u>To be honest</u>, I haven't a clue where I put last week's *New Statesman*.
5 <u>As a matter of fact</u>, St. Boniface did a lot of missionary work in Hesse and Thuringia.

Exercises

6 <u>It was foolish of him to leave</u> the bedroom window open in an inner city area with a high crime rate.
7 <u>To my surprise</u>, her godson lives in North-Rhine Westphalia.
8 <u>Some people maintain that</u> humans are descended from Martians.

5 Writing a reference

Imagine you are a university professor or lecturer. Write a short reference for a student (e.g. somebody in your class), using adverbs where possible. Some words and phrases are given below to help you. If you prefer, you can write a reference for a celebrity, e.g. a film star, well-known politician or sporting personality.

- be involved in extra-curricular activities
- come to class
- express himself/herself
- hand in work
- in contacts with students and staff
- part-time job
- organise his/her time
- prepare for classes
- recommend
- speak several foreign languages
- support a person's application
- take part in class discussions

- active
- careful
- confident
- efficient
- fluent
- imaginative
- pleasant
- punctual
- reliable
- thorough

- articulate
- competent
- conscientious
- energetic
- friendly
- lively
- polite
- regular
- shy
- warm

6 Endings: to add or not to add? That is the question.

Complete the sentences below, using the adverbs given, which can all be used with or without an *-ly* ending, depending on meaning and context. In some cases, more than one answer is possible.

Example

hard / hardly
'Why does Sandy often feel lonely on his remote island?'
'Because he ...'
→ *'Because he hardly sees anybody.'*

1 free / freely
'How did Alex manage to see the play if she's broke?'
'She got in ...'

2 sharp / sharply
'Why did Janet burst into tears in class?'
'Oh, Bugface spoke to her ...'
3 wrong / wrongly
'Did that contestant get the £1 million on "Who wants to be a millionaire?" yesterday?' – 'No, she guessed ...'
4 fair / fairly
'What do you think of the ref's decision in favour of Nokizblokov?'
'The referee was right to call the fight off – in boxing you've got to fight ...'
5 hard / hardly late / lately
'Have you heard the latest? The boss has sacked Greg Browne!'
'I don't blame her. He ... ever turned up at work. And when he did turn up he kept coming ...'
6 sharp / sharply
'When did they say you should turn up for the interview?'
'At 10 o'clock ...'
7 slow / slowly
'What did you say?'
'I said be careful. There's a dangerous bend coming up. For God's sake, go ...'
8 low / lowly
'Why don't you like living near Heathrow?'
'It's so noisy and the planes often fly ...'
9 easy / easily hard / hardly
'Now that you're retired, learning Chinese is something you could ... do.'
'Yes, but all my life I've worked so ... that all I want to do now is take things ...'
10 slow / slowly
Grendel crawled out of the marsh, dragging his stinking body behind him. He saw the hall of Hrothgar's warriors before him. Hungrily, he slithered ... towards the hall of death.

7 Translating auch

Translate the following sentences into English. The more difficult vocabulary is contained in XIII.1 to XIII.3. Before doing the exercise, check the corresponding English focus adverbs in 2.2.

1 Auch in England trinkt man Kaffee.
2 Ich habe leider auch keine Zeit.

3 Auch dieses Geschäft war eigentlich legal.
4 Was er am Montag getan hat, war auch gefährlich!
5 Patrick ist auch Antialkoholiker.
6 Auch Patrick ist Antialkoholiker.
7 Ich habe gestern Nacht auch sehr wenig geschlafen.
8 Meine Frau ist auch am 6. Oktober geboren! So ein Zufall!
9 Übrigens, die DVD-Player sind auch gestern nicht angekommen.
10 Einige Experten machen sich auch über einen stärkeren Euro Sorgen.

8 Focus on adverbs

Put the focus adverbs *alone, even* or *only* in the most natural position in the sentences below.

1 He said that ... people ... who have plenty of money can truthfully say that ... money ... won't make you happy.
2 Actually, ... James ... enjoyed Chicago, and he ... normally ... likes spending his holidays in some remote rural idyll.
3 They say that cats have nine lives and ... humans ... have ... one, but ... cats ... have to die sometime, don't they?
4 What a fantastic wedding cake! If you ask me, ... the cake decorations ... must have cost a fortune! I ... didn't ... know the bride and groom had so much money.
5 You know, ... the most talented writer can't ... be a success if they ... rely ... on ... their genius. In other words, ... talent ... isn't sufficient.

9 The American airman

During World War II Christabel Bielenberg, an Anglo-Irish woman married to a German, takes refuge from the air raids on Berlin in a small village in the Black Forest. One day one of her neighbours discovers a US airman.

Translate the words and phrases underlined, inserting them at the right points in the sentence. Less easy vocabulary is listed below.

a bit flat • against the far wall • at the edge of the woods • bench • cheerful • complete • conspiratorial • cropped close • due • eager • for a moment • from the sudden flatness in his voice • gingerly • gradual • impressed • in the doorway • inevitable • little house • on the other side of the valley • otherwise • over some little town • relaxed •

right and left • right away • (stand) still • sure • thoughtful • wide awake

„Frau Doktor!" Ich deckte gerade den Tisch zum Mittagessen, als
'Frau Doktor,' I ... was ... laying[1] the table for lunch when Hans

Hans Bauschs Kopf im Fenster erschien. Er winkte mir, ans
Bausch's head appeared at the window. He beckoned to me to

Fenster zu kommen, und schaute rasch nach rechts und links.
come to the window and ... glanced ...[2]

„Ich hab was für Sie." „Was ist es denn?" „Es ist ein Amerikaner,
'I've got something for you.' 'What is it?' 'It's an American,

Frau Doktor", flüsterte er verschwörerisch.
Frau Doktor,' he ... whispered ...[3]

Ich versuchte, mich entsprechend beeindruckt zu zeigen.
I tried to look ...[4]

Ich schaute Hans einen Augenblick nachdenklich an.
I looked at Hans ...[5]

„Wo hast du denn diesen Amerikaner gefunden, Hans?" fragte ich.
'Where did you find this American, Hans?' I asked.

„Droben im Wald", antwortete er. „Und wo ist er jetzt?"
'Up in the woods,' he replied. 'And ... where ... is he ...[6]?'

„In meiner Küche, da schläft er." Ich folgte ihm zu seinem
'He's asleep in my kitchen.' I followed him ...[7]

Häuschen am Waldrand auf der anderen Talseite. Hans eilte
... Hans ... hurried

munter vor mir her. Ich blieb einen Augenblick unter der Tür stehen.
... ahead of me ...[8] ...I stood ...[9]

Der Ausdruck, der auf meinem Gesicht lag, war wahrscheinlich
The expression on my face ... was ...[10] no more intelligent than

Exercises

nicht intelligenter als Hans Bauschs Blick, denn auf der schmalen
that of Hans Bausch, for stretched out ...[11]

Bank an der anderen Wand lag völlig entspannt ein großer junger
lay ... a tall young man ...

Mann in einem blauen Fliegeranzug. Ich schaute auf ihn hinunter,
in blue airman's overalls ...[12] *As I looked down at him,*

und allmählich wurde mir klar, dass der Krieg für Deutschland
... I ... realised ...[13] *that ...the war ...was ...lost ...*

unabänderlich verloren war. Es war nicht sein unrasiertes Gesicht –
for Germany ...[14] *It was not his unshaven face –*

ein typisch amerikanisches Gesicht, kurze Nase, großer Mund,
...[15] *short nosed, big mouthed,*

kurz geschnittenes lockiges Haar –, sondern ganz einfach das
...[16] *curly hair –, but ...*[17]

Gesunde, das Wohlbefinden an ihm; sozusagen der Überfluss, die
his general air of health and well being, of affluence; the quality of

Qualität des Stoffes, aus dem sein Overall gemacht war. Plötzlich
the material his overalls were made of. ... I ....

fühlte ich mich schäbig, alt, ramponiert, besiegt. Alles an ihm war
felt ...[18] *shabby, old, dilapidated and defeated. Everything on*

so echt: echte Wolle, echtes Leder, echte Seide – so echt, und er
him was so real: real wool, real leather, real silk – so real, and he

sah so jung aus. Und an mir war alles Ersatz – unecht von meinen
looked so ...[19] *As for me, I was bogus – bogus from the soles of*

Kunstledersohlen bis zum Rand meines Papierstrohhuts, und ich
my synthetic leather shoes to the brim of my synthetic straw hat,

war mir nicht sicher, ob ich mich jemals wieder jung fühlen würde.
and I was not sure if ...I ...would ...feel ...[20]

Source (adapted): Christabel Bielenberg, *The Past is Myself.* London, 1994 (pp. 149–150), and *Als ich Deutsche war 1939–1945.* Munich, 1979 (pp. 156–158)

Quellenangaben:

Umschlagseite 2

① The Observer, 3. 6. 01 (über den Pearl-Harbour-Film)
② © Gareth Llewellyn Williams/ Origin8 Photo Agency, Wales.
③ © The New Yorker Collection 1999 Peter Steiner from cartoonbank.com, appeared in: The New Yorker (Magazine), 17/5/99
④ The Spectator, 13. 6. 1998
⑤ Qantas Australia, in The Observer Life, 29. 3. 1998

Umschlagseite 3

① The Observer, 4. 3. 01
② © David Austin, appeared in The Guardian, 01. 06. 2001
③ The Guardian, 31. 8. 01
④ Sun Datacenter, in The Idependent. 31. 5. 01
⑤ Der Generalanzeiger, 8. 10. 01
⑥ The Observer, 23. 12. 01
⑦ The Independent, 2. 11. 01
⑧ The New Statesman, 24. 10. 1998
⑨ The New Statesman, 20. 12. 1999
⑩ © Peter Macdiarmid/ National Pictures, appeared in: The Guardian, 10.04.1998
⑪ The Independent, 1. 4. 01

XIV The Definite Article

XIV.1 Overview

English uses the definite article less than other Germanic languages, e.g. German and Dutch, and much less than Romance languages like French. Normally the definite article in English is only used for specific reference. Compare :

the = specific
zero = general

1 *Thomas Hobbes once said that the life of man was solitary, poor, nasty, brutish, and short.* (cf. *das Leben des Menschen*)
2 *Life is short, art is long.* (cf. *Das Leben ist kurz, die Kunst ist lang.*)

Example 1 deals with a specific aspect of life, i.e. the life of human beings. By contrast, Example 2 refers to life and art in general and thus has zero article.

History

Germanic and the ancestor of the Romance languages, Latin, had no definite article. The definite article only developed later in the Germanic and Romance languages. It evolved from a demonstrative pronoun in these languages and was originally only used for specific reference. Whereas most Germanic languages and the Romance languages have since extended the use of the article to general reference, English has kept it restricted to specific reference. Use of the article for general reference may be linked to the fact that in most of these languages it also marks gender and/or case, which is not true of English. (cf. for German, Keller 1978, p. 206, 303, 439, cf. for French, Price 1971, p. 116)

XIV.2
Normal pattern

2.1 Common nouns

With common nouns, use of the definite article is frequent. It shows that we are talking about a specific item. Compare the examples in the text below:

Text

> One of the extraordinary things about life is the sort of places it's prepared to put up with living. Anywhere it can get some kind of a grip, whether it's the intoxicating seas of Santraginus V, where the fish never seem to care whatever the heck kind of direction they swim in, the fire storms of Frastra where, they say, life begins at 40,000 degrees, or just burrowing around in the lower intestine of a rat for the sheer unadulterated hell of it, life will always find a way of hanging on in somewhere.
> It will even live in New York, though it's hard to know why. In winter the temperature falls well below the legal minimum, or rather it would do if anybody had the common sense to set a legal minimum. The last time anybody made a list of the top 100 character attributes of New Yorkers, common sense snuck in at number 79. (Adams 1993, p. 7)

The use of the article to select and define is clear from phrases like :

> *One of the extraordinary things about life, the sort of places, and similarly the ... seas of Santraginus V, the ... kind of direction, etc.*

Notice also that *the common sense* is used to talk about a particular type of common sense, whereas *common sense* is used without the article when it means common sense in general.

In the plural of countable nouns, use or non-use of the article also has the function of distinguishing between specific and general reference:

3 *The customers in the supermarket fled in panic when the teenage gunman started shooting at the police.*
4 *Customers are requested not to ask for credit.*

all + article

This distinction is also maintained after *all*, where use of the article marks reference to a specific group. This is different from in German, where the article is often missing in both types:

5 *All the students in this Department prefer Professor Branestawm because her lectures are so lively.* (cf. *Alle Studierenden dieses Seminars ...*)
6 *All students feel nervous before an exam.* (cf. *Alle Studierenden sind nervös vor einer Prüfung.*)

Note

Notice that, as in German and other languages, the definite article can be used with a count noun in the singular to make generalisations. It is then the equivalent of an indefinite plural :

7 *The customer is always right. (= Customers are ...)*
8 *The tiger is an endangered species. (= Tigers are ...)*

This use of the article to denote a class diverges from the normal function of the article, viz. its use for specific reference (see XIV.1 above).

nationality nouns

With nouns referring to nationality, the article implies that the reference is so definite that it includes the whole of the nationality concerned, while the indefinite plural simply means individual members of this group. The use of the article is thus a much stronger generalisation. A similar pattern occurs with nouns formed from adjectives referring to groups of people, e.g. *liberals, Catholics, whites* etc.

9 *The Scots have acquired a reputation for being stingy, which in my experience is totally unjustified.*
10 *Scots don't usually like being taken for English people.*

COLLECTIVES

Some collective nouns referring to specific social groups always have the article:

the aristocracy – the gentry – the bourgeoisie – the working class – the clergy – the public – the press – the Church

11 *The press is often more interested in trivialising events in search of a good story than in giving a balanced picture.*

Note

Some other collective nouns which do not refer to specific social groups, e.g. *the environment* and *the economy (= die Wirtschaft, die Konjunktur)* take the article:

The economy is going through a recession.

When *economy* means 'thrift' *(Sparsamkeit)*, it is used without an article:
For the sake of economy we've turned down the heating.

2.2 Proper nouns

Since proper nouns have unique reference, i.e. they only refer to one person or thing, normally the article is omitted, even with a premodifying adjective of time or place like *medieval* or *southern*:

12 *Jason Brown, 34, is one of London's long-term unemployed.*
13 *Medieval Europe used Latin as its lingua franca.*
14 *Southern Scotland is very similar to the North of England.*

The classes of words below all omit the article:

NAMES AND TITLES

Names, with or without a title, are not used with the article:

15 *Michael Schumacher took second place in the French Grand Prix.* (cf. *Der Michael Schumacher hat den zweiten Platz im Großen Preis von Frankreich gemacht.*)
16 *Prince Charles is very committed to environmental protection.*

When names are preceded by an adjective, especially in emotional contexts, there is normally no article, in contrast to German, where the use of the article is common:

17 *Little Ben's got chicken pox.* (cf. *Der kleine Ben hat Windpocken.*)
18 *Poor old John – he's had a really hard life.*

Parliament, Congress

The collective nouns *parliament* and *congress* can be used as proper nouns. In these cases they have unique reference and therefore no article:

19 *Parliament is divided over the issue of whether to ban hunting.* (i.e. the British parliament)
20 *There will be a debate on the bill in Congress next week.* (i.e. the US Congress)

When they are used as common nouns with an adjective or noun specifying which body is meant, the article is used: cf. *The British parliament is divided* ... and *There will be a debate on the bill in the US Congress next week.*

> Note that in American English *the Congress* can also be used for unique reference.

Note: *Congress*

MONTHS, DAYS, PUBLIC HOLIDAYS

In contrast to German, English does not normally use the article with names of months, days and public holidays:
January, Wednesday, Good Friday, Easter Monday, Christmas Eve, New Year's Day, Whitsun, Independence Day, Thanksgiving.

21 *There's a big parade in Dublin on Easter Monday.*
(cf. *am Ostermontag*)

When referring to a specific day or month, the article is used:

22 *They went off on their honeymoon the Monday after the wedding.*
23 *Sheila was born the April after Mum died.*

GEOGRAPHICAL NAMES

Zero article is the norm in nouns referring to:

1 CONTINENTS, COUNTRIES, STATES, COUNTIES, CITIES, TOWNS, VILLAGES: *Africa* • *New Zealand* • *Maine* • *Devon* • *Brussels* • *Bolton* • *Belmont*

24 *My ancestors emigrated to New Zealand in the 19th century.*

2 LAKES: *Lake Michigan* /ˈmɪʃɪgən/ • *Loch Ness* • *Lough Neagh* /ˈlɒx ˈneɪ/

25 *Chicago is on Lake Michigan.* (cf. *am Michigan-See*)

> Names of lakes sometimes have the article, e.g. *the Great Salt Lake.*

Note

3 MOUNTAINS: *Mount McKinley* • *Ben Nevis* • *Mont Blanc* • *(Mount) Everest*

> Mountains in German-speaking countries usually have the article, e.g. *the Eiger, the Matterhorn,* etc.

Note

26 *The first men to climb <u>Mount Everest</u> were Sir Edmund Hillary and Sherpa Tenzing Norgay in 1953.* (cf. *den Mount Everest*)

4 LOCAL NAMES:
These names usually consist of a proper noun + common noun:
Airports: *Heathrow Airport • O'Hare Airport • Tullamarine Airport*
Bridges: *Tower Bridge • Sydney Harbour Bridge*
Castles: *Windsor Castle • Cardiff Castle • Dublin Castle*
Churches, etc.: *Canterbury Cathedral • Tintern Abbey • York Minster*
Forests: *Epping Forest • Sherwood Forest*
Hills: *Tower Hill • Capitol Hill • Pendle Hill*
Islands: *Canvey Island • Ellis Island • Long Island • Robben Island*
Palaces: *Buckingham Palace • Kensington Palace*
Parks, etc.: *Hyde Park • Clapham Common • Hampstead Heath*
Roads, etc.: *Denton Road • Oxford Street • Fifth Avenue • Times Square • Piccadilly Circus*
Schools: *Charterhouse School • Roedean School • Rugby School • Eton College*
Stations: *Grand Central Station • Euston Station • Manchester Piccadilly*
Universities: *Johns Hopkins University • MIT • Durham University • St. Andrew's University • Trinity College*

Note

The common nouns *Airport, College, School, Station* and *University* are often omitted. Cf. *We landed at Heathrow on time. She studied English at Durham.*

27 *<u>Oxford Street</u> was named after the Earl of Oxford.*
(cf. *Die Oxford Street wurde nach dem Grafen von Oxford benannt.*)

Pronunciation

As a rule, these names have level stress, i.e. both elements are equally stressed or put the main stress on the common noun, e.g. *Hyde Park* /ˈhaɪd ˈpɑːk/ or /ˌhaɪd ˈpɑːk/, *Trafalgar Square* /trəˈfælgə ˈskweə/ or /trəˌfælgə ˈskweə/. However, names with *Street* have single stress on the proper noun, e.g. *Oxford Street* /ˈɒksfəd striːt/.

Many magazines and periodicals take zero article (but see 3.2 p. 271): *Time* • *Newsweek* • *Private Eye* • *Scientific American* • *Language* • *Woman* • *Cosmopolitan*

MAGAZINES, PERIODICALS

28 *I read an interesting article on drugs in Cosmopolitan recently.* (cf. ... *einen interessanten Artikel über Drogen im Cosmopolitan*)

If the proper noun is an acronym, i.e. the name is formed from the initial letters of other words and pronounced as one unit, e.g. /ˈneɪtəʊ/, no article is used. Sometimes the spelling is modified to reflect this feeling that the word is no longer a collection of initials (e.g. *Nato* instead of *NATO*): *NATO* • *UNO* • *UNESCO* • *UNICEF* • *NASA* /ˈnæsə/.

ACRONYMS

29 *After the collapse of communism several East European countries joined NATO.* (cf. ... *traten in die NATO ein.*)

Contrast this pattern with the one for alphabetisms (3.2, p. 272), i.e. *UNO* versus *the UN*.

3.1 Common nouns without the article

XIV.3 Exceptions

Non-use of the article is often a relic of an earlier pattern where the article was less common. It is therefore particularly common in idiomatic usage, which is often a fossilisation of an older pattern.

Some nouns referring to selected human institutions have no article when they are used in idiomatic phrases denoting activities typically connected with the institution in question:

INSTITUTIONS

- *hospital* (BrE only)
- *court, prison, jail*
- *school, college, university*
- *church, chapel*
- *town*
- *bed*

Note

In American English the use of the article is obligatory with *hospital* and is optional with *university*.

30 *Jim's in hospital at the moment, recovering from appendicitis.*
31 *Silence in court!*

32 *The convicted rapist went to prison for five years.*
33 *At primary school we learnt the three R's.*
34 *I always drop off during the sermon in church.*
35 *We had an espresso at a café in town this morning.*
36 *I'm afraid you can't talk to my husband. He's in bed.*

Contrast these with the normal pattern (cf. 2.1), where the article occurs:

37 *The MP went to the prison to look into complaints of corruption.*
38 *Workmen were repairing the roof at the primary school.*
39 *Your T-shirt's where you left it – on the bed.*

PARTS OF THE DAY OR NIGHT

These usually take zero article if they are used in a general sense. After the prepositions *at, by, after, before,* a zero article is especially common: *dawn, sunrise* • *dusk, sunset* • *noon, midday, midnight* • *morning, afternoon, evening, night.*

40 *Dawn and dusk are good times to see deer.*
41 *For me morning is the best time of the day.*
42 *The spy was shot at dawn.*

However, the article is used if a specific occasion is being referred to. When the primary focus is on a specific occasion, even if a generalisation is implied, the article is normally used.

43 *I'll never forget the sunrise that first day in Jamaica.* (specific occasion)
44 *Watching the dawn can be a very moving experience.* (focus on a specific dawn, which is typical of dawns in general)

SEASONS

When words referring to seasons are used in a general sense, the article is omitted or optional:

45 *Spring is my favourite season.*
46 *I hate (the) winter. It's such a depressing time of year.*

When a specific season is referred to, the article is normally used:

47 *The summer this year was cool and rainy in Northern Europe.*

Notice that the normal American word for 'autumn', *the fall*, always takes the article.

Note

MEALS

When names of meals are used in a general sense, they usually have zero article, especially after some verbs (e.g. *have*) and prepositions (e.g. *after, before, at, for*):

48 *Breakfast is available in the hotel restaurant.*
49 *Where are we having lunch today?*
50 *For supper we went out to the local chippie.*

For specific meals, the article is used, though it may also be omitted:

51 *I'm afraid (the) dinner last night didn't agree with me.*

DISEASES

Zero article is the norm with most diseases, e.g. *BSE, foot and mouth disease*:

52 *Come inside and get changed! You'll catch pneumonia!*
53 *AIDS is a huge catastrophe in many African countries.*
54 *Influenza killed millions of people worldwide in 1918.*

However, an older pattern using the article also occurs with common infectious diseases. Use of the article is more common in American English than in British English:

55 *Our Johnny's got (the) 'flu!*
56 *I had (the) measles when I was five.*

ABSTRACT NOUNS

The article is normally omitted with uncountable abstract nouns, unlike in German and many other languages:

57 *History shows that wars don't solve any problems.*
(cf. *Die Geschichte zeigt* ...)
58 *Industry needs to be more environmentally aware.*
(cf. *Die Industrie* ...)

The article is often omitted when the noun is premodified by an adjective. This is particularly common when the adjective refers to time or place:

59 *Human evolution has taken millions of years.*
(cf. *Die menschliche Evolution* ...)
60 *Medieval society was deeply religious.* (adjective of time)
(cf. *Die mittelalterliche Gesellschaft* ...)
61 *One of his special fields is modern history.* (time)
62 *I'm fascinated by Romanesque architecture.*
63 *By the 1980s, Soviet communism was ideologically bankrupt.*
(adjective of place, cf. ... *der sowjetische Kommunismus* ...)
64 *Nowadays British industry is much more competitive.*
(place, cf. ... *die britische Industrie* ...)

Note

But with specific sub-sections of industry, the article is used:
The British car industry contracted enormously in the 1970s and 1980s.

The article is obligatory when the abstract noun is postmodified by

- an *of* phrase,
- a defining relative clause,
- a participle phrase comparable in function to a defining relative clause.

The effect of these three syntactic structures is to select and specify, hence the use of the article:

65 *The evolution of humanity has taken millions of years.*
66 *Of course, the medieval society I'm referring to is that of the higher social classes.*
67 *The Canadian literature dealt with in this course covers the post-war period.*

In 65 we are thinking of a specific evolution, viz. that of humanity.
In 66 the speaker is talking about a specific section of medieval society. In 67 the course deals with a selected period of modern history. Some nouns linked by *of*, e.g. *freedom of speech, right of way* (= *Vorfahrt*) are not seen as specific subcategories of the abstract nouns *freedom* and *right*. They therefore do not take the article.

3.2 Proper nouns with the article

As with abstract nouns, the article is used when the proper noun is postmodified by

- an *of* phrase,

- a defining relative clause,
- a participle phrase similar in function to a defining relative clause.

68 *The Ireland of the mid-1840s was devastated by famine.*
69 *The Jason we've been talking about lives in Edinburgh.*
70 *The Mr Jones mentioned in the article was not Welsh.*

Use of the article is normal in the following cases:

CONTRASTIVE USE

When a proper noun is preceded by an adjective which has a contrastive function, the article is used:

71 *The young Disraeli made a reputation for himself as a novelist.* (contrasted with *the older Disraeli*)
72 *Most tourists never get to see the real China.* (implies a contrast between what they have seen and reality)

PROPER NAMES IN THE PLURAL

1 FAMILIES: *the Blairs • the Marxes • the Smiths*

73 *Keeping up with the Joneses isn't one of our priorities.*

2 GROUPS OF ISLANDS: *the Channel Islands • the Hebrides • the Shetlands • the Canaries*

74 *Scots Gaelic is spoken by most islanders in the Hebrides.*

3 RANGES OF MOUNTAINS/HILLS: *the Himalayas • the Rockies • the Pennines • the South Downs*

75 *The Pennines are traditionally known as the 'backbone of England'.*

4 PLACE NAMES: *the Netherlands • the Midlands • the Highlands • the Great Lakes*

76 *The Netherlands are understandably concerned about the effects of global warming.*

OTHER GEOGRAPHICAL NAMES

1 RIVERS: *the (River) Thames • the (River) Shannon • the (River) Avon • the Missouri (River) • the Hudson (River) • the Murrumbidgee (River) • the Orange River • the (River) Rhine* (BrE)/*the Rhine (River)* (AmE)

Similarly: *the Tennessee Valley* • *the Thames Valley* • *the Mississippi Basin*

77 *The British publishing house Thames and Hudson was founded by the Austrian Jewish émigré Walter Neurath, who named it after the Thames and the Hudson respectively.*

Note

If the common noun *River* is used, it precedes the name in British and Irish place names, but follows it in place names in other English-speaking countries. For names of rivers in non-English speaking countries, usage varies, with British English preferring premodification and American English tending to postmodification. The word River is often omitted. Note also that a few river names take no article, e.g. *Snake River*.

2 OCEANS, SEAS, CANALS: *the Atlantic (Ocean)* • *the Mediterranean (Sea)* • *the Baltic (Sea)* • *the Suez Canal* • *the Panama Canal* • *the Kiel Canal*

78 *The Kiel Canal links the Baltic with the North Sea.*

3 PLACE NAMES with postmodification
Place names with a postmodifying *of* phrase such as *the Isle of Man, the Isle of Wight, the Bay of Naples* take the article.

79 *Among motorcyclists, the Isle of Man is best known for its TT races.*

Note

Place names with a premodifying adjective or noun, by contrast, have no article: cf. *Long Island* • *Coney Island* • *Hudson Bay.*

4 PUBLIC FACILITIES
Art galleries: *the Tate (Gallery)* • *the National Gallery*
Cinemas: *the Odeon* • *the Empire*
Clubs: *the Athenaeum* • *the Reform Club*
Hotels, restaurants: *the Ritz* • *the Waldorf Astoria*
Museums: *the British Museum* • *the Victoria & Albert*
Opera houses: *the Met* • *the Sydney Opera House*
Theatres: *the Globe (Theatre)* • *the Royal Court*

Note

Names of buildings usually have the article unless the name begins with a genitive, e.g. *Guy's (Hospital), St. John's (College)*

80 *The Tate Gallery's collection of international modern art was moved in 2000 to the Tate Gallery of Modern Art, housed in a former power station on London's South Bank.*

5 Some PLACE NAMES: *the Crimea • the Saar • the Ruhr • the Hague • (the) Lebanon • (the) Sudan • (the) Yemen • (the) Tyrol.*

Normally this type of name does not take the article (cf.2.2 GEOGRAPHICAL NAMES 1), but a few place names, especially of countries or regions, do. This may be due to French influence (cf. *la Crimée, le Liban, le Tyrol*). In some cases the article is now optional, as this irregular pattern is gradually being eroded.

81 *The Ruhr is having to cope with the decline in its traditional industries.*

Similarly, some local names take the article, thus contrasting with normal usage, where zero use of the article is prevalent (see 2.2 GEOGRAPHICAL NAMES 4): *the Albert Hall • the New Forest • the Black Forest • the Mall* /mæl/ *• the Strand • the High Street.*

82 *The Mall was lined with people waiting to see the Queen.*

History

In some cases, use of the article probably goes back to the time when the words *mall* ('street where *pallamaglio* is played'), *strand* ('river bank'), *high street* ('main street') were still common nouns. This is a common pattern: place name types like *Chester Road* derive from phrases like *the Chester road* (i.e. 'the road to Chester'). Relics of this pattern still survive, e.g. the London street name *the Old Kent Road*.

SHIPS, PLANES

the Victory, the Titanic, the Spirit of St. Louis

83 *I didn't know that the Titanic had been built in a Belfast shipyard.*

NEWSPAPERS, JOURNALS, PERIODICALS

Some names of newspapers, journals and periodicals take the article: *the Guardian • the Economist • the New York Times • the Washington Post • the British Medical Journal • the Spectator • the New Statesman.*

84 *I've taken out a year's subscription to the Guardian Weekly.*

ALPHABETISMS

Alphabetisms, i.e. words formed from the initials of other words, where the initials are pronounced separately, e.g. /ˌjuː ˈen/, take the article: *the UN* • *the IRA* • *the EU* • *the BBC* • *the RAC* • *the AA* • *the NRA* • *the ANC.*

Note

Names of companies, e.g. *IBM, C&A, ABC, CBS, CNN, NBC* are exceptions, omitting the article.

85 *Unlike the commercial US networks ABC, CBS, CNN and NBC, the BBC, as a public corporation, relies heavily for its funding on the money from TV and radio licences.*

Exercises

1 Starring Robinson Crusoe ...

Robinson Crusoe is being interviewed on a TV chat show. Where necessary, insert the definite article in the gaps below.

'Mr Crusoe, what is _____[1] life really like on a desert island?'
'Well, David, even on a tropical island, _____[2] life certainly isn't just a bowl of cherries. For a start, you have to come to terms with _____[3] nature. We often forget that _____[4] comfortable life we lead in _____[5] Western society has made us oblivious to _____[6] cruelty of _____[7] nature.'
'But this wasn't true of _____[8] England of _____[9] 18th century, surely?'
'Oh yes, people of my social class in _____[10] 18th-century England were also cushioned from _____[11] effects of _____[12] harshness of _____[13] nature, though not to _____[14] same extent as they are today, of course. We had servants to see to the basic necessities of _____[15] everyday life, that sort of thing. It came as quite a shock when I had to face up to _____[16] reality of my situation on the island. I suppose facing _____[17] reality is unpleasant in any circumstances, but you learn to do it pretty quickly on a desert island. Actually, I've always felt Mr Defoe was a bit too lavish in his praises of _____[18] simple life. After all, he didn't experience _____[19] frequent periods of _____[20] hunger that I went through.'
'Mr Crusoe, you've told us about _____[21] hardships of _____[22] life in your tropical paradise. Now that you're back in _____[23] civilisation, is there anything on the desert island that you miss?'
'Well, to be quite frank, I do rather miss _____[24] solitude.'
'Solitude?'

Exercises

'Yes, ever since I've been back everybody's been asking me which I prefer, the bustle and excitement of _____[25] modern society, or _____[26] solitude I was used to on my island. And taking everything into consideration, I think I prefer _____[27] companionship of _____[28] solitude. ...'

2 Flow chart

Use the flow chart below to construct three positive sentences and three critical sentences expressing your opinion, taking the words from the three columns below (NB: Ø means 'zero article'). The following phrases may be useful.

I like • I admire • I love • I enjoy • I'm interested in • I'm fascinated by ...
I dislike • I despise • I hate • I'm bored by • I detest • I'm unimpressed by ...

Determiner Adjective Abstract noun

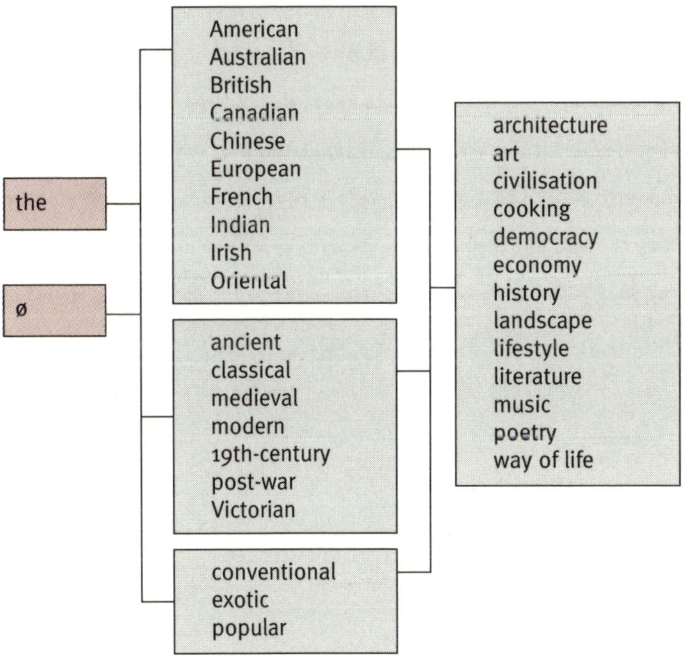

Exercises

3 Error-spotting

The private pupil you tutor in English has asked you to correct the mistakes in the letter she has written to her Welsh penfriend.

Dear Jenny,

are you back at the school yet? We have started the school in the last week. We've just come back from a trip to Tirol and Switzerland. It was a nice change from the Ruhr, where we've had awful weather all the summer. And the spring this year was pretty bad, too. In Tirol we stayed in a hotel with phantastic views over Patscherkofl. It's one of the highest mountains of this part of Austria (much higher than the Snowdon in Wales). We usually went hiking after the lunch. The second week we toured Switzerland, spending most of the time on the Lake Lucerne (in the German it's called "Vierwaldstättersee"). Our hotel, "Wilhelm Tell", was near Altdorf, on the banks of River Reuss. It's named after the swiss national hero, William Tell – you know, the one who shot the apple off the head of his son. While we were there my brother Willy sprained the ankle, so he had to spend the night in the hospital in Altdorf, because they thought he'd broken it. Next day they let him come home, though the poor Willy had to rest it and stay in the bed for a few days, while we were outside in the fresh air enjoying the nature. Now he's at home with the measles! I really feel sorry for him, even though he <u>is</u> my brother ...

Love,

Sabine

4 Quiz: The Big Apple

Answer the questions, using the jumbled names given below. Remember to use the article where necessary.

Exercises

Bronx • Broadway • Brooklyn • Central Park • East River • Ellis Island • Empire State Building • Fifth Avenue • Hudson River • Kennedy Airport • La Guardia Airport • Madison Avenue • Manhattan • Met • Queens • Staten Island • Statue of Liberty • Times Square • Wall Street

1 When you fly to New York from Europe, where would you normally land?
You'd normally land at _____ .
2 What is the name of New York's most famous landmark, which was donated by the French government to commemorate the 100th anniversary of US independence?
It's _____ .
3 About 20 million immigrants entered the US in the 19th and early 20th centuries. Where was the immigration centre in New York which they had to go through?
It was on _____ .
4 What are the names of the five boroughs of New York?
_____ .
5 What two rivers go past the west and east sides of Manhattan?
To the west it's _____ .
To the east it's _____ .
6 What street is the New York Stock Exchange on?
It's on _____ .
7 What's the name of the New York street associated with theatres?
It's called _____ .
8 Which building was the tallest in the world when it was built in 1931?
The world's tallest building was _____ .
9 Where would you go in central Manhattan if you wanted to go to the zoo or listen to an open-air concert?
You'd go to _____ .
10 What street is regarded as the centre of the US advertising industry?
It's called _____ .
11 What's the name of the city's most famous opera house?
It's known as _____ .
12 If you wanted to show someone the centre of the US fashion and publishing industry, which street would you take them to?
I'd take them to _____ .

13 Where is the start of the New Year traditionally celebrated in New York? The celebrations are normally shown on nationwide TV.
It's celebrated in _____ .

14 Which airport in Queens would you be most likely to take a domestic flight within the US from?
From _____ .

5 English and American nationalism

Fill in the gaps in the following text, using the definite article where necessary.

Images and style of _____[1] English nationalism derive from _____[2] Calvinism. And it is from _____[3] struggle of _____[4] Puritan revolution for _____[5] religious liberty that a sense of _____[6] moral duty evolved which saw England as destined not only to fight for its own interests, but also for _____[7] freedom of other nations. John Stuart Mill (1806-1873), one of the proponents of _____[8] philosophy of _____[9] utilitarianism and _____[10] author of *Principles of _____[11] Political Economy*, is a typical example of this. He fought courageously and tenaciously against _____[12] national prejudices. Yet on the other hand he saw his compatriots as having a mission to spread _____[13] idea of _____[14] social and political freedom among _____[15] peoples of _____[16] 19th-century Europe. In the 20th century, however, this messianic aspect of _____[17] English nationalism became much weaker and is now more characteristic of _____[18] American attitudes, which often regard _____[19] American democracy and _____[20] US capitalism as models for the rest of the world. Both forms of _____[21] nationalism, however, have been decisively influenced by _____[22] Calvinism.

6 Headlines

Rewrite the following headlines to make the first sentence of a news story. Take care with tenses and the use of the definite article.

Example

UN TO CUT BUDGET
The United Nations is to drastically reduce its budget, a UN spokesperson announced yesterday.

1 US CUTS DEFENCE BUDGET
2 IOC: ISLE OF MAN TO HOST NEXT OLYMPICS
3 PM SPOTTED IN GAY BAR
4 EU BARS RUSSIAN MAFIA BOSS

5 NASA: OZONE LAYER EXPANDING
6 UK TO JOIN EURO
7 DUTCH QUIT NATO
8 AA: RAIL STRIKE CHAOS ON ROADS LIKELY

7 Quotations

Translate the following quotations into English, taking particular care with the translation of the definite articles.

a „Alles hat sich geändert, nur das menschliche Denken nicht." (Albert Einstein)
b „Die Gewalt lebt davon, dass sie von anständigen Menschen nicht für möglich gehalten wird." (Jean-Paul Sartre)
c „Sich zu Tode zu arbeiten ist die einzige gesellschaftlich anerkannte Form des Selbstmords." (Johann Freudenreich)
d „Die Geschichte der Freiheit ist die Geschichte des Widerspruchs." (Woodrow Wilson)
e „Ich glaube, der Weltraum ist heute weniger gefährlich als die Straßen Berlins." (Wernher von Braun)
f „Die Jugend wäre eine noch viel schönere Zeit, wenn sie erst später im Leben käme." (Charlie Chaplin)

Exercises

8 Car chase

Using the notes and map given below, reconstruct what the police officer is saying in the police patrol car during their car chase through London. Use complete sentences and include the reference points listed in brackets.

Example

'Calling all cars, calling all cars. Two men have just raided a bank in Borough Road, near the Elephant and Castle, around 2.15 a.m. The security guard was shot, but managed to give the alarm. We're giving chase. They're driving a black BMW, registration number 290 BCT ...'

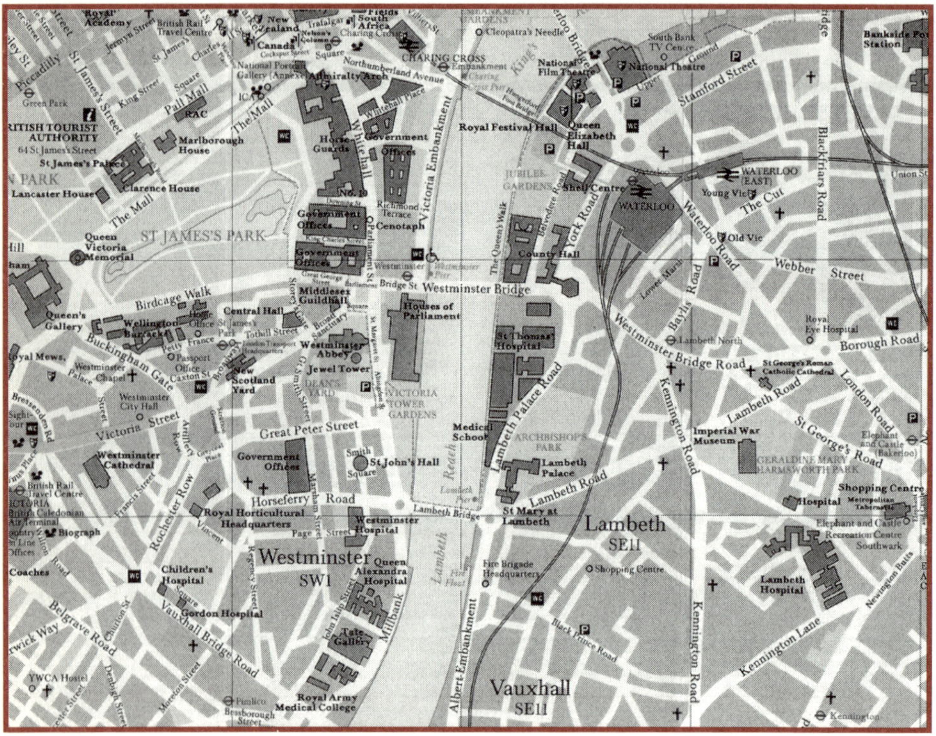

bearing left at roundabout, turning into _____

passing (Imperial War Museum) _____

must be doing about 70 mph, now going past (Lambeth Palace) _____

crossing Thames at (Lambeth Bridge) _____

turning left into John Islip Street , past (Westminster Hospital, Tate Gallery) _____
right into Vauxhall Bridge Road, passing (Children's Hospital) _____
turning right into Victoria Street, past (Westminster Cathedral) _____
left into Buckingham Gate, past (Wellington Barracks), heading for (Green Park) _____
past (Buckingham Palace), changing direction, down Mall _____
past ICA, through Admiralty Arch _____

'... Right, it's all over! The two cars you sent to Trafalgar Square have managed to intercept the car. The suspects are out of the car now. They've been disarmed. Everything's under control. Over and out.'

9 Growing up in Glasgow

Fill in the gaps below, using the definite article where necessary.

I was born in Glasgow, went to _____[1] school in the city and got my first job there. I've always felt that _____[2] Glasgow I know is not one, but several cities. There is _____[3] Victorian Glasgow, which fans of _____[4] 19th-century architecture are so enthusiastic about, or _____[5] art nouveau Glasgow of Charles Rennie Mackintosh. Then there is _____[6] Glasgow torn apart by _____[7] sectarian hatred, _____[8] hatred of Protestants for Catholics and vice versa, reflected in _____[9] hostility of Rangers fans to Celtic supporters. And there is _____[10] violence for which Glasgow's slums are notorious. Take Jimmy Boyle, for instance. He grew up in _____[11] Gorbals, where _____[12] violence was part of _____[13] normal pattern of _____[14] life. In _____[15] mid-Sixties he was in _____[16] court accused of _____[17] murder three times in two years. In 1967 he was convicted of _____[18] murder of a man and sent to _____[19] prison for 15 years. For years newspaper headlines called him 'Scotland's most violent man'. Nothing and nobody could control him, even in _____[20] prison. Then _____[21] prison authorities tried an experiment: they encouraged prisoners to paint and do sculpture. Since then he has never looked back. His sculptures have been exhibited all over the world and he has also written a play. He put _____[22] money earned from _____[23] publication of his autobiography, *A Sense of Freedom*, into a fund to help _____[24] people in a similar situation. 'What worries me most is _____[25] apathy, among kids especially. Kids are using _____[26] heroin in a way that's never been known before in Scotland. Why? They look around and what do they see for _____[27] future? Nothing. And they're right. It's our responsibility to tap _____[28] creativity that's in _____[29] people. Otherwise their future and ours is bleak. As someone said to me the other day, _____[30] apathy is _____[31] frozen violence.'

10 Churchill's early life

Use the notes to write a short sketch of Winston Churchill's early years, taking care with the use of the definite article.

N.B. Harrow is a well-known public school. Sandhurst is Britain's foremost military academy.

- born 1874, Blenheim Palace, Oxfordshire
- young Churchill: unhappy and neglected childhood
- Harrow: weak academically
- Sandhurst: only passed entrance examination at third attempt
- graduated 20th out of a group of 130
- 1895 joined army, serving in India, South Africa
- became famous during Boer War: rescued army train, taken prisoner by Boers /bɔːz/
- subsequent escape from prison: increased fame
- became MP for Oldham after 1900 election
- Parliament: gained reputation for making good speeches

11 How to get to 'Rules'

Wolfram Siebeck, culinary expert at *Die Zeit*, has given you the directions to his favourite restaurant. You are trying to find it with an English friend. Translate the following directions, taking special care with the use of the definite article.

Bei der Ankunft am Victoria-Bahnhof müssen Sie rechts in die Victoria Street einbiegen.
Sie gehen dann die Victoria Street hinunter.
Am Ende der Victoria Street gehen Sie an der Westminster-Abtei vorbei.
Am Parliament Square dann links in die Whitehall.
Gehen Sie dann an den Regierungsgebäuden vorbei – übrigens, auf der linken Straßenseite sehen Sie die Downing Street, wo der Premierminister wohnt.

Sie gehen weiter die Whitehall hinunter, bis Sie den Trafalgar Square erreichen, da wo die großen steinernen Löwen stehen – da gibt es immer viele Touristen, die die Tauben füttern.
An der Nordseite vom Trafalgar Square sehen Sie die Nationalgalerie. Da gehen Sie aber nicht hin – das ist die falsche Richtung.
Statt dessen geht es zur Strand.
Auf der Strand biegen Sie links vor dem Adelphi-Theater in die Bedford Street ab, dann rechts in die Maiden Lane. Die Maiden Lane ist die Fortsetzung des Chandos Place.
Rules ist die Nr. 35 in der Maiden Lane. Es ist das älteste Restaurant Londons und steht an diesem Platz seit 1798.

12 Liberalism and fascism

Fill in the gaps in the text below, inserting the definite article where necessary.

At the end of _____[1] medieval times the new spirit of _____[2] liberalism arose in Europe. Its aims were _____[3] opening up of the world, _____[4] liberation of _____[5] mind and _____[6] release of _____[7] business enterprise. It was exemplified in such movements as _____[8] Renaissance, _____[9] Reformation, _____[10] rise of _____[11] capitalism and _____[12] struggle for _____[13] democracy. The hard core of this tradition involved _____[14] belief in _____[15] reason, _____[16] universal suffrage, tolerance of widely differing religious and political views, _____[17] basic sanctity of _____[18] human life, _____[19] freedom of _____[20] thought and _____[21] desirability of _____[22] universal peace. These values became widely accepted until they were challenged by _____[23] fascism in the 20th century. In fact, _____[24] European fascism was the negation of every aspect of this tradition, with _____[25] emotion taking the place of _____[26] reason. It believed in _____[27] right of a self-appointed élite to rule the state, persecuted those with different political and religious beliefs, suppressed _____[28] freedom of _____[29] speech, and regarded _____[30] war as desirable if it advanced _____[31] power of _____[32] state.

XV Relative Clauses

XV.1 Overview

definition

Relative clauses are subordinate clauses which modify nouns and noun groups (and sometimes clauses, see 2.2). They follow the noun or noun group and contain a finite verb (i.e. not a participle or infinitive). In their function, though not their position, they are similar to adjectives.

Relative clauses are introduced by words like *who* and *which*, which otherwise function as interrogative pronouns. Some types of relative clauses can also begin with *that* or occur without a relative pronoun. The latter is known as the zero relative, the clause which it introduces being called a contact clause. The relative pronouns *who, whom, which, that* and the zero relative are restricted in the contexts where they can be used. Which pronoun is used depends on the following factors:

- whether the pronoun refers to animates or inanimates
- the function of the pronoun in the relative clause (e.g. subject, object, etc.)
- whether the clause is a defining or non-defining relative clause (see XV.2)
- which register (i.e. formal versus informal style) is being used.

Note

The relevance of these factors can be seen from their distribution in the table below. In the table, and in this chapter in general, pronouns which introduce defining relative clauses are marked in red, whereas pronouns introducing non-defining relative clauses are underlined.

	animates			inanimates		
	subject	object	genitive	subject	object	genitive
defining	who *(that)*	whom *who* *that* ZERO	whose (of which)	which that	which that ZERO	of which (whose) *(that ... of)*
non-defining	, who ...,	, whom ..., , *who* ...	, whose ...,	, which ...,	, which ...,	, of which ..., (,whose...,)

Note

In the table, brackets mean that these items are less common. Words in italics in the table are typical of informal register. ZERO denotes the zero relative.

By animates we mean living beings, i.e. humans and animals, although the use of *who(m)* is normally restricted to the higher animals or animals to which people personally have an emotional relationship. In the case of young humans and animals, speakers alternate between the use of *who(m)*, treating them like persons, and *which*, treating them like things. This usage is the same as that in the common noun class (see X.2.3 and X.3.1). Compare:

1 *That child who's standing over there seems to have lost her mummy.*
2 *Any child which is left alone will soon feel bored and lonely.*
3 *Our rabbit, who we thought was a male, has just had babies.*
4 *The rabbit which ran in front of our car was plainly dead.*

The same alternation occurs with collective nouns referring to groups of human beings, which either collocate with *who* followed by a plural verb, because they refer to a group of people, or by *which* followed by a singular verb, because they are regarded as a single abstract unit. The former pattern (an example of notional concord, see IX.3.9 COLLECTIVE NOUNS) is much more common in British English than in

American English. The latter pattern is the most frequent type even in British English, and in American English is often the only type acceptable. In German only the latter pattern is normal.

5 *My family, who are vegetarians, can't stand the sight of meat.*
6 *Harris's family, which has a long army tradition, remains unperturbed.*

After quantifiers like *all, anything, everything, something, nothing, only* and superlatives, the normal relative pronoun is *that* (see Swan 1995, §474.4, for other examples):

7 *All that's missing is my gold watch.*
8 *Something that she would really like is a dish-washer.*
9 *The only solution that springs to mind is to buy a new video.*
10 *The craziest thing that's ever happened to me was when I was a student in Sweden, at Gothenburg University.*

In non-standard usage, other relative pronouns such as *what* and (in British dialects) *as* are also common:

11 *The geezer what we bought the car off was a loony!* (non-standard)

History

The modern restriction of *that* to defining relative clauses and the use of *who(m)* for animates, *which* for inanimates is a recent development. In the 18th century *that* was so common that the playwright Richard Steele wrote the essay *The Humble Petition of Who and Which*, advocating the use of these pronouns instead of *that*. In fact, the use of *that* as a relative pronoun is much older, going back to the 8th century, and was the normal relative pronoun in Middle English. The interrogative pronouns only start to be used as relative pronouns under Latin influence during the 16th century, when the modern restriction of *which* to inanimates was not yet the norm (see Faiß 1989, §3.8.1., §3.8.3. and §3.8.4., and Lass 1999, §4.6.2.2.1.). The Lord's Prayer in the 1611 Authorised Version of the Bible, for example, still has '*Our Father, which art in heaven ...*'. The zero relative is first recorded in Old English, but did not become common until Modern English. A similar construction occurs in Norwegian, Swedish and Danish (see König 1994, p.263, p.301, p.345).

XV.2 Normal pattern

There are two main types of relative clause, defining and non-defining. They need to be carefully distinguished, because the use of relative pronoun and pronunciation or punctuation are dependent on which type is being used.

2.1 Defining and non-defining relative clauses

Although defining and non-defining relative clauses occur in other languages, including German, the difference is not necessarily reflected in the punctuation. In German the distinction is blurred because German uses commas to mark off any relative clause. By contrast, in English, French or Spanish commas are only used in non-defining relative clauses.

DEFINING RELATIVE CLAUSES
definition

Defining relative clauses define or identify more exactly which persons or things are referred to in a specific context. They are also known as *restrictive* or *identifying* relative clauses.

Defining relative clauses are not marked off by pauses in speech or by commas in writing. This is because the noun or noun phrase would not be complete without the relative clause, with the result that the sentence would either make no sense or would have a different meaning. There is, in other words, a close link between the noun and the relative clause. Defining relative clauses answer the question 'Which person or thing is meant?' They usually imply a potential contrast with other persons or things. Compare:

12 *The man who's standing over there looks like a wino.* ('Which man?')
13 *The person whom we appoint is required to submit proof of his or her qualifications.*
14 *The man who I marry will have to do his share of the housework.*

With animates, *who* is normally used for the subject of the relative clause. Use of *that* is less common, being restricted to colloquial English. The pronoun *whom* is frequently used for the object of the relative clause in formal register, especially in writing. Colloquially, both in speech and writing, it is usually replaced by *who*.

15 *He visited the village which he had grown up in during the 1960s.* ('Which village?')

The pronoun *which* is used for inanimates, both when they are the subject or the object of the relative clause and when the pronoun is dependent on a preposition, as in 15 (i. e. *in*)

16 *The woman whose car he crashed into was very angry.* ('Whose car?')
17 *The car whose gears were faulty had to be towed away.*

The genitive pronoun *whose* can refer back to either an animate antecedent (in 16, *the woman*) or an inanimate one (in 17, *the car*), although it is more common with animates.

18 *The book that was on special offer only cost £1.50.* ('Which book?')
19 *The semi that they bought was a snip at £50,000.*

The pronoun *that*, which only occurs in defining relative clauses, is most often used with an inanimate antecedent. It is used both as the subject and object of the relative clause, as in 18 and 19 respectively.

20 *Have you met the girl __ Chris wants to marry?*
21 *I've just seen the stranger __ I was talking to on the bus yesterday!*

The zero relative is only used when it is the object of the relative clause (as in 20) or is dependent on a preposition (i. e. *to* in 21).
Notice the position of the prepositions *in, into* and *to* which are located at or towards the end of the relative clauses in 15, 16 and 21. In informal English, this 'preposition stranding' (see Kortmann 1999, p.141) is the most frequent pattern. It can also occur in non-defining relative clauses.

NON-DEFINING RELATIVE CLAUSES

Non-defining relative clauses tell us more about a person or thing that has already been identified or defined. They are far more common in formal than in informal contexts. Clauses like these have two features:

- They are marked off by pauses in speech and by commas in writing.
- They can only be introduced by *who(m), whose, which*.

22 *The man wearing glasses, who was standing at the bar, looked nervous.*

23 *The red-haired student, whom Jim had seen at the theatre the previous evening, was buying a book on Restoration comedies.*

Note that the preceding noun phrase which the relative pronoun refers to often contains elements which identify the person or thing, e.g. *wearing glasses, red-haired* in 22 and 23 respectively. This is also true of the following types of noun phrase:

- personal names *(Jenny, the Joneses)*
- place names *(London)*
- possessive adjectives like *my, your, their,* etc.
- usually the demonstrative pronouns *this, that* and their plural forms

All these are an indication that the relative clause may be non-defining. They are not, however, infallible proof that the clause is bound to be non-defining (see also XV.3.3).

24 *Jenny, who he was later to marry, had in fact known him at school.*
25 *London, which is one of Europe's biggest cities, is a fascinating place.*
26 *My car, which I sold for 2100 euros, had 90,000 kilometres on the clock.*
27 *I recently visited the Joneses, whose children I used to look after.*
28 *That man, who must be at least seventy, doesn't look very healthy, does he?*

Notice that in 29 and similar cases the accompanying quantifier *many* precedes the relative pronoun, whereas in German *viele* follows it:

29 *The football fans, many of whom were drunk, were in an ugly mood after their team's defeat.*
30 *Die Fußballfans, von denen viele betrunken waren, waren nach der Niederlage ihrer Mannschaft schlecht drauf.*

2.2 which referring to preceding clause

One special type of defining relative clause is used to refer back to the whole of the preceding clause. It is always introduced by *which* and corresponds to the German relative pronoun *was*:

31 *He broke his right hand while skiing in the Pyrenees, which meant that he couldn't sit the exam.* (= *was bedeutete ...*)

32 *She's very shy, which I think is a great pity, because she's a lovely person to talk to.* (= *was ich sehr schade finde, ...*)

2.3 when, where, why used as relative pronouns

The interrogatives *when* and *where* can be used as relative pronouns to introduce either defining or non-defining relative clauses (see also Sinclair 1990, §8.103ff.). Compare:

33 *There was a time when I would never have touched veal.*
34 *I saw Karen last week, when we met at a party.*
35 *The place where I grew up was a small town in New Hampshire.*
36 *They live in Morecambe, where we used to go on holiday as kids.*

The interrogative *why* can also be used to introduce a defining relative clause after the word *reason*. Notice that alternative constructions with *that* and a zero relative are also possible (see Swan 1995, §473.3, and Sinclair 1990, §8.107f.):

37 *The reason why I decided not to come with you to Vienna was the cost.*
38 *The main reason that we chose Norway was the unspoilt scenery.*
39 *She said that the reason __ she preferred Malta was the climate.*

XV.3 Exceptions

3.1 Defining relative clauses after names, etc.

Although nouns implying unique reference, e.g. names, usually only co-occur with non-defining relative clauses (see 2.1, NON-DEFINING RELATIVE CLAUSES), they can be followed by a defining relative clause when a contrast is involved:

40 *The London which I'm referring to is the one in Ontario, Canada.*
41 *The Joneses that I was talking about are the family from Norwich.*

As can be seen from the above examples, in these cases the names do not in fact imply unique reference. If they did, a contrast would not be possible. Similarly, defining relative clauses are possible after the demonstrative adjectives *this, that*, and their plural forms, provided a contrast is implied:

42 *That man who is standing on the corner looks rather suspicious.*
43 *Those people __ we met in Ibiza were Canadian, weren't they?*

Exercises

1 Definitions

In this section, answer the question in the space provided, using a relative clause which includes one of the alternatives given. Take care with punctuation and the use of the relative pronouns *that, when, who, which, where:*

Example

What's a mammoth? *A mammoth is an animal* _____.

a lives in South America
b a type of marsupial
c extinct
→ *A mammoth is an animal which is extinct.*

1 What's a shoplifter? *A shoplifter is a person* _____
 a lifts shops
 b steals from shops
 c steals shops
2 What's a teetotaller? *A teetotaller is somebody* _____
 a sells T-shirts
 b works in a bank
 c doesn't drink alcohol
3 What's peritonitis? *Peritonitis is a disease*
 a a person becomes deaf
 b people have bladder problems
 c the inside wall of the body becomes infected
4 What's a curate? *A curate is a person* _____.
 a assists a vicar
 b looks after the exhibits in a museum
 c helps a doctor's patients
5 What's a percolator? *A percolator is something*
 a is made to carry people between floors in a tall building, e.g. department store
 b is for making coffee
 c is used for giving sexual stimulation
6 What's xenophobia? *Xenophobia is* _____.
 a frightened of foreigners
 b fear of women
 c afraid of the letter x
7 What's a vegan? *A vegan is* _____.
 a a type of rhyme, invented by the Spanish poet Lope de Vega
 b an alien, from the planet Vega
 c a vegetarian, refuses to eat animal products, e.g. milk or eggs

8 What's mistletoe? *Mistletoe is something _____.*

a you hang it in a room at Xmas

b you put it in soup

c you rub on your feet if they are aching

Exercises

2 Weird!

In this exercise, use your imagination to make a (preferably humorous) definition of the following words, none of which really exist.

Example

tompepper → *A tompepper is a vegetable which is a genetically modified cross between a tomato and a pepper.*

1 a mushwinger 2 hyphenitis 3 a punspickle 4 pompocracy 5 to shinwoggle sb.

3 Adding information

Use a non-defining relative clause to combine each of the two sentences.

1 Guernsey lies west of Normandy. It has a population of about 56,000.
2 The island is 63 square kilometres in area. It is the second largest of the Channel Islands.
3 The island is self-governing. It is not a part of the British state.
4 Guernsey has its own parliament. It is known as the States.
5 The island is very prosperous. Its main industries are tourism, horticulture and dairy farming.
6 A major attraction for tourists is the island's sandy beaches. Most of them are safe.
7 One prominent resident of the island was Victor Hugo. He moved to the island in 1852.
8 Victor Hugo wrote *Les Misérables* during his exile in Guernsey. His house in the capital, St. Peter Port, is maintained as a museum by the city of Paris.
9 Guernsey has long been a tax haven for people who wish to avoid paying U.K. income tax. In recent decades it has become an important offshore financial centre.
10 Guernsey does not have VAT (value-added tax). It is not a member of the EU.
11 The island issues its own banknotes, coins and stamps. None of them can be used in mainland Britain.

Exercises

4 My memory fails me!

You are seventy years old, trying to remember with an old school friend what you did when you were a child. Use the clues given in the call-outs. You should use informal register for this exercise.

Example

He lived next door → *What was the name of the man who lived next door?*

1 She taught us Physics. *What was the name of the teacher _____?*

2 Their children used to walk around barefoot. *What was the name of the family _____?*

3 You used to go fishing with him. *What was the friend called _____?*

4 We lived there. *What was the name of the street _____?*

5 You sat next to him in class. *What was the boy called _____?*

6 She always used to give you sweets on your birthday. *What was the little old lady called _____?*

Exercises

5 Preposition – stranded!

Combine the basic sentence with the sentence in brackets by using a relative clause which contains preposition stranding (see 2.1, 287).

Example

This is our new car. (We're very proud of it)
→ *This is our new car, which we're very proud of.*

1 I've just bought a brilliant CD-ROM on architecture. (I'm fascinated by architecture.)
2 This is a picture of my aunt. (We often used to stay with her when we were little.
3 We've now booked our holiday in Majorca. (I'm really looking forward to it.)
4 Unpunctuality is bad for the firm's reputation. (I will not put up with it.)
5 Jimmy is now a multi-millionaire. (I used to knock around a lot with him as a kid.)
6 I like watching that soap. (I don't even mind getting up early for it.)
7 At the moment there are a lot of corruption scandals in politics. (The police are looking into them.)

6 Commenting on things

Add a comment to the sentences below, using the most suitable elements in the box to form the relative clause, as shown in the example. The comment should always be introduced by *which* in this exercise. Take care with the punctuation.

Example

He has absolutely no sense of humour.
→ *He has absolutely no sense of humour, which is a pity.*

> That's very generous • That was very disappointing. • It was difficult. • It's a nuisance. • The kids thought it was marvellous. • It means he'll have to go on a diet • thought it was very stingy of them. • It's a pity.

1 They haven't got e-mail.
2 He's lending me his sports car.
3 I had to climb in through the bathroom window.
4 The hotel didn't even have a swimming pool.
5 My dad's overweight.

Exercises

6 They didn't even offer us a biscuit.
7 It's been snowing all day.

7 Improving the style

Improve the style of the two sentences in each case by combining them with a relative clause. Be careful with the punctuation and use of relative pronouns.

1 I like your accent. It sounds very authentic.
2 My paper in fact only employs four blacks. It is proud of its equal opportunities policy.
3 The man didn't believe I had grown up in London. I was talking to him last week.
4 Gary Younge is a black journalist. He was born in London.
5 The NAACP fights for equal rights for blacks. I attended its convention recently.
6 Baton Rouge is a deep-water port on the Mississippi. It's in Louisiana.
7 John Brown had used force to free black slaves. He was hanged in 1859.
8 Frederick W. Douglass was a runaway slave. He was the first great black political leader in the US. He died in 1895.

8 Translating relative clauses

Translate the relative clauses into English, using the vocabulary provided. Take care with the punctuation.

ein Risiko eingehen = *to take a risk*

1 Ein Manager, der niemals Risiken eingeht, wird letzten Endes den Bestand des Unternehmens gefährden.
An executive _____ will in the end be a danger to the firm's existence.

ziemlich = *fairly*
links = *left-wing*

2 Londons neuer Bürgermeister, der ziemlich links ist, kritisiert die Regierung wegen ihrer Pläne für die Londoner U-Bahn.
London's new mayor _____ is criticising the government because of its plans for the London Underground.

streichen = *to cancel sth.*

3 Die ganze Nation klagt schon seit längerem über Operationen, die in den Krankenhäusern oft in letzter Minute „wegen fehlenden Personals" gestrichen werden müssen.

The entire nation has been complaining for some time about operations _____ at the last minute 'due to staff shortages'.

Exercises

4 In New York findet man kaum eine Straße, die nicht in die Literaturgeschichte eingegangen ist.
In New York there is hardly any street _____.

in die Geschichte eingehen = *to go down in history*

5 Edith Wharton, die später den Pulitzerpreis erhielt, wohnte auch am Washington Square.
Edith Wharton _____ also lived in Washington Square.

Pulitzerpreis = Pulitzer Prize
erhalten = *to be awarded (a prize)*

6 Das Haus von Henry James' Großmutter, in dem sich der junge Henry James länger aufhielt, steht leider nicht mehr.
The house belonging to Henry James' grandmother _____ is unfortunately no longer standing.

sich aufhalten = *to stay*
länger = *for quite a while*

7 Die alten Herrenhäuser rund um den Platz, der heute in der Hand von Studenten, Touristen und Drogenhändlern ist, sehen immer noch sehr gepflegt aus.
The old townhouses around the square _____ still look very well maintained.

Drogenhändler = *drug dealer*

8 Dieser Stadtteil von New York hat jene etablierte Gelassenheit, die in anderen Ecken der Stadt rar ist.
This district of New York possesses that established composure _____ in other parts of the city.

9 Megan's Law, das seit 1995 in vielen US-Bundesstaaten eingeführt wurde, ermöglicht, dass die persönlichen Daten von Sexualstraftätern im Internet veröffentlicht werden.
Megan's Law _____ enables the personal particulars of sexual offenders to be published on the Internet.

einführen = *to introduce sth.*

10 Das Gesetz wurde nach einem siebenjährigen Mädchen benannt, das vor sechs Jahren entführt, vergewaltigt und ermordet wurde.
The law was named after a 7-year-old girl _____ six years ago.

entführen = *to abduct sb.*
vergewaltigen = *to rape sb.*

11 Der Klient des New Yorker Rechtsanwalts ist ein junger Mann, der selbst als Fünfjähriger von einem männlichen Babysitter sexuell missbraucht worden ist.

sexuell missbrauchen = *to sexually abuse sb.*

The New York lawyer's client is a young man _____ by a male babysitter.

12 Nur eine Plakette an einer Hauswand erinnert an jenen Slum, in dem zu Engels' Zeiten irische Einwanderer wohnten.
Only a plaque on the wall of a house reminds us of the slum _____.

Appendix

Linguistic Glossary

NB: Cross-references are marked with an asterisk (*).

adjective, premodifying
A premodifying adjective is any adjective placed in front of the noun it modifies. Premodification is the norm in English and other Germanic languages.

affirmative
A statement or question is affirmative if it is not negated, i.e. not in the negative.

allomorph
An allomorph is a phonemic variant of a morpheme, i.e. of the same unit of meaning. In English the allomorphs of the past tense morpheme are /d/, /t/ and /ɪd/, as in *called*, *kicked* and *mended* respectively (see also p. 169 and 203).

allophone
An allophone is a phonetic variant of a phoneme*. In German the phoneme /x/ has two allophones [x] and [ç], often called the *ach-Laut* and *ich-Laut* respectively, as in *lachen* and *Licht* (see also Kortmann 1999, p.33).

analytic
An analytic language is one where the form of words does not change, i.e. words do not have inflections. Chinese is a typical example of an analytic language.

animate
Any living being is known as animate. Things are inanimate.

antecedent
The antecedent of a relative clause is the noun or noun phrase about which the relative clause provides more information, e.g. *The milk which I bought was sour.*

attitudinal use
Attitudinal use of a tense or aspect means that the category concerned is used to show the speaker's attitude to something, e.g. the Past or Progressive to indicate politeness, as in *We were hoping you could help us* (referring to the present).

attributive
An adjective is used attributively when it is placed next to a noun. In English this usually means that the adjective is before the noun.

clause, temporal
A temporal clause is a subordinate clause referring to time.

closed class
A closed class is a class of words with a fixed number of items, e.g. the pronouns of a language (see also p. 37 and p. 170).

common case
The basic form of the noun, contrasting with the *-s* genitive.

complement
The complement is an element of the sentence which follows verbs like *be, become, seem*, where this element is not an object, e.g. *He seems fine.*

complement, extended adjectival
An extended adjectival complement is frequently used in German before nouns in formal register. The adjectival phrase preceding a

noun is expanded, e.g. by adding an adverbial: *die damals vorherrschende Kälte.*

complement, object

The object complement tells us more about the object of a sentence, e.g. *They saw the ghost walking across the room.*

complement, subject

The subject complement tells us more about the subject of a sentence, e.g. *He lay dreaming in the hot sun.*

conjunction, temporal

A temporal conjunction is one referring to time, e.g. *When I arrived, he'd left.*

copula

A copula is a verb with little meaning of its own which is used to link the subject and complement, e.g. *be, become, seem* (see Kortmann 1999, p.102f.)

determiner

A determiner is a grammatical element placed before nouns to express concepts like definiteness, indefiniteness, quantity etc., e.g. *the, a, some, our*.

Early Modern English

Early Modern English (EMnE) is the English spoken between the mid-15th and the 18th centuries. Shakespeare was a speaker of Early Modern English.

final(ly)

Sounds in final position occur at the end of a word (German *im Auslaut*)

gradable

An adjective or adverb is gradable if it can be put into the comparative and superlative or can be modified by an intensifier, e.g. *very*. Thus, *slow* and *slowly* are gradable, whereas the adverb *outside* is non-gradable.

hypercorrect
A hypercorrect form is one where speakers, usually of a non-standard variety, overgeneralise a form regarded as typical of the standard variety, e.g. when Rhinelanders pronounce *englisch* as if it ended in *-ich* [ç], in an attempt to avoid non-standard pronunciations like *isch weiß et nischt*, with [ʃ].

inanimate, see *animate*

initial(ly)
Sounds occurring initially are at the beginning of a word (German *im Anlaut*).

marked
Something is described as *marked* if it contains a feature which is missing in a comparable item, e.g. *boy's* is marked for the genitive case by having the ending /z/ in contrast to the unmarked common case without ending. The term is also used to mean that one of two forms or categories has a more specific meaning, in contrast to the unmarked or neutral form (cf. p. 32ff., p. 104).

medial(ly)
Sounds occurring medially are in the middle of a word (German *im Inlaut*).

Middle English
Middle English (ME) is the English spoken between the early 12th and mid-15th centuries. Chaucer (c. 1345-1400) belongs to the Middle English period.

Modern English
Modern English (MnE) is the English spoken between approx. 1800 and today.

morpheme
A morpheme is the smallest distinctive unit of meaning in a language, e.g. *smallest* and *meaning* consist of the morphemes {small}, {est}, {mean}, and {ing}.

non-gradable, see *gradable*.

Old English

Old English (OE) is the English spoken between the mid-5th and the late 11th centuries. The first written records date from the 8th century. Perhaps the best known piece of literature from this period is the heroic epic *Beowulf.*

phoneme

A phoneme is the smallest unit at the level of sounds which distinguishes meaning, e.g. in English /ð/ in *they* contrasts with /d/ in *day*. In Spanish the same sounds, as in *un dedo* 'a finger' [un 'deðo], are variants of the same phoneme and do not distinguish meaning.

predicative

An adjective is used predicatively when it follows the copula*, e.g. *She is happy.*

prescriptive

A prescriptive approach to languages is the authoritarian view, common among non-linguists, that some forms of language (e.g. the standard language) are 'better' than others (e.g. dialects). This attitude is also extended to grammar, e.g. prescriptivists claim that *Whom did you see?* is 'better' than *Who did you see?*, or that *größer als* is 'correct', while *größer wie* is 'wrong' (see p. 66, p. 207).

register

Register means the type of language suitable for a specific situation, e.g. formal register for a more formal occasion, informal for a more relaxed situation.

suppletive form

A suppletive form fills gaps in the grammatical pattern of a word, e.g. *went* is a suppletive form to the forms *go, goes, going, gone* (cf. p. 105, p.108).

synthetic

A synthetic language is one where grammatical functions are expressed by inflectional endings which express several different meanings at the same time, e.g. the *-o* of Latin *amo* shows that it is first person, singular, present tense etc.

unmarked, see *marked*

verb, intransitive, see *verb, transitive*

verb, lexical
A lexical verb, also known as a *full* verb, which denotes actions, events or states. It contrasts with auxiliary verbs, which mainly have grammatical functions.

verb, strong
Strong verbs in English, German and other Germanic languages form their past tense and past participle by changing the vowel of the stem, e.g. sing – sang – sung. Weak verbs use a suffix, e.g. *play – played*, *spielen – spielte – gespielt*.

verb, transitive
A transitive verb is one which is followed by an object, e.g. *repair*. If it does not take an object it is intransitive, e.g. *sit*.

verb, weak, see *verb, strong*

zero article
Zero article means that no definite or indefinite article occurs before a noun.

Bibliography

Adams, Douglas, *Mostly Harmless*. London, 1993.
Allen, W.S., *Vox Latina. The Pronunciation of Classical Latin*. Cambridge, 1970.
Berlin, Isaiah, *Karl Marx*. Oxford, 1978.
Biber, Douglas, et al., *Longman Grammar of Spoken and Written English*. Harlow, 1999.
Blake, Norman, *The Cambridge History of the English Language*, vol. II. Cambridge, 1992.
Broughton, Geoffrey, *Penguin English Grammar A-Z*. London, 1990.
Campbell, A., *Old English Grammar*. Oxford, 1959.
CIDE = *Cambridge International Dictionary of English*. Cambridge, 1995.
Close, R.A., *A reference grammar for students of English*. London, 1975.
Comrie, Bernard, *Aspect*. Cambridge, 1976.
Comrie, Bernard, *Tense*. Cambridge, 1985.
Corbett, Greville, *Gender*. Cambridge, 1991.

Crystal, David, *The Cambridge Encyclopedia of the English Language*. Cambridge, 1995.
Crystal, David, *The Penguin Dictionary of Language*. London, 1999 (2nd ed.).
Diderichsen, Paul, *Elementær Dansk Grammatik*. Copenhagen, 1976.
Duden, *Grammatik der deutschen Gegenwartssprache*. Mannheim, 1984 (4th ed.).
Faiß, Klaus, *Englische Sprachgeschichte*. Tübingen, 1989.
Fleischhack, Erich, Hellmut Schwarz, *Cornelsen English Grammar*. Berlin, 2001.
Gethin, Hugh, *Grammar in Context*. London, 1983.
Greenbaum, Sidney, and Janet Whitcut, *Guide to English Usage*. London, 1998.
Hellinger, Marlis, *Kontrastive feministische Linguistik. Mechanismen sprachlicher Diskriminierung im Englischen und Deutschen*. Munich, 1990.
Hewings, Martin, *Advanced Grammar in Use*. Cambridge, 1999.
Hoffmann, Hans and Marion, *Große Lerngrammatik*. Munich, 2001.
Hogg, Richard, *The Cambridge History of the English Language*, vol. I. Cambridge, 1992.
Keller, R.E., *The German Language*. London, 1978.
König, Ekkehard, Johan van der Auwera (eds.), *The Germanic Languages*. London, 1994.
Kortmann, Bernd, *Linguistik: Essentials*. studium kompakt Anglistik • Amerikanistik. Berlin, 1999.
Lamprecht, Adolf, *Grammatik der englischen Sprache*. Berlin, 1989 (9th ed.).
Lass, Roger (ed.), *The Cambridge History of the English Language*, vol. III. Cambridge, 1999.
Leisi, Ernst, Christian Mair, *Das heutige Englisch: Wesenszüge und Probleme*. Heidelberg, 1999 (8th ed.) .
Levinson, Stephen, *Pragmatics*. Cambridge, 1983.
Lyons, John, *Introduction to Theoretical Linguistics*. Cambridge, 1968.
Mindt, Dieter, *An Empirical Grammar of the English Verb System*. Berlin, 2000.
Mitchell, Bruce, Fred C. Robinson, *A Guide to Old English*. Oxford, 1982 (2nd rev. ed.).
Price, Glanville, *The French language: present and past*. London, 1971.
Quirk, Randolph, et al., *A Comprehensive Grammar of the English Language*. London, 1985.

Rug, Wolfgang, Andreas Tomaszewski, *Grammatik mit Sinn und Verstand*. Munich, 1993.
Sinclair, John, *Collins Cobuild English Grammar*. London, 1990.
Strang, Barbara, *A History of English*. London, 1970.
Swan, Michael, *Practical English Usage*. Oxford, 1995 (2nd ed.).
Ungerer, Friedrich, *Englische Grammatik heute*. Stuttgart, 2000.

Index

I Word Order

1 1 YES: a Cats don't like dogs. b Dogs don't like cats. It's cats that dogs don't like. c plural nouns

2 NO: a b The girl was able to find the house easily. c sense (animate subject necessary)

3 YES: a Jennifer met Tom at a party. b Tom met Jennifer at a party. It was Jennifer that Tom met at a party. c names

4 YES: a The doctor looked sceptically at the patient. b The patient looked sceptically at the doctor. It was the doctor that the patient looked sceptically at. c feminine nouns

5 YES: a The girl thinks the guard is cute. b The guard thinks the girl is cute. It's the girl that the guard thinks is cute. c neuter and feminine nouns

6 NO: a b Most women don't like Frank. c plural form of verb

7 YES: a The gangsters saw you, didn't they? b You saw the gangsters, didn't you? It was the gangsters you saw, wasn't it? c plural noun, *Sie*

8 YES: a Berliners don't like you, do they? b You don't like Berliners, do you? You don't like doughnuts, do you? It's Berliners/doughnuts you don't like, isn't it? c plural noun, *Sie*

2 *Enter Oswald and Sir Edgar.*

O Why does Your Grace look so serious today?

E The night was stormy/storm-tossed. Strange cries were heard, and ghosts, people say, were walking.

O Yes, some people say that the earth was feverish and shook. This is how the Fates reveal the evil that humans try to hide. Is the king leaving today?

E Yes, he is, before two.

O Are you going with him this afternoon?

E I am, if all goes well.

A servant enters.

S O horror! Horror!

O & E What's the matter?

O How did you get here?

S Haven't you heard the news/Don't you know what's happened? The king, the king, the king is dead. Viciously murdered while he was still in bed. Wake up! Wake up! Sound the alarm! Murder and treason! Sound the alarm!

3 1 'I don't like Tchaikovsky.' 'I don't either.'
2 She only remembered the answer to the last question after the exam.
3 It didn't become clear until Tuesday that the earthquake's death toll would run into the thousands.
4 'We didn't go on holiday last year.' 'We didn't either.'
5 There haven't been such massive expressions of popular grief since Winston Churchill died.
6 Jim didn't grasp how much she had loved him until he read her suicide note.
7 We can only provide the funding you require if these conditions are met.
8 He wasn't aware at any time that he was actually committing a crime.
9 I've seldom experienced such crass stupidity.
10 We had no sooner entered the haunted castle when the lights went out.

4 Never has this country been in such dire straits as under the present government.
Nowhere else in the EU has the economy been neglected to the same extent. Not since the Wilson government of the 1970s has the number of multi-national firms leaving the U.K. been so high.
Nor is this surprising.
Scarcely had the present party come into office when it began to frighten away foreign investors with its taxes on profits.
Rarely in the post-war period has there been any party which has matched the government's hamfistedness in its timing and tactics.
It is my considered opinion that only if the government bites the bullet and sends the Chancellor of the Exchequer packing will this change for the better.
In no time a large part of our financial problems would be solved.
Not only would we be rid of an incompetent administrator, we would also be saying a tearless farewell to a government minister who was better known for his love affairs than for his debating skills in the House.
At no time does he seem to have been aware of the gravity of the country's financial situation.
Therefore, under no circumstances should the government permit such a mediocre minister to remain one month longer in office.

5 [2] my girlfriend I'm going with [3] we're doing is flying [4] Marbella where we're going (to)/Marbella that we're going to [5] she's studying is speech therapy [6] who's/that's studying at Keele [7] I need is

6 Dear Professor Hogshead,
We are now putting the finishing touches to our programme (*BrE*)/program (*AmE*) for Oxford. We were very grateful for your kind offer to show us round your college and gladly accept.
I have one or two questions. I was wondering whether it would be convenient for us to come on the morning of Tuesday, 22 September (*BrE*)/September 22. We are hoping to visit St. Edward's School in the afternoon, but we are not going there till/until 2 p.m., so that there will probably be enough time in the morning to visit your college. However, on no account should you change your plans if Tuesday is not convenient. We are very flexible, except on Wednesday and Friday. We are visiting (the town of) Stratford-upon-Avon on Wednesday. We have a guided tour round the Royal Shakespeare Theatre (*BrE*)/(theater *AmE*) from 10 to 12, and we will spend the afternoon walking around the town and visiting Shakespeare's birthplace. Of course we will also see a play by Shakespeare in Stratford. We have bought tickets for 'The Merchant of Venice' in the evening. So we will have no time on Wednesday. And for Friday morning we have arranged a visit to Cheney School. In the afternoon we will be leaving for Germany. Please let me stress once more that under no circumstances should you cancel any plans you may have for Tuesday morning. I am sure we can fit most other times you suggest into our schedule. Looking forward to hearing from you.
Yours sincerely, Heinz Katzenellenbogen

II Tense & Aspect: The Progressive

1 [1] I think he's trying to break into the factory. [2] He appears to be having difficulties. [3] A security guard is shouting to him. [4] Now the guard's German shepherd is running towards the man. [5] The man's running away. [6] The dog's pinning him to the ground. [7] The guard seems to be calling for help on his mobile.

3 1 Tom's taking (<u>today</u>) 2 she's working (<u>today</u>) 3 I'm having (<u>today</u>) 4 I <u>rarely</u> use ... (<u>at the moment</u>) I'm taking ... is being repaired 5 seems to be getting (<u>now</u>) 6 <u>often</u> has 7 <u>always</u>

recommend ... (occasionally) come across 8 currently appears to be experiencing 9 (Whenever) I phone ... she's having 10 is just being given

4 ① I was having a wash. – Actually I was making love to Emma.
② I was reading the paper. – Actually I was listening at the door.
③ I was getting ready to go out. – Actually I was in bed with Simon.
④ I was watching TV.– Actually I was having an argument with Anita.

Note: In Exercise 4 the answers after *Actually* in the thought bubbles are the only correct ones. In the speech bubbles any answer is possible, e.g. 'I was having a wash' could occur in 1, 2, 3 or 4.

5 1 I We had 2 I was taking 3 I dropped 4 I ran 5 I got 6 Andrea was phoning 7 he wanted 8 I was preparing 9 Dave rang 10 Angie was expecting 11 he was taking 12 Andrea came 13 I went 14 I was getting 15 the first guests arrived 16 Andrea was still putting 17 Andrea opened 18 she burst 19 they were 20 they thought 21 they were coming 22 one of them was wearing 23 was pretending 24 she certainly looked 25 we were still laughing 26 the next guests turned up 27 it definitely broke 28 we were swapping 29 really took off 30 started

6 1 Have you been running? 2 Have you been gardening? or Have you been working in the garden? 3 Have you been drinking (beer)? 4 Have you been painting? 5 Have you been waiting long?

7 1 I've been revising 2 has won 3 I've been reading ... I haven't finished 4 Have you been eating 5 I've been looking 6 They've been touring ... They've visited 7 you've been working 8 Have you seen

8 1 It was announced yesterday by Jamaica's prime minister
2 Similar measures are being considered by several Commonwealth countries 3 The Queen is seen as 4 It is being predicted by many observers (*also*: It is predicted ...) 5 A possible move to a republic is also being currently debated by Barbados ... and 6 although republicanism was rejected by a majority of Australian voters ... 7 it is being assumed by political

experts (also: it is assumed ...) [8] Developments are being closely monitored by Buckingham Palace.

9 [1] That looks [2] Can you see (*esp. AmE*: Do you see) [3] who he's talking to? [4] he seems [5] to be having [6] I feel [7] what's going on [8] You're being nosey [9] You really are

10 1 Can you see/Do you see *(esp. AmE)* 2 Do you mean 3 who's standing 4 who's wearing 5 who's smoking 6 calls 7 speaks 8 met 9 was talking 10 introduced 11 thought 12 have been seeing 13 likes 14 don't seem 15 think 16 often see 17 Jessica's told/Jessica tells 18 has been acting 19 seems 20 be avoiding 21 rings/phones/calls 22 hangs up 23 sounds 24 says 25 is currently/at present being investigated 26 is starting/beginning 27 is wondering

Note: In 17 and 18 it is also possible to say 'Jessica told ... had been acting'.

III Tense and Aspect: The Perfective

1
1. 'Have you seen Paul lately/recently?' 'Yes, I met him in town yesterday.'
2. 'When I arrived in Venice last week, it was very hot.'
3. 'I was so hungry this morning that I made myself a fried egg.'
4. Johnny made/was making himself a fried egg while he talked/was talking to Jennifer.
5. On Monday I baked a cake, and then I drove/went to town.
6. We left the old fridge behind when we moved out.
7. Did you leave the cooker/stove there, too, when you moved out?

2 1 We've sold our caravan. 2 I've forgotten the name of Jane's fiancé. 3 I've broken this vase. 4 Marleen's gone on holiday to Rome. 5 Leonard's been to Switzerland. 6 I've caught a cold.

3
1. It's been snowing hard since about 6 p.m.
2. Ralph's been playing football for three hours.
3. I've been reading this book since this morning.
4. He's been on the phone with his girlfriend for an hour.
5. They've been climbing Mount Everest since last Tuesday.

4 1 I was standing in the bank waiting to be served when two masked men entered.
2 They made the customers stand on one side of the room.
3 While one of the men forced/was forcing the cashier to hand over the money,
4 the other kept/was keeping the customers covered with a sawn-off shotgun.
5 The man who was covering us with the shotgun was wearing jeans and a suede jacket.
6 I didn't have a chance to see what the other man was wearing.
7 The man in jeans was talking to the other one when they left/were leaving the bank.

5 1a 2b 3a (also 3b in *AmE*) 4c 5b 6b

6 1 Have you heard ... Fiona is having ...
When did that happen?
It hasn't happened yet ... (*AmE also:* It didn't happen ...)
No, I mean(t), I didn't know she was going out ...
Oh yes, she has known ...
They met when she was working ...
2 I saw ...
He seems to have been going/have gone ...
He's been ..., his girlfriend's just left him (*AmE also:* his girlfriend just left him ...), and he's had/been having ...
Yes, I saw ...
He looked/was looking ...
3 I've been looking ...
Don't you remember that we arranged ...
Where were you/have you been?
Camilla rang me ... while I was talking ... and I just forgot what we had arranged earlier
4 She's never been ... since she fell ...
When I first came... she was... and she has been... has remained/remains...
At least, she has always seemed ... for as long as I've known
she has been getting/has got (*AmE*: gotten) more and more peculiar
Recently she even asked ... if she fancied ...

7 1 Have you ever climbed ... 2 Did you ever play ... 3 Have you ever thought ... 4 Have you ever worked ... 5 Have you ever been ... 6 Did you ever eat ... 7 Did you ever meet ...

8 1 ... who ruled ...built
2 I haven't visited ...
3 Serena's father ... 'Did you see ...'
4 ... So far we've been lucky, but I'm sure that Otho and Rautio will soon be ...
5 ... says that the British king Cassivelaunus has already told the Britons ...
6 How did Nipius Ascanius find out that Marcus knew ...?
7 ... 'Since Britain became part of the Roman Empire 50 years ago, life has become easier for many Britons.'

9 1 Since 1st January I've stopped smoking. *(prep.)*
2 For six months (now) he's been meeting his best friend's girlfriend in secret. *(prep.)*
3 Somebody brought her some chocolates from Belgium recently. She's been stuffing herself/her face with Belgian chocolates ever since. *(adv.)*
4 Since he's had the new Porsche, he's been driving far/much too fast. *(conj.)*
5 Oliver's been drinking like a fish ever since Sarah left him. *(conj.)*
6 For years he's refused/been refusing to disclose where the money came from. *(prep.)*
7 Since Boris stopped drinking so much vodka, he's felt/been feeling much/far better. *(conj.)*
8 Since he's been in love with her, he's seen/been seeing the world through different eyes. *(conj.)*

10 1 It was built between 1891 and 1895 in honour (*BrE*)/honor (*AmE*) of Emperor William I.
2 During the Second World War it was badly damaged in 1943 in an air raid.
3 After the war there were plans/it was planned to demolish the church.
4 However, public opinion was in favour (*BrE*)/favor (*AmE*) of keeping the original church.
5 The architect Egon Eiermann solved it by integrating the ruined church and the new church.

6 The new church was completed in 1961, the same year as the Berlin Wall was built.
7 Since that time it's been one of Berlin's major landmarks.
8 Most of the original church has been demolished.
9 Only part of the church steeple has remained intact.
10 The square surrounding the church, Breitscheid Square, has been enlarged.
11 Trams (*BrE*)/streetcars (*AmE*) have been superseded by buses.
12 The Romanisches Café east of the church has been replaced by the 22-storey (*BrE*)/22-story (*AmE*) Europa Centre (*BrE*)/Center (*AmE*).

11 1 British policemen hurt in street fighting
In clashes between the police and Asian teenagers two policemen have been hurt and 25 vehicles set on fire. Four demonstrators were arrested. A police spokeswoman/spokeswoman for the police confirmed that the two policemen only had/have minor injuries.

2 Israel shoots down Lebanese plane
The Israeli air force has shot down a Lebanese Cessna which had entered Israeli air space. According to Israeli army reports the pilot of the aircraft did not react to several attempts by Israeli helicopters to make contact. The plane was shot down off the coast north of Tel Aviv. The pilot was killed.

3 Anthony Quinn dies/dead
The US actor Anthony Quinn died on Sunday at the age of 86 in a Boston hospital. He was best known for his leading role in the film *Zorba the Greek*, which was shot in 1964.

4 7 bn mark(s) fine for tobacco firm
A record fine has been imposed on the US tobacco firm Philip Morris after it was sued by a smoker who had contracted cancer. The Los Angeles court/court in Los Angeles instructed the company to pay 56-year-old Richard Boeken more than 3 billion dollars. Philip Morris announced that it would appeal.

5 ETA: no new truce
The Basque terrorist organisation ETA yesterday announced that it was continuing its strategy of violence. An ETA spokesman said in an interview that no new 'truce' was planned. He added that a renunciation of violence would only be feasible as part of a peace process.

IV Future Time

1 1 a was cycling to work b is cycling to work c will be cycling to work
2 a was walking b is walking c will be walking

2 1 is getting 2 are going/will be going 3 will be living 4 will be playing 5 will be widening 6 are taking 7 will be lying

3 1 Will you be staying in tonight?
2 Mum, will you be passing a postbox?
3 Laura, how long will you be needing those CDs I lent you?
4 When will you be sending me the next chapter of your book?
5 Will you be coming to my graduation party on 17th July?
6 When exactly will you be visiting me/us?

4 1 won't bite *(prediction)* 2 won't rain *(prediction)* 3 I'm going *(plan)* 4 will get *(prediction)* 5 we're selling *(plan)*
6 I'm looking after *(plan)* 7 will see *(prediction)* 8 She's having *(plan)* 9 We're staying *(plan)*

5 1 is going to (stay) 2 I'll (show) 3 I'm going to (cry)
4 There's going to (be)/There'll (be) 5 is going to/will (have to)
6 'I'm going to (do)' 'Good! I'll (come) ...' 7 I'll (phone) 8 I'm going to (hoover) ...

6 1 are you going to be *(intention/prediction)* – I'm going to be *(intention/prediction)* – are you doing *(plan)*/are you going to do *(intention)* – I'm going *(plan)*/I'm going to go *(intention)* 2 I'm going to find *(intention)* 3 is going to have *(prediction)* 4 it's going to explode *(prediction)* 5 We're moving *(plan)*/We're going to move *(intention)* 6 is going to be *(prediction)*
7 Who's coming *(plan)* 8 it's going to leave *(prediction)*

7 1 are you/will you be/are you going to be
2 are you visiting/will you visit/will you be visiting/are you going to visit
3 takes off/is taking off/will take off/will be taking off
4 land/will (*also*: shall *BrE*) be landing
5 starts/is starting/will start/will be starting/is going to start
6 go/are going/will (*also*: shall *BrE*) be going/are going to go
7 visit/are visiting/will (*also*: shall *BrE*) be visiting/are going to visit

8 is/will be/is going to be
9 leave/are leaving/will (*also*: shall *BrE*) leave/are going to leave
10 get/will get/will be getting

V Other Tense Uses

1 [1] had been found [2] had [3] was passed [4] was [5] was [6] would not happen [7] was/had been [8] had taken up [9] those senseless killings of his [10] would like to make [11] should realise [12] was [13] wished [14] was appreciated

2
1 (The US ship requested that) we change our course by 15 degrees north to avoid a collision.
2 (We replied) that they should change their course 15 degrees south to avoid a collision.
3 (The captain of the US ship then repeated) that we should change our direction,
4 (and we repeated) that they should change their direction.
5 (They then pointed out that) they were the USS Lincoln,... (the second biggest ship in the US Atlantic fleet)
6 (and that they) were being accompanied (by three destroyers, three cruisers and several ancillary vessels).
7 (They demanded that) we change our course or counter-measures would be taken to ensure the safety of their ship.
8 (We then informed them that) we were a lighthouse and it was their move.

3 [1] had been barking [2] the night before/the previous night [3] could only have been [4] had been/was [5] had been/was [6] had [7] recognised [8] was [9] started barking [10] began to bark [11] opened [12] didn't even wake up [13] happened [14] went for [15] was [16] woke up

4 *Richard Townsend said that Pennsylvania* was/had been a wilderness when they arrived. The main inhabitants were/had been Indians and some Swedes, who (had) received them in a friendly manner. *He stressed that* although there were a lot of people, Providence was/had been kind to them, *explaining that provisions* were/had been found for them by the Swedes and Indians at very reasonable rates.
He explained that their first concern was/had been to maintain their religious worship, *adding that as* they had had nothing but love

and goodwill in their hearts towards each other they had (had) very comforting meetings. *Furthermore, he said, after* their meeting was over they assisted each other in building little houses for their shelter.

He described how William Penn treated the Indians with extraordinary humanity, *with the result that they* became very polite and friendly to them, and brought in plenty of venison. *He concluded that just as, in other countries, the Indians* had been exasperated/frustrated by harsh treatment, which (had) resulted in a lot of bloodshed, *so the opposite kind of treatment* there i.e. in Pennsylvania, had resulted in them showing love and affection.

5 *Possible sample answers*

1 a If the tram hits it, it'll be smashed.
  b If the tram ran into the cyclist, he'd be very badly injured.
  c If Jordan hadn't shouted to him, he wouldn't have noticed the tram approaching.

2 a They would give him/her directions to the nearest youth hostel.
  b They would tell him the meter was checked last week.
  c They would lend her a packet of sugar.

3 a There wouldn't be/have been any churches, a Pope, bishops, archbishops, the Crusades etc.
  b There wouldn't have been a Russian Revolution, at least not in 1917. Russia might have remained a monarchy. Lenin and Stalin would probably not have come to power.
  c Perhaps the Second World War would/could have been avoided.
  d Japan would have surrendered later.

6 1 If she was/were deprived of insulin ...
2 If you are about to drive ...
3 ...if it had been contacted in time.
4 If you're depressed ...
5 If it had been diagnosed at an early stage ...
6 ... if it was/were starved of oxygen for such a long time.
7 If she had been asked politely ...

7 1 It would contain ...
2 There would be ...

3 Six persons would own 59% of the village's entire wealth and all 6 would be from the US.

4 Eighty would live/be living in dilapidated housing, 70 would be illiterate, 50 would be suffering from malnutrition, one would be dying, one would be being born, one would possess a computer, and one would have graduated from university.

8 1 a führe ... verbrauchte 1 c drove ... would use
2 a rechnete ... 2 c counted ... would be
3 c would have been avoided ... had been invented
4 a vorzöge ... 4 c preferred ... would be making
5 a fragte ... 5 c asked ... would say
6 a vergäbe ... 6 c did not forgive ... would be

9 1 didn't have 2 try/are trying ... succeed ... did you do? 3 wouldn't have ... didn't have ... would be 4 would have been ... hadn't filled/(*AmE also:* wouldn't have filled) 5 was/were ... would be ... would pick up 6 are grown/are being grown ... are/will be 7 doesn't have ... is it 8 had been ... would have wanted 9 wasn't/weren't ... would be 10 Q: would have happened ... had been A: would have asked

VI Modal Verbs

1 *Sample answer:*

Personality: My ideal partner must be affectionate.
He/She should be intelligent.
He/She can be untidy.
He/She doesn't have to be adventurous.
He/She mustn't be arrogant.

Interests: My ideal partner must love motorcycling.
He/She should like children.
He/She can enjoy (going to) the opera.
He/She doesn't have to like dancing.
He/She mustn't like folk music.

2 1 Could we ... 2 Should I ... 3 Would/Could you ... 4 We would like to ... 5 Could/May/Might I ... 6 Should we ... 7 could I/may I/might I ... 8 I would like (*NB:* 'want' *would be very impolite*)

3 1 will not 2 cannot 3 should/ought to 4 must not (*BrE*)/cannot (*AmE*) 5 could/might 6 would like to 7 must (*BrE*)/(will) have to 8 must not (*BrE*)/cannot (*AmE*)

4 1 may not 2 can't/may not 3 can't 4 can't/may not 5 may not 6 can't

5 1 was able to save – *konnte* 2 could be – *könnten* 3 could speak – *konnte* 4 was able to catch – *konnte* 5 could lead – *könnte* 6 was/were (*BrE*) able to reduce – *konnte* 7 could swim – *konnte* 8 Brian could/might be going – *könnte*
9 were able to fend off – *konnten*

6 1 could/may/might have been 2 can't 3 must (*BrE*)/has to (*AmE*) 4 can/could/would be able to 5 can't 6 must (*BrE*)/have to (*AmE*) 7 may/might 8 might 9 can/should 10 must (*BrE*)/have to (*AmE*)

7 1 mustn't (*BrE*)/cannot (*AmE*) park there. You might get towed away by the police.
2 have to stop. You might crash into a vehicle on the major road.
3 may be queues/tailbacks (*BrE*). You might crash/run into the car in front.
4 mustn't (*BrE*)/cannot (*AmE*) drive faster than 40 m.p.h. You might get fined for speeding/get caught in a radar trap.
5 may be cattle on the road. You might run into them.
6 may be pedestrians on the road. You might run into/over them.
7 may be slippery. You might skid.
8 may be low-flying aircraft overhead. You might be startled by planes and lose control of your car.

8 1 are said/supposed to be – *sollen* 2 should be/ought to be – *solltest* 3 Should I lend – *soll* 4 *correct, also:* are supposed to be – *sollen* 5 is said/supposed to be – *soll* 6 was supposed to ring/be ringing – *sollte* 7 *correct* (*BrE*)/Should (*AmE*) – *sollen* 8 shouldn't be – *sollten*

9 1 may be 2 all need to 3 do not dare to/dare not 4 we may/might 5 not want to 6 we must 7 we should not/ought not to 8 we must 9 should we 10 We therefore need to 11 can/will be able to 12 may 13 do not want to 14 should 15 we must 16 can

10 1 You should take anti-malaria tablets with you.
2 Would you like to sit here?
3 You mustn't go down there – it's a one-way street!
4 You really must go and see *Invasion of the Blob Monsters*, Steve. It's brilliant!
5 You don't have to/need to change planes in Singapore or Sydney. You can take a through flight to New Zealand.
6 Would you like to come along to the restaurant with us?
7 Will you get me a bag of salt and vinegar crisps and a packet of peanuts, please?
8 Shall I get some crisps for the rest of you, too?

11 1 do not want their wives to 2 should/ought to 3 doesn't have to/doesn't need to/needn't 4 must (*BrE*)/has to 5 should 6 simply can't 7 has to 8 might/could 9 was able to/managed to 10 should/ought to 11 doesn't want Jessica to 12 can 13 is said/supposed to be 14 used to

VII The Participle

1 1 working in the garden 2 lying on the beach 3 having a relaxing bath 4 playing on the computer 5 using my mobile 6 tinkering with the car

2 1 We saw people standing at the windows in the smoke-filled building, trying to attract attention.
2 Don Corleone sat outside the café watching the people on the piazza.
3 They lay in bed smoking.
4 He stood there, dazed by the impact of the explosion.
5 The guerrillas watched the soldiers coming out of the barracks.
6 She heard her name being called out by the man at the bar.
7 We could smell the food burning.
8 They were standing at the corner gossiping as usual.
Or: They were standing gossiping at the corner as usual.

3 1 The team, headed by the embryologist James Thomson, used human embryos created by artificial insemination in order to treat childless couples.
2 Before operating, the team has to localise the source of the epileptic attacks.

3 The data obtained while doing this can then be used for other purposes.
4 They removed the remaining internal cell mass, transferring it into special cultures.
5 The lectures held at the Physics Department were part of an experiment aimed at trying out new teaching methods. One important tool used was an electronic whiteboard. Two video cameras filmed the lecturer, with the sound being recorded by using cordless microphones.
6 The researchers transplanted the oligodendrocytes obtained in the laboratory into the spinal cord of rats suffering from a genetic defect in the formation of their myelin sheaths. The cells attached themselves to nerve cells, producing myelin there.

4 1 A barking dog never bites. b
2 A shut mouth catches no flies. c
3 Threatened men live long. b
4 A rolling stone gathers no moss. d
5 Nothing ventured, nothing gained. a
6 First come, first served. f

5 1 While I was crossing the street at a zebra crossing, a car nearly ran me over.
2 While I was lying in bed, my thoughts ranged back over my past life.
3 As a rule my kids won't touch apples, but if the apples are dipped in chocolate they lap them up.
4 When parking their cars, hotel guests are advised to remove all their valuables.
5 A dog bit the postman while he was delivering letters.
6 Dolphins can be taught some very clever tricks, if properly trained.

6 The bus driver brought the bus to a gradual halt by the bus-stop outside a row of thatched cottages. Two old women dressed in black waited until the bus was quenched of all motion before clutching each other and edging cautiously towards it. 1: 2.1 B 2: 2.3 B

In a moment he heard their voices crying unintelligibly to the conductor. Then activity seemed to cease. At least five seconds passed. Dixon looked 3: 2.2 B

out of the bus to see what the cause of the delay
might be. Was the driver slumped in his seat, the 4: 2.1 A
victim of a stroke, or had he suddenly got an idea for
a poem? Then, at last, the picture of sleepy rustic calm
was modified by the fairly sudden emergence from
a cottage some yards further of a third woman in a
lilac costume. She looked keenly towards the bus
and identified it without obvious difficulty, then 5: 2.1 A
approached it with a kind of bowed shuffle. The bus
now set off, nosing its careful way on to the crown of 6: 2.3 A3
the road, and the gap between it and the lorry in front
began to narrow. Dixon found that his whole being
had become centred on the matter of the bus's
progress. He just sat there galvanised by the pitchings 7: 2.2 A
of the bus into the appearance of seismic laughter,
sweating stealthily in the heat and the apprehension, 8: 2.2 A
stretching his face in a fresh direction at each over- 9: 2.2 A
taking car. Suddenly the lorry moved off into a lay-by.
Now was the time, he thought, with a reviving hope, 10: 2.1 A
for the driver to start making up for lost time, but the
driver seemed blissfully unaware of this. Dixon lit
another cigarette, jabbing with the match at the 11: 2.3 A3
sandpaper as if it were the driver's eye. Just then the
bus rounded a corner and slowed abruptly, then
stopped. Making a lot of noise, a tractor was labori- 12: 2.3 A3
ously pulling, at right angles across the road,
something that looked like the springs of a giant bed,
caked in places with earth and decked with ribbon- 13: 2.1 B
like grasses. Dixon thought he really would have to go 14: 2.1 B
downstairs and knife the drivers of both vehicles;
what next? what next? a masked hold-up, a crash, 15: 2.1 A
floods, an electric storm with falling trees and meteor- 16: 2.1 A
ites, a diversion, a low-level attack by Communist
aircraft, sheep, the driver being stung by a hornet? If 17: 2.3 D1
consulted, he'd choose the last of these. Grinding its 18: 2.3 B
gears, the bus crept on, while every few yards troupes 19: 2.3 A 3
of old men waited to make their quivering way 20: 2.1 A
aboard.

VIII The Gerund

1 1 Censoring newspapers ... 2 Collecting beer mats 3 ... is that smoking ... 4 ... against banning soft drugs 5 Being operated on ... 6 ... against executing murderers 7 Publicising the names of ... 8 Accusing somebody ... 9 Being accused of ...

2 1 Smoking 2 Collecting stamps 3 writing 4 surfing 5 zapping through 6 Rock-climbing 7 skiing 8 travelling (*BrE*)/traveling (*AmE*)

3 1 ✓ 2 I really mean to turn over ... 3 He went on playing ... 4 Please try to be ... 5 I'll never forget going ... 6 ✓ 7 Did you forget to switch off ... 8 ✓ 9 ✓ 10 Have you ever stopped to think ... 11 Have you tried reading ... ✓ ✓ ✓

4 1 going (to places where there are lots of people.)
2 borrowing/to borrow (money when I'm broke.)
3 to driving (on the right-hand/wrong side of the road.)
4 to ask (his boss for a pay-rise (*BrE*)/pay-raise (*AmE*).)
5 using (the shampoo for greasy hair.)
6 buy (each other loads of presents.)
7 to own (a big dog like that.)
8 listening (to sanctimonious speeches by boring politicians.)
9 waiting (here for a couple of minutes.)
10 mowing/to be mown (soon.)
11 (to be)(rather risky.) (NB: Use of *to be* is optional.)
12 meeting (in a bar off Grafton Street.)
13 to repair (the telephone lines.)
14 of (me/my) getting (her autograph.)
15 moving (it.)

5 (1) To be frank (2) being (3) working/to work (4) being (5) of being/to be (6) being/to be (7) to go (8) being (9) to being (10) to being (11) sniggering (12) overheating (13) to use up (14) jamming up (15) singing/to sing (16) committing (17) of fretting (18) in getting (19) moping/to mope (20) looking/to look (21) copying/to copy (22) crying

6 *Dear Sue,*
Thanks for your letter. I apologise for taking such a long time in replying/to reply, but I have been revising hard for my exams. Thanks for telling me about the book

on David Lodge. I'll try to buy a copy at our local bookshop. I'm so scared of failing English in my exams that having it will make me feel much more confident. My teacher also suggested getting a PC program to improve my English grammar. What would you advise me to do? Is it worth getting one? Do you know of a good one? I hope you don't mind me asking you all these questions, but I know that you had similar problems preparing for your exams.

I'm not only worried about failing my exams. Do you remember me telling you about meeting Mario at that party? My parents don't approve of me going out with him. They say he's on drugs. That's rubbish. I know he's not, and I enjoy being with him. I just wish my parents would stop treating me like a child. Unfortunately I forgot to tell Mario that my parents are against me going out with him. He came to our house yesterday to take me to a party at Sandra's, and my parents found out that I hadn't stopped seeing him. We had a big fight about it at home. So now they won't allow me to go out at the weekends. I'm so angry. But there's no point in getting too worked up. Anyway, I still manage to meet him at a friend's house. But I do miss going to discos with him. He's such a good dancer.

You asked me in your last letter if I felt like coming over in summer. Yes, I'd like that. I'm looking forward to going on holiday when I've finished doing my exams, and seeing you again would be great.

Love, Jasmin

7
1 You could practise using key vocabulary.
2 I think we should postpone celebrating the club's 20th anniversary.
3 Would you advise me to take out insurance cover for doctors' fees?
4 Did your client deny stealing the money from the safe?
5 Do you miss eating borshch?
6 Excuse my asking, but where do you come from?
7 Did you allow Ian to go on holiday with his friends?
8 I'd prefer (not) to go to the Taj Mahal again.
9 I enjoy water-skiing and scuba-diving.

8 *Suggested advice:*

Ann Barker for the Yorkshire Dales (She likes history and enjoys cycling and potholing).

Len Barlow for the Lake District (He is interested in poetry and likes angling, hiking, fell-walking and mounteneering)

Steve Carré for Northumberland (As a Latin teacher he will probably want to see Hadrian's Wall. He can do angling, golfing, hiking, sailing and water-skiing)

9 1 I'm against students buying ...
2 advocates abolishing/is in favour (*BrE*)/favor (*AmE*) of abolishing
3 recollect/recall/remember ever having seen/having ever seen
4 keeps coming ... sick and tired of having to
5 Quit moaning/Stop complaining ... smoking
6 chances of something like that happening
7 driving ... drinking/downing

IX Number

1 1 Ten years is a long time.
2 Curly kale with sausage is Dieter's favourite food.
3 These jeans are too tight for me. I've put on weight, you see.
4 The USA wants to protest against this measure.
5 Half of those interviewed were for the death penalty.
6 I think 50 euros is a lot of money for an entrance ticket.
7 Did you know that about 60 per cent (*BrE*)/percent (*AmE*) of all Irish people live in towns?
8 I like these shorts. I'll take them.

2 1 What experience have you got/had in the field of electronics?
2 I'd like some information about cheap flights for students to Australia.
3 Can you give me some advice on/about whether to choose the module on post-war British history or the American Civil War?
4 Billy, how much homework have you got?
5 Have you made any progress with your job applications?
6 I don't think the evidence is sufficient to persuade a jury of Boothby's guilt.
7 Angus, have you had any luck with getting a vacation job?

3 1 b, c 2 b 3 a, b 4 d 5 a 6 c 7 a 8 b 9 b 10 a, d

4 1 Those deer look graceful. 2 This furniture is ugly. 3 These binoculars are expensive. 4 Those calves look cute. 5 Those Japanese look happy. 6 Those sunglasses are cool. 7 That hair is greasy. 8 Those sheep look healthy. 9 Those pyjamas look silly.

5 1 Most analyses of the censuses held in Britain since 1801 show that there is no correlation between the phenomena of population size and prosperity.
2 The lives of the larvae of the water boatman are a constant battle against predators.
3 Economic criteria alone are not always decisive in the success of new products – ethics are also an important factor in some cases, e.g. in cosmetics which have not been tested on animals.
4 The hunters of the tribe used their knives to cut up the carcasses of the two water buffalo before giving their wives the meat.
5 Inaccurate diagnoses by doctors have proved to be one factor in the excessive number of appendixes which have been removed in hospital operations.
6 The data available on the curriculums (*also:* curricula) of European universities confirm (*or:* confirms) that there are enormous differences between universities in different parts of the EU, the disparity being partly due to the wide variation in syllabuses (*also:* syllabi) used.

6 1 The US is to support a new peace initiative in ...
2 Hundreds of tourists are feared dead after a collision in mid-air over ...
3 A scientist has claimed/is claiming that five rare species are becoming extinct every day ...
4 The Financial Times says that British Telecom are (*BrE*)/is making huge/enormous profits.
5 Scissors have been named as the murder weapon in the trial ....
6 XY, the EU Commissioner, has warned that R&D is vital for the EU's future.
7 The minister of agriculture claims that poultry are not in any danger from the current outbreak of salmonella.
8 The government is/are (*BrE*) planning to abolish the education regulatory body ...

7 1 alumnae 2 lice 3 cod

8 ... .in the 190-metre band ... the 550-metre band
Here is the news.
The United States has imposed ... on European wines ... of food.
... the Europeans' refusal ... of genetically modified cows
... that the EU are (*BrE*)/is considering ...

... two million people ... a 50-mile stretch
... have had to be evacuated.
the cattle are feared drowned
The United Nations has offered
... 6 million euros ...
'Six million euros does not ...
... this year's ...
Darts has been gaining ... over the past few years in several European countries
Ireland were/was ... last year's championship ... are (*BrE*)/is Denmark
Denmark's chances ... his six-year-old son
Luckily measles was ...
... aircraft ...
... the Porz residents' association ...
The data ... shows/show
The police have arrested eight youths ...
Ten people were ... two of them seriously.
The police say ... five flick-knives, three knuckle-dusters ...
... group ... are/is ...
... freshwater fish ... trout, pike and bream.
... four French people ... two Irish people, four Nepalese ... three Pakistanis
... Radio Gummersbach's ... Our next news ... is at 9 p.m.

X Gender

1
1 person – he
2 neighbor – he (*BrE:* neighbour)
3 clerk – she
4 co-worker – she (*BrE:* colleague, workmate)
5 manager – he
6 employee – she
7 mechanic – he

2
1 Humans/Human beings are tool-making animals.
2 Most executives ...
3 husband and wife
4 the camera operator ... Ms Hurley
5 chair/chairperson ... to air their views
6 Most firefighters ...
7 Isn't it brilliant!

8 When patients enter a GP's surgery, the doctor stands up, goes towards the patients and addresses them ... As soon as they are sitting down, the doctor asks them to explain why they have come to the surgery.
Or: As soon as the patient is sitting down, the doctor asks the patient to explain why he or she has come to the (doctor's) surgery.

3 1 c (*a is impolite, b is clumsy*) 2 a, b 3 a (*c is also possible; b is strange – personification would be unusual here*) 4 c *most normal* (*b also possible*) 5 c 6 b (*a possible, but in colloquial speech unusual*) 7 c

4 1 The pupil (*BrE*)/student was crying because the teacher had criticised (*BrE*)/criticized her.
2 If anybody asks for me, tell them I'll be back in two hours' time/two hours.
3 Frank, ask your girlfriend if she can order the book. She's a librarian, isn't she?
4 France recalled her/its ambassador from New Zealand on Monday.
5 Who's left their pullover/sweater/jumper here?
6 Nobody would do that on purpose, would they?
7 On Fridays she always goes dancing with her friend/girlfriend (*AmE*) .
8 Anyone wishing/Anyone who would like to take part in this seminar must (*BrE*)/has to register by 1st March (*BrE*)/March 1st.
9 Among students of English/English students female/women students are in the majority.

XI Case

1 1 b 2 a 3 c 4 a 5 a, b 6 c 7 b 8 c 9 b 10 a, c

2 1 that man from Chicago's daughter 2 that girl over there's boyfriend 3 in a month or so's time 4 that guy in the leather jacket's crash helmet 5 the President of Peru's daughter 6 the pop singer we met last night's partner 7 Charles II's coronation robes 8 the Bank of England's governor 9 somebody else's pen

3 1 b 2 b 3 b 4 b 5 a, c 6 b 7 b, c 8 b 9 a, c

4 Thanks ... // ... according to its postmark ... // Jean Lennox's little girl ... // ... in St. Thomas's hospital ... // cases like Doris's/Doris ..., ... a couple of weeks' time. // ... the one whose hair ..., ... like a bird's nest. // ... over the coals ... // ... to got to Jim's. // ... the boss's husband ... // He's a colleague of Jim's ... // One's a new edition of Shakespeare's history plays. // The other's a book about Beethoven's symphonies. // ... I'm at my wits' end ... // In four weeks' time/four weeks we're off to the Canaries with a few friends of Keith's. // I must go to C&A's soon.

5
1 GERMANY'S FASTEST ROLLER COASTER OPENED IN RUHR
2 EDINBURGH'S PRINCES STREET TO GET FACE-LIFT
3 EU'S FOREIGN MINISTERS SEEK CLOSER LINKS
4 PM'S THINK-TANK WARNS AGAINST/WARNING OF GOVERNMENT'S PLANS FOR PUBLIC SERVICES
5 ORCHESTRA FACES BANKRUPTCY AFTER RATTLE'S EXIT
6 TEACHERS' STRIKE SHELVED

XII The Adjective

1 1 heavier 2 shallower 3 more exact ... likelier 4 drier 5 more spry 6 more naive 7 posher 8 untidier 9 nobler

2 1 a small, black, leather one 2 more expensive/dearer one 3 annoying thing 4 gold ones 5 a tall/big one ... 6 a small/short one 7 smaller one 8 other one 9 old, dirty ones 10 strange/peculiar thing 11 das einzige

3 2 the lovers 3 people are the comedians 4 people are the bank managers 5 people are the cooks 6 people are the policemen. (NB: Other combinations are possible.)

2 the French 3 the Irish 4 the British 5 the Dutch 6 the Italians
(NB: Other combinations are possible.)

4 1 Many elderly people ... 2 Most deaf people ... 3 A lot of young people ..., and many old people ... 4 the homeless ... 5 A few unemployed people ... 6 The Naked and the Dead

5 1 a der getöteten Missionarin
b Missionarin, die getötet wurde,
c who was killed
2 a an zehn der geprüften Seen
b an zehn der Seen, die geprüft wurden,
c which/that were tested
3 a des seit Ende September andauernden Palästinenser-Aufstandes
b des Palästinenser-Aufstandes, der seit Ende September andauert.
c (uprising), which has been continuing since the end of September.
4 a des schon zu normalen Zeiten sehr flachen Plattensees
b des Plattensees, der schon zu normalen Zeiten sehr flach ist,
c (Lake Balaton), which even in normal times is very shallow,
5 a auch die noch in Bonn verbliebenen Ministerien
b auch die Ministerien, die noch in Bonn verblieben sind,
c those/the ministries which/that have remained in Bonn
6 a Der von indischen Experten sorgfältig gewebte Stoff dieses Madras-Hemdes
b Der Stoff dieses Madras-Hemdes, der von indischen Experten sorgfältig gewebt wurde,
c The material of this Madras shirt, which was carefully woven by Indian experts,
7 a eine von Prinz Charles gegründete Akademie für Architektur und Kunst
b eine Akademie für Architektur und Kunst, die von Prinz Charles gegründet wurde.
c an academy of architecture and art which was founded/set up by Prince Charles.
8 a Das von Norbert Oellers geleitete Projekt
b Das Projekt, das von Norbert Oellers geleitet wurde,
c The project, which is headed by Norbert Oellers,
9 a Dieses mit Klimaanlage und Air-Bags ausgestattete Modell ... einen für Autos seiner Klasse äußerst niedrigen Benzinverbrauch.
b Dieses Modell, das mit Klimaanlage und Air-Bags ausgestattet ist ... einen Benzinverbrauch, der für Autos seiner Klasse äußerst niedrig ist.
c This model, which is equipped with air conditioning and air

bags, has a petrol consumption which is extremely low for cars of its class.

6 [1] the people involved/concerned/responsible [2] the present government [3] the persons responsible/involved/concerned [4] such involved processes [5] The government departments concerned/responsible/involved [6] the proper procedures [7] for responsible behaviour [7] the journalists present

7
1 The rarest disease in the world is smallpox.
2 The commonest/most common cause of sudden death in the developed countries is coronary heart disease.
3 The most fatal epidemic in the world is AIDS.
4 The bloodiest battle in history was the Somme, with 1.22 million dead and wounded.
5 The male emperor moth has the most acute sense of smell in the world.
6 The heaviest man in the US, Jon Minnoch, was 362 kg when he died in 1983.
7 London has the most extensive underground railway in Europe, with a total length of 408 km.
8 The most complex motorway interchange in the U.K. is the M6 at Spaghetti Junction at Gravelly Hill, near Birmingham, with 18 routes at six levels.
9 The narrowest street in the EU is Vicolo della Virilità in Italy, which at one part is only 38 cm wide.
10 The biggest and most famous department store in London is Harrods, with a total selling floor space of 10.5 hectares.

XIII The Adverbial

1
1 She looked at me shyly.
2 This guitar sounds pleasant.
3 Janice behaved in a terribly silly way.
4 They protested publicly against the motorway.
5 They were involved in selling designer drugs illegally.
6 Manipulating humans genetically opens up frightening possibilities.
7 You acted in an extremely cowardly way/fashion.
8 Publishing the casualty figures weekly had a devastating effect on national morale.
9 The new professor lectured in a lively way.

10 Cassius looks lean and hungry.

2 [1] really scared (real scared = *AmE*) [2] looked very posh [3] I waited patiently [4] looked at me curiously [5] asked me politely [6] seemed very learned /ˈlɜːnɪd/ [7] felt pretty shy [8] these unfamiliar surroundings [9] our local primary school [10] looked at me kindly/in a kindly way [11] as ably as I could [12] sounded pretty sensible [13] were significantly better [14] at how simple [15] much more cheerful.

3
1 ... Hungarian fluently
2 ... silently in the corridor
3 ... their team wildly in Reebok Stadium
4 ... quietly just after midnight through the Strait of Gibraltar (2, 1, 3, but also 2, 3,1 possible)
5 ... on holiday in the Czech Republic next spring (3, 1, 2, but also 3, 2, 1 possible)
6 ... several members of the Heligoland Liberation Front last week.
7 ... the newspaper slowly over breakfast
8 ... Tony and Kate in Hungary last October

4 1 Understandably, ... 2 Frankly,... 3 Unfortunately, ... 4 Honestly, ... 5 Actually, ... 6 Foolishly, he left ... 7 Surprisingly, ... 8 Allegedly, ...

5 *Possible sample*
X comes to class punctually. She speaks several foreign languages fluently and uses language articulately. She prepares for classes conscientiously and takes part actively in class discussions. My impression is that she organises her time efficiently. Nor are her interests merely academic. She is in addition actively involved in extra-curricular activities: sport, amateur drama, dancing and travel. She is friendly, pleasant and polite in her contacts with students and staff. I can warmly recommend her as an excellent student and have no hesitation in supporting her application.

6 1 ... free. 2 ... sharply 3 ... wrong. 4 ... fair. 5 ... hardly ... late. 6 ... sharp. 7 ... slow. (*also:* slowly) 8 ... low. 9 easily. hard ... easy 10 ... slowly

7 1 In England, too, people drink coffee.
People drink coffee in England, too/as well.
Coffee is also drunk in England.
2 Unfortunately I haven't got any time, either.
3 Actually, this transaction was legal, too.
This transaction was also legal, actually.
4 What he did on Monday was dangerous, too.
What he did on Monday was also dangerous.
5 Patrick is a teetotaller, too/as well.
Patrick is also a teetotaller.
6 Patrick, too, is a teetotaller.
7 I didn't sleep very much last night, either.
Last night I didn't sleep very much, either.
8 My wife was born on 6th October (*BrE*)/October 6th, too!
What a coincidence!
9 By the way/Incidentally, the DVD players didn't arrive yesterday, either.
10 Some experts are also worrying about a stronger euro.

8 1 only people // money alone
2 even James // only likes
3 humans only have (*or:* humans have only one) // even cats
4 the cake decorations alone // I didn't even know
5 even the most talented writer // if they only rely on // talent alone

9 [1] I was just laying [2] and quickly glanced/glanced quickly right and left [3] he whispered conspiratorially [4] duly impressed [5] thoughtfully for a moment [6] And where is he now? [7] I followed him to his little house at the edge of the woods on the other side of the valley [8] cheerfully hurried/hurried cheerfully [9] I stood still for a moment in the doorway. [10] was probably no more intelligent [11] stretched out on the narrow bench against the far wall [12] lay, completely relaxed, a tall young man *or:* a young man, completely relaxed, in blue ... *or:* in blue overalls, completely relaxed. [13] gradually I realised *or:* I gradually realised *or:* I realised gradually [14] that, inevitably, the war was lost for Germany. *or:* that the war was inevitably lost for Germany. [15] a typically American face [16] close cropped curly hair [17] but quite simply [18] Suddenly I felt *or:* I suddenly felt [19] he looked so young. [20] if I would ever feel young again *or:* if I would ever again feel young

XIV The Definite Article

1 [1] life [2] life [3] nature [4] the comfortable life [5] Western society [6] the cruelty [7] nature [8] the England [9] the 18th century [10] 18th-century England [11] the effects [12] the harshness [13] nature [14] the same extent [15] everyday life [16] the reality [17] reality [18] the simple life [19] the frequent periods [20] hunger [21] the hardships [22] life [23] civilisation [24] the solitude [25] modern society [26] the solitude [27] the companionship [28] solitude

2 *All combinations are without article (i.e. Ø) except:*
the economy, the landscape, the lifestyle, the way of life

3 *Are you back at school yet? We started school last week. We've just come back from a trip to (the) Tyrol and Switzerland. It was a nice change from the Ruhr, where we've had awful weather all (the) summer. And (the) spring this year was pretty bad, too. In (the) Tyrol we stayed in a hotel with fantastic views over the Patscherkofl. It's one of the highest mountains in this part of Austria (much higher than Snowdon in Wales). We usually went hiking after lunch. The second week we toured Switzerland, spending most of the time on Lake Lucerne (in German it's called 'Vierwaldstättersee'). Our hotel, the 'Wilhelm Tell', was near Altdorf, on the banks of the River Reuss. It's named after the Swiss national hero, William Tell – you know, the one who shot the apple off his son's head.. While we were there my brother Willy sprained his ankle, so he had to spend the night in hospital in Altdorf, because they thought he'd broken it. Next day they let him come home, though poor Willy had to rest it and stay in bed for a few days, while we were outside in the fresh air enjoying nature. Now he's at home with (the) measles! I really feel sorry for him, even though he is my brother...*
Love, Sabine

4 1 Kennedy Airport 2 the Statue of Liberty 3 Ellis Island 4 the Bronx, Brooklyn, Manhattan, Queens, Staten Island 5 the Hudson River, the East River 6 Wall Street 7 Broadway 8 the Empire State Building 9 Central Park 10 Madison Avenue 11 the Met 12 Fifth Avenue 13 Times Square 14 La Guardia (Airport)

5 [1] English nationalism [2] Calvinism [3] the struggle [4] the Puritan revolution [5] religious liberty [6] moral duty [7] the freedom [8] the philosophy [9] utilitarianism [10] the author [11] *Political Economy* [12] national prejudices [13] the idea [14] social and political freedom [15] the peoples [16] 19th-century Europe

[17] English nationalism [18] American attitudes [19] American democracy [20] US capitalism [21] nationalism [22] Calvinism

6 1 The US is reducing its defence budget, a government spokesman has announced.

2 The IOC has confirmed that the Isle of Man is to be the host for the next Olympic Games.

3 The Prime Minister has been seen with a male friend in an exclusive bar in Mayfair which is frequented by gays.

4 The EU has decided to ban the notorious Russian mafia boss Vladimir Popimov from entering the European Union.

5 NASA claims that recent studies it has carried out show that the ozone layer is in fact expanding.

6 The UK has announced that it intends to join the euro within the next two years.

7 The Dutch government has confirmed that it will withdraw from NATO as soon as possible.

8 The AA is warning motorists that the rail strike is likely to cause chaos on Britain's roads as people take to their cars.

7 a 'Everything has changed except human thinking.'

b 'Violence feeds on the fact that it is not thought possible by decent people.'

c 'Working yourself to death is the only socially acceptable form of suicide.'

d 'The history of freedom is the history of dissent.'

e 'I think nowadays space is less dangerous than the streets of Berlin.'

f 'Youth would be a much nicer time if it came later in life.'

8 They're bearing left at the roundabout, turning into Lambeth Road. Now they're passing the Imperial War Museum. They must be doing about 70 m.p.h. Now they're going past Lambeth Palace. I can just see them crossing the Thames at Lambeth Bridge. They're turning left into John Islip Street, going past Westminster Hospital and the Tate Gallery. Now they've turned right into Vauxhall Bridge Road and they're passing the Children's Hospital. They're turning right into Victoria Street and they're going past Westminster Cathedral. Now they've gone left into Buckingham Gate. They've just gone past Wellington Barracks and they seem to be heading for Green Park. They're going past Buckingham Palace. Oh, and now they're changing direction. They're going down the Mall past the ICA, and they're passing through Admiralty Arch.

9 1 school 2 the Glasgow 3 Victorian Glasgow 4 19th-century architecture 5 the art nouveau Glasgow 6 the Glasgow 7 sectarian hatred 8 the hatred 9 the hostility 10 the violence 11 the Gorbals 12 violence 13 the normal pattern 14 life 15 the mid-Sixties 16 court 17 murder 18 the murder 19 prison 20 prison 21 the prison authorities 22 the money 23 the publication 24 people 25 the apathy 26 heroin 27 the future 28 the creativity 29 people 30 apathy 31 frozen violence

10 Winston Churchill was born in 1874 at Blenheim Palace in Oxfordshire. The young Churchill had an unhappy and neglected childhood. At Harrow he was weak academically. In fact, at Sandhurst he only passed the entrance examination at the third attempt. This changed, however, and when he graduated he was 20th out of a group of 130. In 1895 he joined the army, serving in India and South Africa. He became famous during the Boer War, when he rescued an army train. However, he was taken prisoner by the Boers. His subsequent escape from prison increased his fame. He became the MP for Oldham after the 1900 election. In Parliament he gained a reputation for making good speeches.

11 When you arrive at Victoria Station you have to turn right into Victoria Street. Then you go down Victoria Street. At the end of Victoria Street you go past Westminster Abbey. At Parliament Square take a left into Whitehall. You then go past the government buildings – by the way, on the left hand side of the road you'll see Downing Street, where the prime minister lives. You continue down Whitehall until you reach Trafalgar Square, where there are the big stone lions – there are always a lot of tourists there feeding the pigeons. On the north side of Trafalgar Square you'll see the National Gallery. But don't go there – that's the wrong direction. Instead you go towards the Strand. In the Strand turn left before the Adelphi Theatre into Bedford Street, then right into Maiden Lane. Maiden Lane is the continuation of Chandos Place. *Rules* is no. 35 in Maiden Lane. It's the oldest restaurant in London and has been there since 1798.

12 [1] medieval times [2] liberalism [3] the opening up [4] the liberation [5] the mind [6] the release [7] business enterprise [8] the Renaissance [9] the Reformation [10] the rise [11] capitalism [12] the struggle [13] democracy [14] the belief [15] reason [16] universal suffrage [17] the basic sanctity [18] human life [19] freedom [20] thought [21] the desirability [22] universal peace [23] fascism [24] European fascism [25] emotion [26] reason [27] the right [28] freedom [29] speech [30] war [31] the power [32] the state

XV Relative Clauses

1
1 a person who/that steals from shops.
2 somebody that/who doesn't drink alcohol.
3 a disease where the inside wall of the body becomes infected.
4 a person who/that assists a vicar.
5 something which/that is used for making coffee.
6 is when somebody is frightened of foreigners.
7 a vegetarian who/that refuses to eat animal products, e.g. milk or eggs.
8 something (that) you hang in a room at Xmas.

2
1 a mushwinger: a small, poisonous flying reptile which/that lives on Eos, a planet in the Vegan solar system (Lyra constellation) – its bite is fatal to humans
2 hyphenitis: a disease that involves excessive use of hyphens by students of English
3 a punspickle: someone who frequently uses puns in their conversation
4 pompocracy: a state where pompous politicians dominate the country's affairs
5 to shinwoggle sth. or sb.: an activity where you dance so closely with your partner that your shins are touching (*see also:* to chinwoggle: *ditto*, using the chins)

3
1 Guernsey, which has a population of about 56,000, lies west of Normandy.
2 The island, which is the second largest of the Channel Islands, is 63 square kilometres in area.
Or: The island, which is 63 square kilometres in area, is the second largest of the Channel Islands.

3 The island, which is not part of the British state, is self-governing.
Or: The island, which is self-governing, is not part of the British state.
4 Guernsey has its own parliament, which is known as the States.
5 The island, whose main industries are tourism, horticulture and dairy farming, is very prosperous.
6 A major attraction for tourists is the island's sandy beaches, most of which are safe.
7 One prominent resident of the island was Victor Hugo, who moved to the island in 1852.
8 Victor Hugo, whose house in the capital, St. Peter Port, is maintained as a museum by the city of Paris, wrote *Les Misérables* during his exile in Guernsey.
9 Guernsey, which in recent decades has become an important offshore financial centre, has long been a tax haven for people who wish to avoid paying U.K. income tax.
10 Guernsey, which is not a member of the EU, does not have VAT.
11 The island issues its own banknotes, coins and stamps, none of which can be used in mainland Britain.

4 1 of the teacher who taught us Physics?
2 of the family whose children used to walk barefoot?
3 the friend called (who) you used to go fishing with?
4 the name of the street where we lived?
5 the boy called (who) you sat next to in class?
6 the little old lady called who always used to give you sweets on your birthday?

5 1 on architecture, which I'm fascinated by.
2 my aunt, who we often used to stay with when we were little.
3 our holiday in Majorca, which I'm really looking forward to.
4 Unpunctuality, which I will not put up with, is...
5 Jimmy, who I used to knock around a lot with as a kid, is...
6 that soap, which I don't even mind getting up early for.
7 corruption scandals in politics(,) which the police are looking into.

6 1 e-mail, which is a nuisance.
2 sports car, which is very generous.
3 window, which was difficult.

4 a swimming pool, which was very disappointing.
5 overweight, which means he'll have to go on a diet.
6 a biscuit, which I thought was very stingy of them.
7 all day, which the kids thought was marvellous.

7 1 I like your accent, which sounds very authentic.
2 My paper, which is proud of its equal opportunities policy, in fact only employs four blacks.
3 The man (that/who) I was talking to last week didn't believe I had grown up in London.
4 Gary Younge is a black journalist who was born In London. Or: Gary Younge, who is a black journalist, was born in London.
5 The NAACP, whose convention I attended recently, fights for equal rights for blacks.
6 Baton Rouge, which is in Louisiana, is a deep-water port on the Mississippi. *Or:* Baton Rouge, which is a deep-water port on the Mississippi, is in Louisiana.
7 John Brown, who was hanged in 1859, had used force to free black slaves.
8 Frederick W. Douglass, who died in 1895, was a runaway slave who was the first great black political leader in the US.

8 1 executive who never takes risks
2 mayor, who is fairly left-wing,
3 operations, which often have to be cancelled
4 which has not gone down in literary history.
5 Edith Wharton, who was later awarded the Pulitzer Prize,
6 grandmother, in which the young Henry James stayed for quite a while,
7 square, which today is in the hands of students, tourists and drug dealers,
8 which is rare
9 Megan's Law, which has been introduced since 1995 in many US states,
10 a 7-year-old girl who was abducted, raped and murdered
11 a young man who was himself sexually abused as a 5-year-old
12 the slum in which Irish immigrants lived in Engels'(s) time.